Contents

PART ONE
"The Dead":
The Complete Text

PART TWO
"The Dead":
A Case Study in Contemporary Criticism

PART ONE

"The Dead":
The Complete Text

Introduction:
Biographical and
Historical Contexts

James Augustine Aloysius Joyce was one of twelve children, only eight of whom lived past childhood. He was born in Rathgar, a suburb of Dublin, on February 2, 1882. Due to a combination of sloth, drink, and financial imprudence, his father, John Stanislaus Joyce, took the family fortunes from prosperity to near poverty. He was pensioned at the age of 42 by the Dublin Corporation but never was able to live on his pension or the odd jobs he held after that. James Joyce blamed his father for the decline in the family economic fortunes and even more so for the premature death of his mother, May Joyce, at the age of 44. James Joyce was shaped by his Irish Catholic upbringing and the cultural repression of the Irish by the ruling British. Joyce's fictional surrogate, Stephen Dedalus, says in the opening chapter of *Ulysses*, "I am the servant of two masters . . . an English and an Italian . . . and a third there is who wants me for odd jobs." Joyce meant that as an Irish writer he had to serve the British Empire, the pope, and do "odd jobs" for his mother country, which he felt did not appreciate his genius.

While Joyce relied heavily on autobiography in presenting his protagonist, Stephen Dedalus, in *A Portrait of the Artist as a Young Man* (1916), he does not follow facts with blind obedience. More likely to take part in family song and festivities than the sullen and intransigent Stephen, young James was known as "sunny Jim." In 1888 Joyce was sent to boarding school at Clongowes Wood College, a Jesuit preparatory school with considerable prestige. Despite the discomfort he

dramatized in the early pages of *Portrait*, Joyce at times recalled the
school with fond memories. But because of his father's financial difficulties, James had to withdraw.

In 1893 Joyce entered Belvedere College, another Jesuit preparatory school, and won a prize for excellence in a national competition.
For a time the Jesuits encouraged him to consider becoming a priest,
but his reading and his sexual experimentation with prostitutes deflected him from that course. The substance of his disillusionment with
Catholicism is graphically dramatized in *Portrait*. Yet Joyce disbelieved
as intensely and obsessively as only a former believer can; his imagination was informed by his Catholic education throughout his life. In *Portrait* and *Ulysses* Joyce frequently refers not only to Catholic rites and
prayers, but to Catholic philosophy; he also owes to his Jesuit years
some of his classical training in Aristotle and Plato.

In 1898 he graduated from Belvedere and entered University College in Dublin, where he studied foreign languages as well as English.
University College was a Catholic institution founded by Cardinal
Newman as an alternative to Trinity College, the college for Protestants, but by his university days Joyce had completely turned his back on
Catholicism. After graduating in 1902 he went to Paris to study medicine but pursued nightlife more diligently than his courses.

Joyce's father was an enthusiastic follower of Charles Stewart Parnell (1846–91), the Irish nationalist and political leader of the Irish Parliamentary Delegation. Known as "The Uncrowned King of Ireland,"
Parnell was a major influence during Joyce's childhood. Although a
Protestant, Parnell became the leader of the Irish members of the British Parliament and by 1879 the leader of the Irish Home Rule Movement. Along with Michael Davitt, he formed the Land League to redis-
tribute farm land. But, in part because of Parnell's religion, the
Catholics turned on him when his adulterous relationship with the wife
of Captain O'Shea — one of his colleagues in the Home Rule Party —
was revealed. He was removed as head of the Irish Parliamentary Delegation and, under the onslaught of a variety of charges, his health de-
clined, and he died at the age of 45. His legend was such that rumors
abounded that he was not dead and would return.

Early on, Parnell's influence is evident in Joyce's work. At the age of
nine, Joyce wrote a poem, "Et Tu, Healy," which denounced Parnell's
betrayer, Tim Healy, and equated him with Brutus; this so pleased John
Joyce that he had his son's poem printed, although copies of the poem
have not survived. Joyce identified with Parnell as a figure of exceptional
brilliance and ability whose merit was finally unappreciated by the Irish

people. In a short piece (written originally in Italian) entitled "The Shade of Parnell" (1912), he wrote:

> The ghost of the "uncrowned king" will weigh on the hearts of those who remember him when the new Ireland in the near future enters into the palace . . . but it will not be a vindictive ghost. . . .
> In his final desperate appeal to his countrymen, he begged them not to throw him as a sop to the English wolves. . . . They did not throw him to the English wolves; they tore him to pieces themselves.[1]

In "Ireland, Island of Saints and Sages" (1907), Joyce wrote: "[T]o deny the name of patriot to all those who are not of Irish stock would be to deny it almost to all the heroes of the modern movement — Lord Edward Fitzgerald, Robert Emmet, Theobald Wolfe Tone . . . and, finally, Charles Stewart Parnell, who was perhaps the most formidable man that ever led the Irish, but in whose veins there was not even a drop of Celtic Blood" (*Critical Writings of James Joyce* 162). In *Ulysses*, both Stephen, the putative artist hero who will someday write the work that will raise the consciousness of Ireland, and Bloom, the pacifistic, humanistic hero, are versions of Parnell. By referring frequently to Parnell, by hinting at Bloom's involvement in political affairs, and, most of all, by having Bloom think of Parnell quite often, Joyce arouses our expectations that Parnell is a prefiguration of Bloom. Parnell's life is one of the major contemporary patterns of allusions to which Joyce juxtaposes the action of June 16, 1904, the date on which the entire action of *Ulysses* takes place.

Just as Joyce was aware of his political heritage, he was aware of contemporary Irish literature and the Irish writers who came before him, particularly Jonathan Swift, Oscar Wilde, and William Butler Yeats. When Joyce reached maturity, the prominent figure in Irish literature was Yeats (1865–1939), who encouraged Joyce but whom Joyce regarded as something of a rival. Seventeen years older than Joyce, Yeats dominated Irish literary culture from 1890 to 1922, the year of the founding of the Irish Free State, and beyond. He wanted to create an Irish literary culture that drew upon indigenous Irish myths, legends, and heroes. Yeats was influenced by the nationalism of John O'Leary and Maud Gonne as well as by the spiritualism of AE (George Russell), Madam Blavatsky, and the Theosophists, who claimed a mystical insight into the divine nature of the universe. Along with Lady Gregory, Yeats

---

[1]Ellsworth Mason and Richard Ellmann, eds., *The Critical Writings of James Joyce.* (New York: Viking, 1959) 162.

founded the Irish Literary Theatre, later known as the Abbey Theatre, to give voice to various playwrights in the movement.

Joyce supported the right of Yeats and his colleagues to express themselves (in 1899 he refused to sign a University College students' protest against Yeats's *The Countess Cathleen*), but he believed that the appropriate direction for Ireland was to join the European intellectual and cultural community. Joyce became increasingly impatient with Ireland's parochialism and turned toward Europe. He very much admired the realistic domestic dramas of Henrik Ibsen (1828–1906) and published in 1900 an important defense of Ibsen in the British *Fortnightly Review*. He even attacked members of the Irish Literary Theatre as Irish Philistines in a 1901 essay "The Days of the Rabblement." Joyce disagreed with the idea that Ireland should or could be a Celtic nation with its own language and that Ireland should focus only on its myths and heroes while ignoring the European cultural tradition. The very title *Ulysses* — the Roman name of the hero of the Greek epic poem the *Odyssey* — announces this position. So does his insistence in *Ulysses's* crucial "Scylla and Charybdis" chapter on defining Shakespeare as his literary father. Joyce also parted ways with the various forms of the occult to which Yeats and his followers subscribed. To Joyce, Yeats's idealization of Irish culture represented a kind of neo-Platonic narcissism that interferes with the artist's intercourse with the real world. In *Ulysses* Stephen Dedalus mocks the folk literature being published at the turn of the century by Yeats's sisters in projects under Yeats's auspices: "Five lines of text and ten pages of notes about the folk and the fishgods of Dundrum. Printed by the weird sisters in the year of the big wind" (*Ulysses* I. 11. 365–66). Joyce was uncomfortable, too, with the fact that most of the major figures in the Irish movement were Protestants and that Yeats had deferred to the aristocracy of the "Great Families" such as that of Lady Gregory. Joyce identified with the urban Catholic middle class.

In "Circe," the climactic chapter of *Ulysses*, Stephen acknowledges Bloom as father, and Bloom perceives Stephen as a son in terms that allude to the work and identity of Yeats and Oscar Wilde. The reader understands then that Joyce is acknowledging Yeats and Wilde as his artistic fathers. Joyce identified with Wilde as an outsider (Wilde had been persecuted for his homosexuality); yet Joyce could also speak of Wilde as one of the Irish writers who became a "court jester to the English" (*Critical Writings of James Joyce* 202). Just as Yeats was vilified because of the literary nonconformity of his *The Countess Cathleen*, Wilde was ostracized for his personal and sexual nonconformism. Joyce identified with both his fellow victims of middle-class parochialism. That Stephen's definition of Irish art as "The cracked lookingglass of a servant" is partially indebted to the preface in Wilde's *The Decay of Lying* (1889), shows that Joyce wants us to see that Stephen is in danger of becoming inculcated with Wilde's cynicism. (Wilde had written: "I can quite understand your objection to art being treated as a mirror. You think it would reduce genius to the position of a cracked looking glass."[2]) We should not forget the links between Stephen's aestheticism in *Portrait* and Wilde's theories and behavior; as Darcy O'Brien has noted, "resemblances between Stephen's aestheticism and the art for art's sake movement of the eighties and the nineties are obvious enough in the search for the beautiful; in the scorn of bourgeois society; in the love of the languorous, the self-conscious, the elegantly eccentric, even in Stephen's (and Joyce's) walking stick."[3] And Joyce was influenced by Wilde's theory of masques and fictions in essays such as "The Decay of Lying." Joyce's desire to objectify part of himself in Bloom (a character who seems to be the diametric opposite of Stephen, the artist based on his younger self), probably was influenced by Wilde's theory of masques: Wilde believed that we must assume a masque in order to liberate ourselves from our customary conventional daytime selves.

In his fantasy of his son, Rudy, at the end of "Circe," Bloom the watchful, thoughtful, humanistic Mason evokes a figure that is his opposite, his anti-self, his masque. The bizarre vision of his deceased son is the kind of extravagant figure Wilde would have imagined. The ivory cane held by Rudy suggests Stephen's ashplant, which Bloom is holding, but the bizarre costume further suggests the dandyish Oscar Wilde. In this scene, Joyce affirms his ties not only to the Romantic tradition of Blake and Yeats, but to the decadent Romanticism of Wilde.

In April 1903 he returned home to visit his dying mother, but after her death on August 13, 1903, he remained in Ireland, living in a tower at Sandymount with Oliver St. John Gogarty, who became the model for Malachi Mulligan. The first chapter of *Ulysses* captures the tension between Gogarty and Joyce, and Stephen's bitterness, resentment, cynicism, and intransigence reflect Joyce's attitudes at this time.

In June 1904, Joyce met his future wife Nora Barnacle — on June 10 in all probability — and on about June 20, following a drunken spree in Dublin, he was taken home by Alfred Hunter, a man who may

---

[2]Don Gifford and Robert J. Seidman, *Notes for Joyce: An Annotation of James Joyce's "Ulysses"* (New York: Dutton, 1974) 8.
[3]Darcy O'Brien, *The Conscience of James Joyce* (Princeton: Princeton UP, 1968) 11.

have been both Jewish and an unfaithful husband. When writing *Ulysses,* Joyce's imagination assigned both dates to June 16, 1904, the day Joyceans celebrate as Bloomsday. Hunter became the source for Leopold Bloom, the humanistic Jewish hero of *Ulysses,* from whom Stephen learns about family, courage, caring, and life. In 1904 Joyce published early versions of several stories in *Dubliners* ("The Sisters," "Eveline," and "After the Race"); "The Dead," the final story to be written, was completed in 1907.

While writing *Dubliners,* Joyce had many audiences in mind: Dublin's drowsing citizens whose consciences and consciousness needed arousing; the Catholic hierarchy; the Irish artistic and intellectual elite, including Yeats; the British public; and perhaps a prospective publisher for his story. In the first three stories — "The Sisters," "An Encounter," and "Araby" — Joyce uses the young boy to demonstrate the values of a representative preadolescent in Dublin and to show what forces — notably Catholicism and British domination of Ireland — shape the boy's epistemology and language, even as the speaker performs for us the consequences of that upbringing.

The reader, too, is the object of Joyce's artistry, the figure whose lapsed soul must be restored to his imagination and who must rediscover his humanity so that Dublin can become healthy and whole. Joyce wants to teach imperfect Irish readers to make sense of Dublin by showing them what *Dublin* really is. What Giuseppe Mazzotta has written about in Dante's *Divine Comedy* is just as true of *Dubliners:* it "dramatizes in a fundamental way the activity of interpretation — it recounts the effort of the poet-exegete to read the book of the world."[4] Joyce is reading the book of Dublin for us. Like Dante, we are pilgrim-spectators, and Joyce is Virgil showing us the inferno of contemporary Dublin. The reader, accompanied by the narrator-guide, sees the landscape of Dublin and is urged to think of the possibility for renewal. The reader in his sense-making must establish not only hierarchies among his critical approaches, but also hierarchies among the details. Our reading iterates the characters' efforts to make sense of the world, but our reading must go beyond their sense-making. *Dubliners* teaches the reader that he must abandon Dublin-think and Dublin-speak if he is to find meaning. Because the reader's sense-making involves fulfilled expectations and understood patterns, his activity is at odds with the frustrated quests of most of the figures in *Dubliners.* But because the speaker's telling reveals that he is only at a resting place and that he has the resources of

[4]Quoted by Mary Reynolds, *Dante and Joyce* (Princeton: Princeton UP, 1981) 220.

language and imagination to resume the struggle to discover meaning in his quest, the reader may have more in common with the speaker in "Araby" than with the other protagonists.

In *Dubliners* we see the totality of Dublin life and the evolving patterns that hold Joyce's visions of the city together even when aspects of that pattern are in different stories. We see stories in a spatial configuration as if they were stars in a constellation held together by what might be called the magnetism of significance. We should think of *Dubliners* as an evolving series of stories, a kaleidoscope in which each story takes turns as the centerpiece in the pattern. The episodes cohere into the mindscape of Dublin and enact the repetitious cycle of blunted aspiration and frustration, of crass materialism, of sexual repression, of drunkenness, of moral idiocy. *Dubliners* is a cityscape, a representation of Dublin; as such it looks forward to, and becomes part of, Joyce's later depictions of Dublin's characters in *Ulysses* and *Finnegans Wake*.

The first three stories of *Dubliners* might be called "A Portrait of the Artist as a Very Young Man"; they speak of the transformation of consciousness that Joyce experienced as he became disillusioned with what he felt was Catholicism's rigorous, repressive, and hypocritical attitudes toward sexuality. Because of the continuity among these three stories, the young man becomes a shadowy version of a portrait of the artist as a *very* young man. Indeed, these first three stories are part of a fictional sequence, including *A Portrait of the Artist* and *Ulysses*, about a young man growing up in Dublin. Thus, "Araby" enacts a dialectical linguistic drama in which realistic language describing the pedestrian world of Dublin struggles with the language of the romance world. Within the boy's mind the language of sexual desire, religious education (especially the ritual of confession), Irish songs, and literary naturalism struggle not only with one another but also with his own desire and efforts as a putative artist to invent stylized and mannered forms to render his past experience. The boy's charged language — the language borrowed from reading rather than experience — is transformed and undermined by the pedestrian world of Dublin and the obsessive hold of the Church.

That "Araby" is the third of a series of stories in which boys wander through Dublin looking for meaning, and in which sexuality seems debased and corrupt, creates a context for our response. Yet the stylistic signature of the speaker is different from the first-person speaker's alienated detachment from his subject in "The Sisters" — where spaces between anecdotes enact his anaesthetized condition — and the relatively straightforward account of "An Encounter" where the speaker's obsession with the homosexual flagellant is in stark contrast with the distancing of "The Sisters." Unlike the other characters in the first three stories, the boy in "Araby" is a magician with words. Yet his speech, like the pervert's in "An Encounter," finally "circles round and round in the same orbit" as if he cannot leave the Church's epistemology. Just as he is constrained by his English and Catholic masters in action, he iterates his past experience. He flagellates himself as (to recall a key phrase from "An Encounter") a "rough and unruly" boy who has, as he puts it in his reminiscence, been "driven and derided" by vanity. He "whips" himself for having a "sweetheart." Indeed, at the end of "Araby" isn't he accusing himself of simony, the worldly traffic in spiritual things of which the priest in "The Sisters" was supposedly guilty?

The engaged first-person speakers of the first three stories create an identification, an empathy, that makes the ironic detachment of the following stories — "Eveline," "After the Race," "Two Gallants" — all the more striking. We may link the young boy's sexual repression with the frustrated and guilty sexuality of the title character of the subsequent story, "Eveline." Eveline is a version of the aged spinster in "The Sisters." She is a warning not only of what Mangan's sister might become but also of what the boy might become should he not have the imaginative resources to create his own world. "Eveline," a more flagrant and indeed pathological story of reflexive self-imprisonment, retells "Araby" in the third person. Not only is the speaker much older than the speaker of "Araby", she also lacks the latter's imaginative power — a power that has the potential to transform the drab world of Dublin. The final image of her leaning on the rail is a metonym for imprisonment by the Catholic epistemology and by Irish traditions and conventions, both of which define pleasure and self-gratification as sinful; that definition of sin creates damaged psyches, which feed on repression, sublimation, and projection. In the face of the systems of cognition embedded in her psyche, Eveline becomes catatonic when she has a chance for escape: "She set her white face to him passive, like a helpless animal. Her eyes gave him no sign of love or farewell or recognition." At this crucial moment she recoils to religion ("her lips moved in silent prayer"); we recall her promise to her dead mother ("she prayed to God to direct her, to show her what was her duty"). Her unintelligible Irish speech — "Derevaun Seraun! Derevaun Seraun!" — reminds us that Joyce was very skeptical even in 1904 of Yeats and the Irish Renaissance and that he felt Ireland's future lay with the European community.

In 1904 Joyce submitted to the journal *Dana* an essay story entitled "A Portrait of the Artist"; although it was rejected, he would later expand and rewrite it as *Stephen Hero*. That same year, opposed to marriage as a convention, he and Nora left Ireland to live out of wedlock. Their existence was a peripatetic one for some months until they settled in Trieste, where they lived most of the time for the next several years. First Joyce taught languages in the Berlitz school and then gave private lessons in English. In 1905 his son Giorgio was born, and his brother Stanislaus joined him in Trieste. While Stanislaus and James had occasional fallings-out, Stanislaus (whose posthumous volume, *My Brother's Keeper: James Joyce's Early Years*, is a useful source for Joyce's biography), often helped Joyce find adequate writing conditions and domestic tranquility. In 1907, after finishing "The Dead," Joyce began to rewrite *Stephen Hero* as *A Portrait of the Artist as a Young Man*. Also in 1907 his daughter Lucia Anna was born and his poetry collection, *Chamber Music*, was published.

Joyce twice returned to Ireland, once to organize the first Irish cinema in 1909 and for the last time in 1912 with Nora and their five-year-old daughter Lucia to visit Nora's home in Galway and Dublin. So discouraged was he with *Portrait* that in 1911, he would have deliberately burned the manuscript had his sister Eileen not pulled it from the fire. Finally, in 1914 the London journal *The Egoist* began to serialize *Portrait*, and in the same year Grant Richards finally published *Dubliners* after years of delay due to misgivings about the propriety of certain subjects and phrases.

A Portrait of the Artist as a Young Man is a *kunstlerroman*, a novel about the development of a young artist. The major figure is Stephen Dedalus, whose life is dramatized from his earliest verbal understanding:

> Once upon a time and a very good time it was there was a moocow coming down along the road and this moocow that was coming down along the road met a nicens little boy named baby tuckoo. . . .
> His father told him that story: his father looked at him through a glass: he had a hairy face.
> He was baby tuckoo. The moocow came down the road where Betty Byrne lived: she sold lemon platt.[5]

Each of the five chapters ends with a moment of illumination or epiphany. Originally an epiphany was a manifestation of Christ to the Gentiles

[5] James Joyce, *"A Portrait of the Artist as a Young Man,"* ed. R. B. Kershner. Case Studies in Contemporary Criticism Series, ed. Ross C Murfin (Boston: Bedford–St. Martin's, 1993) 19.

in the person of the Magi. Joyce's religion of art gives a secular and aesthetic meaning to this term. The novel's climax is the point when Stephen imagines himself as poet-priest of art who will go into exile and write the great Irish epic. "Welcome, O life! I go to encounter for the millionth time the reality of experience and to forge in the smithy of my soul the uncreated conscience of my race. *27 April:* Old father, old artificer, stand me now and ever in good stead" (*Portrait* 218).

Wayne Booth has discussed the difficulty of locating Joyce's attitudes toward his protagonist/surrogate Stephen:

> The truth seems to be that Joyce was always a bit uncertain about his attitude toward Stephen. Anyone who reads Ellmann's masterful biography with this problem in mind cannot help being struck by the many shifts and turns Joyce took as he worked through the various versions. . . .
>
> It is only when Joyce places at the center of a long work a figure who experiences epiphanies, an epiphany-producing device, as it were, who is himself used by the real author as an object ambiguously distant from the norms of the work, that the complications of distance become incalculable. If he treats the author-figure satirically, as he does in much of *Stephen Hero,* that earlier, windier version of *Portrait,* then what happens to the quality of the epiphanies that *he* describes? Are they still genuine epiphanies or only what the misguided, callow youth *thinks* are epiphanies?[6]

In a sense Joyce is dramatizing his inability to resolve the problem of whether Stephen is, as Booth puts it, "a portrait of the prisoner freed" or a "portrait of the soul placing itself in chains." While readers have alternated between stressing Joyce as a surrogate Joyce and seeing him ironically, perhaps one can have it both ways and see that Joyce is regarding his egoism with poignance and sympathy.

Certainly when Joyce returns to Stephen in *Ulysses,* he distances himself from him as a narcissistic, emotionally paralyzed, and self-deluding figure. Because *Portrait* had moved teleologically toward Stephen's escape from Ireland and his self-definition as an artist, the opening chapters of *Ulysses* are all the more poignant and bathetic. If, in *Portrait,* the narrator had viewed with gentle irony both Stephen's concluding dialogue with Cranly and his subsequent diary entries, now Stephen regards himself with bitter self-conscious irony. In place of the ebullient brilliance and confidence in his role as an artist (which we saw

---

[6] Wayne C. Booth, *The Rhetoric of Fiction,* 2nd ed. (Chicago: U of Chicago P, 1983; orig. ed. 1961) 330, 332.

in his dialogue with Cranly in the last section that precedes the diary entries in *Portrait*), Stephen reveals, in his opening dialogue with Mulligan, self-hatred, loneliness, and cynicism.

Why did Joyce choose for his surrogate self the name Dedalus? Unlike his mythical namesake Daedalus, the Greek inventor who adapted the arts to the reality of experience, Stephen is lost in the world of his own dreams. Stephen is also the name of the first Christian martyr. Like Daedalus and his son Icarus, who were imprisoned by the Cretan King Minos in their own labyrinth because they helped Minos's wife have intercourse with a bull to produce the hybrid monster Minotaur, Stephen is imprisoned in a labyrinth of his own making. Daedalus plans to escape Minos's wrath by making for himself and Icarus wings fashioned of wax and feathers; Icarus flies too close to the sun and falls into the sea. At times Stephen is an Icarus figure who has flown too near the sun rather than, like his namesake Daedalus, a man who has flown successfully. Stephen had wanted to adopt Daedalus as his mythic father without taking on the inevitable identity of the drowning Icarus.

In 1914 Joyce began to write his masterwork *Ulysses* — which, with Stephen Dedalus playing a central role, is a kind of sequel to *Portrait* — and in 1915, he finished his play *Exiles,* a domestic drama that was rejected by the Abbey Theatre but was published in 1918 and finally performed in Munich in 1919. Because of the world war, he moved to neutral Zurich. In 1919 he briefly returned to Trieste before moving in 1920 to Paris at the strong urging of the American poet Ezra Pound, who had corresponded with him and had been his friend since 1913. Joyce tended to live on the economic edge and often lacked funds to pay his rent. He was often helped by the generous gifts of Harriet Weaver and, for a time, Mrs. Harold McCormick. In 1917 he had his first eye operation; problems with his sight would bedevil him off and on, and he was nearly blind at his death in 1941, following abdominal surgery for a perforated ulcer. He lived in Paris the rest of his life, except for his final year in Zurich after the fall of France. In 1931, Joyce went to London briefly, where he and Nora finally were married on July 4, but they soon returned to Paris. In 1932 his son Giorgio and his wife gave him a grandchild, Stephen James Joyce; and his daughter Lucia had the first of her schizophrenic breakdowns. Her illness was another burden for Joyce's later years.

Let us return to *Ulysses. Ulysses* was serialized from 1918 to 1920 in an American journal, *The Little Review,* but it was not until 1922 that it was published as a book in Paris. After a court ruled that it was not pornographic, *Ulysses* was published in 1934 by Random House in the

United States. As noted, *Ulysses* takes place on June 16, 1904, com-memorating both the day Hunter befriended Joyce in Dublin's red light district and the day Joyce remembered falling in love with Nora. *Ulysses* is first and foremost a novel about three individuals — Stephen Dedalus, Leopold Bloom, and Molly Bloom — who live in turn-of-the-century Dublin. It is a paradox of *Ulysses* that it is the most temporally and spatially ambitious of epic novels as it ranges far and wide through human experience, even as it is the most nigglingly nominalistic and compulsively naturalistic novel in its focus on the pedestrian details of life in Dublin on one day. Convincing his readers that Stephen and Bloom are universal figures embodying significant cultural values is an artistic problem that Joyce had to solve to create the national epic that he wished desperately to write.

As a realist, Joyce has the characters think in terms appropriate to 1904 Dublin; yet the characters resonate for the reader with historical and cultural implications. Joyce's allusions bring the weight of past eras and historical contexts into the very texture of our reading experience. *Ulysses* is based on Joyce's view that at any random point in time, one can evoke through allusions what has been significant in human history. His elaborate references to Homeric, biblical, and Elizabethan anteced-ents become extended metaphors in which contemporary events ac-quire additional significance through connections to absent literary and historical figures, even as they in turn lend some of their own signifi-cance to the figures to whom they are being compared. Because history, Joyce believed, repeats itself in crucial ways, literature is a central re-source for discovering how people lived in past eras.

Within *Ulysses,* history is a series of concentric circles proceeding outward from the centerpoint of June 16, 1904. For Joyce *any* one day could be defined as the center of a series of concentric circles proceed-ing outward. We might examine history, Joyce believed, the way we examine the rings of a redwood tree. The closer circles at any one mo-ment are those that can be shown to most resemble the events being dramatized, while the more distant ones provide less important paral-lels. Thus, in the section entitled "Lestrygonians," with the exception of the opening evocation of Elijah, the Homeric parallel is the closest cir-cle; in "Aeolus," the Homeric parallel is gradually superseded by the Passover story; and in "Scylla and Charybdis," the Shakespeare era dis-places the Homeric one as the closest circle.

Joyce chose literary and historical sources that present what he be-lieved to be the central recurring issues that appear within each cycle and that illustrate the universal values on which man's survival depends. Joyce chose Homer's *Odyssey* as his primary model because it is the one major European epic that emphasizes the centrality of family and personal relationships: parent and child, particularly father and son; male friendship and rivalry; and heterosexual lovers, especially the complex ties between a long-married husband and wife. Indeed, the *Odyssey* begins with a son's quest for his missing father and soon turns to the hero's quest to displace a rival for his wife's affections and resume his proper place in the home.

But he also chose the *Odyssey* as a model because it was the epic that stresses how an individual uses his intelligence, judgment, and inner strength to overcome obstacles and, finally, to accomplish his goal. By announcing in the title *Ulysses* that his subject is a retelling of the Greek prototype, Joyce is consciously substituting what he regarded as this more civilized European tradition for the emphasis of Yeats and the Celtic Renaissance on the folk legends and the myths of the Irish gods. Joyce is interested far less in physical prowess than in moral courage. Unlike the mythic Irish hero Cuchulain, who physically expands and contracts at will when he is challenged, Ulysses is a hero who lives by his wits. (Of course, one might object that his reading of the classical tradition is idiosyncratic, for had he chosen the *Iliad* or the Greek tragedies, he would have found models for bellicose behavior.) In *Ulysses* Joyce also focuses on *Hamlet,* the Shakespearean tragedy most concerned with family relations and the mental and emotional life of the individual; this is consistent with his focus on private lives and interior space. His version of *Hamlet* hardly attends to the original work's aspects as revenge tragedy.

In his quest for meaning, the fictionalized Joyce — the speaker and writer of the events within the imagined world — becomes an Odysseus figure within the novel. While Odysseus goes from place to place, Joyce goes from style to style. For Joyce, no one perspective could represent or do justice to the diversity of plausible views of reality. Thus, each of the eighteen chapters has its own unique technique, colors, organs, and Homeric correspondences. Indeed, Joyce kept an evolving chart before him as he wrote the book. Thus he required multiple perspectives to create what he calls *parallax,* a mathematical term that describes how an object can look different if perceived from different places. Wolfgang Iser remarked, "Joyce wanted to bring out, if not actually overcome, the inadequacy of style as regards the presentation of reality, by constant changes of style. For only by showing up the relativity of each form could he expose the intangibility and expansibility of observable reality."[7]

Ulysses is Joyce's inquiry into the question: What values are viable in the twentieth-century urban world where, according to Joyce's view, God does not exist, and traditional notions of heroism are obsolete? Among other things, *Ulysses* is an effort to redefine the concept of the hero. Joyce uses Bloom, the marginal Jew, to redefine heroism in secular humanistic terms. As he examines recent Irish history and culture, Joyce proposes Bloom both as an alternative to the xenophobia and fantasies of the Celtic Renaissance and as a successor to Parnell.

The novel redefines the traditional concept of heroism to emphasize not only pacifism, but commitment to family ties, concern for the human needs of others, sense of self, tolerance, and decency. Heroism for Joyce is a set of personal values that makes it possible to improve the quality of life ever so slightly for others — as Bloom does for the Dignam family, for Mrs. Purefoy, and, most of all, for Stephen and Molly. In stressing Bloom's commitment to home and family, Joyce believes he is returning to the original spirit of the Homeric source. Yet he retains something of Tennyson's stress on the need for courageously facing the struggles of life. Joyce continues the tendency of the later nineteenth-century English novel to make its heroes (Dobbin, Alan Woodcourt, Clym Yeobright) into domestic figures committed to family values.

We recall Joyce's own discussion of genre in *Portrait:*

[A]rt necessarily divides itself into three forms progressing from one to the next. These forms are: the lyrical form, the form wherein the artist presents his image in immediate relation to himself; the epical form, the form wherein he presents his image in mediate relation to himself and to others; the dramatic form, the form wherein he presents his image in immediate relation to others. . . . The lyrical form is in fact the simplest verbal vesture of an instant of emotion. . . . He who utters it is more conscious of the instant of emotion than of himself as feeling emotion. The simplest epical form is seen emerging out of lyrical literature when the artist prolongs and broods upon himself as the centre of an epical event and this form progresses till the centre of emotional gravity is equidistant from the artist himself and from others. The narrative is no longer purely personal. The personality of the artist passes into the narrative itself, flowing round and round the persons and the ac-

---

[7]Wolfgang Iser, *The Implied Reader: Patterns of Communication in Prose Fiction from Bunyan to Beckett* (Baltimore: Johns Hopkins UP, 1974) 192.

tion like a vital sea. . . . The dramatic form is reached when the vitality which has flowed and eddied round each person fills every person with such vital force that he or she assumes a proper and intangible esthetic life. The personality of the artist, at first a cry or cadence or a mood and then a fluid and lambent narrative, finally refines itself out of existence, impersonalises itself, so to speak. The esthetic image in the dramatic form is life purified in and reprojected from the human imagination. (186–87)

In applying Joyce's aesthetic to his own works, we should think of literary works not as purely lyrical, epical, or dramatic, but as mixed modes that contain aspects of more than one genre. *A Portrait of the Artist as a Young Man* begins in the lyrical mode, but, to the degree to which it is ironic, it approaches the epical mode. If we understand the relationship in *Ulysses* between the three genres as a dynamic process — as a trialogue among them — we can better understand the novel's form and meaning. Thus, in *Ulysses* Joyce progresses from the lyrical to the epical and finally to the dramatic. The first three chapters oscillate between the lyrical perspective of Stephen and the epical perspective of Joyce's omniscient but not entirely distanced narrator, a narrator who is never far from Stephen's consciousness and who does not enter into the consciousness of any other characters. By using the lyrical mode in *Portrait*, Joyce establishes the continuity of both Stephen and of the narrative presence, and calls attention to the process of fictionally reexamining and recreating his own life. By allowing the lyrical mode to dominate the epical mode with which *Portrait* had concluded, he shows that Stephen has taken a step backward in his artistic development, for the mature artist needs the objectivity Stephen lacks.

Reading the first three chapters of *Ulysses*, we inevitably refer to *Portrait*. Put another way, *Portrait* is a special case of Joyce's use of the literary and historical past. That is, we not only measure Stephen against Telemachus and Hamlet, but we hold him up against the younger version of himself who had first left Ireland in spring 1902 and returned in August 1903 to see his dying mother. The richness of these first three chapters depends in part on our responding to echoes of prior language and incidents. When we recall the euphoric expectations of the penultimate diary entry in *Portrait*, we realize that Stephen's artistic career is at a standstill. Because he lacks the reality of experience in the form of passionate feelings and empirical knowledge of life, he is not yet ready to be the writer of the epic that Ireland requires. For Joyce, Stephen's apostasy is his inability (one could say a refusal based on immaturity) to transform his personal and cultural experience into epical and dramatic art. Before Stephen can write an epic of modern Ireland, he must reject various forms of aestheticism that preach "art for art's sake" and glorify a separation between life and art. In his 1922 *Ulysses*, Joyce is rejecting the aestheticism and solipsism of Stephen's credo in the 1916 *Portrait*: "I will try to express myself in some mode of life or art as freely as I can and as wholly as I can, using for my defence the only arms I allow myself to use — silence, exile, and cunning" (*Portrait* 213).

In 1923 Joyce began to write "Work in Progress," the book that became *Finnegans Wake*. In 1925 he began to publish fragments from that work, but it was not published as a complete novel until 1939. *Finnegans Wake* lacks a traditional narrative and characterization. Indeed, the first sentence starts in the middle and is the end of the sentence with which the novel concludes. Joyce was influenced by both Giovanni Battista Vico and Sigmund Freud, both of whom were interested in the unconscious. Joyce found confirmation of his cyclical theory in Vico. Like Vico, Joyce believed that history is cyclical rather than progressive. Vico was a model for Joyce's vision of a recurring pattern in social history; at the same time he believed that languages, literature, and myths of a culture are the best sources of its values, beliefs, and customs. Vico's *The New Science* (1725) is, like *Finnegans Wake*, predicated on etymological studies. In *Finnegans Wake* and *Ulysses* Joyce's subject, like Vico's, is the disruption of family and the need for its restoration.

Of H. C. Earwicker, the central figure of *Finnegans Wake*, John Bishop writes,

> As HCE, then, the "belowes hero" of *Finnegans Wake* is not at all a "character," possessed of reified properties like "personality," "individuality," and "identity," but a body, inside of which, "tropped head," there is no consciousness of anything much outside, except as it has been cargoed and reformed in memory; on top of and throughout which, in wakefulness, the man-made constructs of character, personality, individuality, identity, and ego have been layered.[8]

One way of understanding *Finnegans Wake* is to see it in terms of Joyce's prior novels and to understand H. C. Earwicker and Anna Livia Plurabelle as developments of Bloom and Molly. Thus, many difficult passages can be better understood by reference to *Ulysses*, *Portrait*, and *Dubliners*. Another way of enjoying *Finnegans Wake* is simply to submit

---

[8]John Bishop, *Joyce's Book in the Dark: "Finnegans Wake"* (Madison: U of Wisconsin P, 1986) 27.

to the elaborate play on language. We cannot always distinguish among the male figures — Finnegan, HCE, Adam, Osiris, and Finn Macool — although we can see that the female figure ALP, or Anna Livia Plurabelle, is the female counterpart to the male HCE and an echo of Eve. *Finnegans Wake* resists our usual practice of reading linearly for plot and character and invites us to see it as a disruption of narrative expectations if not as a complex, linguistic, indecipherable puzzle. For we cannot even look to the title character, Finnegan, as a figure to help us make sense of the plot, although the title is based on the legend of a drunken man who has fallen off a ladder and apparently dies, only to arise at his wake.

Isn't Gabriel Conroy, the protagonist of "The Dead," another figure who falls off the ladder of his hopes and illusions only to awaken and recover in his final epiphany of the common humanity that binds human beings together? Our focus in this volume is on "The Dead," that magnificent short novel of tenderness and passion but also of disappointed love and frustrated personal and career expectations. Gabriel's narrative reminds us of what happens when we translate our personal lives into self-sustaining but ultimately narcissistic myths, for Gabriel, as we shall see, has lost intimate touch with his wife Gretta and has sought refuge in his positions as family patriarch, teacher, and book reviewer. Furthermore, the elegiac disposition of the Irish characters at the Misses Morkans' party demonstrates what happens when we create cultural myths that are indifferent to reality. The Morkans are not the Three Graces but three spinsters, and the Irish obsession with past heroes and musical luminaries interferes with the possibility of overcoming social and political paralysis in Ireland.

Daniel R. Schwarz

WORKS CITED

Bishop, John. *Joyce's Book in the Dark: "Finnegans Wake."* Madison: U of Wisconsin P, 1986.

Booth, Wayne C. *The Rhetoric of Fiction,* 2nd ed. Chicago: U of Chicago P, 1983; orig. ed. 1961.

Gifford, Don, and Robert J. Seidman. *Notes for Joyce: An Annotation of James Joyce's "Ulysses."* New York: Dutton, 1974.

Iser, Wolfgang. *The Implied Reader: Patterns of Communication in*

Prose Fiction from Bunyan to Beckett. Baltimore: Johns Hopkins UP, 1974.

Joyce, James. *"A Portrait of the Artist as a Young Man."* Ed. R. B. Kershner. Case Studies in Contemporary Criticism Series. Ed. Ross C Murfin. Boston: Bedford–St. Martin's, 1993.

——. *Ulysses.* 1922. Ed. Hans Walter Gabler, Wolfhard Steppe, and Claus Melchior. New York: Vintage, 1986.

Mason, Ellsworth, and Richard Ellmann, eds. *The Critical Writings of James Joyce.* New York: Viking, 1959.

O'Brien, Darcy. *The Conscience of James Joyce.* Princeton: Princeton UP, 1968.

Reynolds, Mary. *Dante and Joyce.* Princeton: Princeton UP, 1981.

"The Dead"

Lily, the caretaker's daughter, was literally run off her feet. Hardly had she brought one gentleman into the little pantry behind the office on the ground floor and helped him off with his overcoat than the wheezy hall-door bell clanged again and she had to scamper along the bare hallway to let in another guest. It was well for her she had not to attend to the ladies also. But Miss Kate and Miss Julia had thought of that and had converted the bathroom upstairs into a ladies' dressing-room. Miss Kate and Miss Julia were there, gossiping and laughing and fussing, walking after each other to the head of the stairs, peering down over the banisters and calling down to Lily to ask her who had come.

It was always a great affair, the Misses Morkan's annual dance.° Everybody who knew them came to it, members of the family, old friends of the family, the members of Julia's choir, any of Kate's pupils that were grown up enough and even some of Mary Jane's pupils too. Never once had it fallen flat. For years and years it had gone off in splendid style as long as anyone could remember; ever since Kate and Julia, after the death of their brother Pat, had left the house in Stoney Batter° and

---

annual dance: The party took place after New Year's Eve and before Twelfth Night, the Feast of Epiphany.   **Stoney Batter:** A mixed street of small shops, tenements, and a few houses; located northeast of central Dublin.

taken Mary Jane, their only niece, to live with them in the dark gaunt house on Usher's Island,° the upper part of which they had rented from Mr Fulham, the cornfactor on the ground floor. That was a good thirty years ago if it was a day. Mary Jane, who was then a little girl in short clothes, was now the main prop of the household for she had the organ in Haddington Road. She had been through the Academy° and gave a pupils' concert every year in the upper room of the Ancient Concert Rooms. Many of her pupils belonged to better-class families on the Kingstown and Dalkey line.° Old as they were, her aunts also did their share. Julia, though she was quite grey, was still the leading soprano in Adam and Eve's,° and Kate, being too feeble to go about much, gave music lessons to beginners on the old square piano in the back room. Lily, the caretaker's daughter, did housemaid's work for them. Though their life was modest they believed in eating well; the best of everything: diamond-bone sirloins, three-shilling tea and the best bottled stout. But Lily seldom made a mistake in the orders so that she got on well with her three mistresses. They were fussy, that was all. But the only thing they would not stand was back answers.

Of course they had good reason to be fussy on such a night. And then it was long after ten o'clock and yet there was no sign of Gabriel° and his wife. Besides they were dreadfully afraid that Freddy Malins might turn up screwed. They would not wish for worlds that any of Mary Jane's pupils should see him under the influence; and when he was like that it was sometimes very hard to manage him. Freddy Malins always came late but they wondered what could be keeping Gabriel: and that was what brought them every two minutes to the banisters to ask Lily had Gabriel or Freddy come.

— O, Mr Conroy, said Lily to Gabriel when she opened the door for him, Miss Kate and Miss Julia thought you were never coming. Good-night, Mrs Conroy.

— I'll engage they did, said Gabriel, but they forget that my wife here takes three mortal hours to dress herself.

Usher's Island: A not very fashionable area on the south bank of the Liffey, west of the center of Dublin. It is near an industrial section dominated by the Guinness Brewery. **the Academy:** The Royal Academy of Music, founded in 1848 and located at 6 Merrion Square, a fashionable area. **Kingstown and Dalkey line:** Kingstown and Dalkey were, at the turn of the century, fashionable areas on the southeast outskirts of Dublin. **Adam and Eve's:** The popular name for the Franciscan church in Merchants Quay in Dublin; the name of the church fascinated Joyce, and he opens *Finnegans Wake* with a reference to it. **Gabriel:** Bret Harte had entitled a novel *Gabriel Conroy* (1876); one major parallel is the pervasive snow in both "The Dead" and in the opening of Harte's novel.

He stood on the mat, scraping the snow from his goloshes, while Lily led his wife to the foot of the stairs and called out:

— Miss Kate, here's Mrs Conroy.

Kate and Julia came toddling down the dark stairs at once. Both of them kissed Gabriel's wife, said she must be perished alive and asked was Gabriel with her.

— Here I am as right as the mail, Aunt Kate! Go on up. I'll follow, called out Gabriel from the dark.

He continued scraping his feet vigorously while the three women went upstairs, laughing, to the ladies' dressing-room. A light fringe of snow lay like a cape on the shoulders of his overcoat and like toecaps on the toes of his goloshes; and, as the buttons of his overcoat slipped with a squeaking noise through the snow-stiffened frieze, a cold fragrant air from out-of-doors escaped from crevices and folds.

— Is it snowing again, Mr Conroy? asked Lily.

She had preceded him into the pantry to help him off with his overcoat. Gabriel smiled at the three syllables she had given his surname and glanced at her. She was a slim, growing girl, pale in complexion and with hay-coloured hair. The gas in the pantry made her look still paler. Gabriel had known her when she was a child and used to sit on the lowest step nursing a rag doll.

— Yes, Lily, he answered, and I think we're in for a night of it.

He looked up at the pantry ceiling, which was shaking with the stamping and shuffling of feet on the floor above, listened for a moment to the piano and then glanced at the girl, who was folding his overcoat carefully at the end of a shelf.

— Tell me, Lily, he said in a friendly tone, do you still go to school?

— O no, sir, she answered. I'm done schooling this year and more.

— O, then, said Gabriel gaily, I suppose we'll be going to your wedding one of these fine days with your young man, eh?

The girl glanced back at him over her shoulder and said with great bitterness:

— The men that is now is only all palaver and what they can get out of you.

Gabriel coloured as if he felt he had made a mistake and, without looking at her, kicked off his goloshes and flicked actively with his muffler at his patent-leather shoes.

He was a stout tallish young man. The high colour of his cheeks pushed upwards even to his forehead where it scattered itself in a few formless patches of pale red; and on his hairless face there scintillated restlessly the polished lenses and the bright gilt rims of the glasses which screened his delicate and restless eyes. His glossy black hair was parted in the middle and brushed in a long curve behind his ears where it curled slightly beneath the groove left by his hat.

When he had flicked lustre into his shoes he stood up and pulled his waistcoat down more tightly on his plump body. Then he took a coin rapidly from his pocket.

— O Lily, he said, thrusting it into her hands, it's Christmas-time, isn't it? Just . . . here's a little. . . .

He walked rapidly towards the door.

— O no, sir! cried the girl, following him. Really, sir, I wouldn't take it.

— Christmas-time! Christmas-time! said Gabriel, almost trotting to the stairs and waving his hand to her in deprecation.

The girl, seeing that he had gained the stairs, called out after him:

— Well, thank you, sir.

He waited outside the drawing-room door until the waltz should finish, listening to the skirts that swept against it and to the shuffling of feet. He was still discomposed by the girl's bitter and sudden retort. It had cast a gloom over him which he tried to dispel by arranging his cuffs and the bows of his tie. Then he took from his waistcoat pocket a little paper and glanced at the headings he had made for his speech. He was undecided about the lines from Robert Browning for he feared they would be above the heads of his hearers. Some quotation that they could recognise from Shakespeare or from the Melodies would be better. The indelicate clacking of the men's heels and the shuffling of their soles reminded him that their grade of culture differed from his. He would only make himself ridiculous by quoting poetry to them which they could not understand. They would think that he was airing his superior education. He would fail with them just as he had failed with the girl in the pantry. He had taken up a wrong tone. His whole speech was a mistake from first to last, an utter failure.

Just then his aunts and his wife came out of the ladies' dressing-room. His aunts were two small plainly dressed old women. Aunt Julia was an inch or so the taller. Her hair, drawn low over the tops of her ears, was grey; and grey also, with darker shadows, was her large flaccid face. Though she was stout in build and stood erect her slow eyes and parted lips gave her the appearance of a woman who did not know where she was or where she was going. Aunt Kate was more vivacious. Her face, healthier than her sister's, was all puckers and creases, like a shrivelled red apple, and her hair, braided in the same old-fashioned way, had not lost its ripe nut colour.

They both kissed Gabriel frankly. He was their favourite nephew, the son of their dead elder sister, Ellen, who had married T. J. Conroy of the Port and Docks.

— Gretta tells me you're not going to take a cab back to Monkstown° to-night, Gabriel, said Aunt Kate.

— No, said Gabriel, turning to his wife, we had quite enough of that last year, hadn't we? Don't you remember, Aunt Kate, what a cold Gretta got out of it? Cab windows rattling all the way, and the east wind blowing in after we passed Merrion.° Very jolly it was. Gretta caught a dreadful cold.

Aunt Kate frowned severely and nodded her head at every word.

— Quite right, Gabriel, quite right, she said. You can't be too careful.

— But as for Gretta there, said Gabriel, she'd walk home in the snow if she were let.

Mrs Conroy laughed.

— Don't mind him, Aunt Kate, she said. He's really an awful bother, what with green shades for Tom's eyes at night and making him do the dumb-bells, and forcing Eva to eat the stirabout.° The poor child! And she simply hates the sight of it! . . . O, but you'll never guess what he makes me wear now!

She broke out into a peal of laughter and glanced at her husband, whose admiring and happy eyes had been wandering from her dress to her face and hair. The two aunts laughed heartily too, for Gabriel's solicitude was a standing joke with them.

— Goloshes! said Mrs Conroy. That's the latest. Whenever it's wet underfoot I must put on my goloshes. To-night even he wanted me to put them on, but I wouldn't. The next thing he'll buy me will be a diving suit.

Gabriel laughed nervously and patted his tie reassuringly while Aunt Kate nearly doubled herself, so heartily did she enjoy the joke. The smile soon faded from Aunt Julia's face and her mirthless eyes were directed towards her nephew's face. After a pause she asked:

— And what are goloshes, Gabriel?

— Goloshes, Julia! exclaimed her sister. Goodness me, don't you know what goloshes are? You wear them over your . . . over your boots, Gretta, isn't it?

Monkstown: In 1904, a prosperous village to the southeast of Dublin.   **Merrion:** A village on Dublin Bay.   **stirabout:** Porridge, usually made of oatmeal.

— Yes, said Mrs Conroy. Guttapercha things. We both have a pair now. Gabriel says everyone wears them on the continent.

— O, on the continent, murmured Aunt Julia, nodding her head slowly.

Gabriel knitted his brows and said, as if he were slightly angered:

— It's nothing very wonderful but Gretta thinks it very funny because she says the word reminds her of Christy Minstrels.°

— But tell me, Gabriel, said Aunt Kate, with brisk tact. Of course, you've seen about the room. Gretta was saying . . .

— O, the room is all right, replied Gabriel. I've taken one in the Gresham.

— To be sure, said Aunt Kate, by far the best thing to do. And the children, Gretta, you're not anxious about them?

— O, for one night, said Mrs Conroy. Besides, Bessie will look after them.

— To be sure, said Aunt Kate again. What a comfort it is to have a girl like that, one you can depend on! There's that Lily, I'm sure I don't know what has come over her lately. She's not the girl she was at all.

Gabriel was about to ask his aunt some questions on this point but she broke off suddenly to gaze after her sister who had wandered down the stairs and was craning her neck over the banisters.

— Now, I ask you, she said, almost testily, where is Julia going? Julia! Julia! Where are you going?

Julia, who had gone halfway down one flight, came back and announced blandly:

— Here's Freddy.

At the same moment a clapping of hands and a final flourish of the pianist told that the waltz had ended. The drawing-room door was opened from within and some couples came out. Aunt Kate drew Gabriel aside hurriedly and whispered into his ear:

— Slip down, Gabriel, like a good fellow and see if he's all right, and don't let him up if he's screwed. I'm sure he's screwed. I'm sure he is.

Gabriel went to the stairs and listened over the banisters. He could hear two persons talking in the pantry. Then he recognised Freddy Malins' laugh. He went down the stairs noisily.

— It's such a relief, said Aunt Kate to Mrs Conroy, that Gabriel is here. I always feel easier in my mind when he's here. . . . Julia, there's

---

Christy Minstrels: The stereotypical minstrel show in blackface, organized by Edwin T. Christy and originating in Buffalo, New York.

Miss Daly and Miss Power will take some refreshment. Thanks for your beautiful waltz, Miss Daly. It made lovely time.

A tall wizen-faced man, with a stiff grizzled moustache and swarthy skin, who was passing out with his partner said:

— And may we have some refreshment, too, Miss Morkan?

— Julia, said Aunt Kate summarily, and here's Mr Browne and Miss Furlong. Take them in, Julia, with Miss Daly and Miss Power.

— I'm the man for the ladies, said Mr Browne, pursing his lips until his moustache bristled and smiling in all his wrinkles. You know, Miss Morkan, the reason they are so fond of me is —

He did not finish his sentence, but, seeing that Aunt Kate was out of earshot, at once led the three young ladies into the back room. The middle of the room was occupied by two square tables placed end to end, and on these Aunt Julia and the caretaker were straightening and smoothing a large cloth. On the sideboard were arrayed dishes and plates, and glasses and bundles of knives and forks and spoons. The top of the closed square piano served also as a sideboard for viands and sweets. At a smaller sideboard in one corner two young men were standing, drinking hop-bitters.

Mr Browne led his charges thither and invited them all, in jest, to some ladies' punch, hot, strong and sweet. As they said they never took anything strong he opened three bottles of lemonade for them. Then he asked one of the young men to move aside, and, taking hold of the decanter, filled out for himself a goodly measure of whisky. The young men eyed him respectfully while he took a trial sip.

— God help me, he said, smiling, it's the doctor's orders.

His wizened face broke into a broader smile, and the three young ladies laughed in musical echo to his pleasantry, swaying their bodies to and fro, with nervous jerks of their shoulders. The boldest said:

— O, now, Mr Browne, I'm sure the doctor never ordered anything of the kind.

Mr Browne took another sip of his whisky and said, with sidling mimicry:

— Well, you see, I'm like the famous Mrs Cassidy, who is reported to have said: *Now, Mary Grimes, if I don't take it, make me take it, for I feel I want it.*

His hot face had leaned forward a little too confidentially and he had assumed a very low Dublin accent so that the young ladies, with one instinct, received his speech in silence. Miss Furlong, who was one of Mary Jane's pupils, asked Miss Daly what was the name of the pretty waltz she had played; and Mr Browne, seeing that he was ignored, turned promptly to the two young men who were more appreciative.

A red-faced young woman, dressed in pansy, came into the room, excitedly clapping her hands and crying:

— Quadrilles! Quadrilles!

Close on her heels came Aunt Kate, crying:

— Two gentlemen and three ladies, Mary Jane!

— O, here's Mr Bergin and Mr Kerrigan, said Mary Jane. Mr Kerrigan, will you take Miss Power? Miss Furlong, may I get you a partner, Mr Bergin. O, that'll just do now.

— Three ladies, Mary Jane, said Aunt Kate.

The two young gentlemen asked the ladies if they might have the pleasure, and Mary Jane turned to Miss Daly.

— O, Miss Daly, you're really awfully good, after playing for the last two dances, but really we're so short of ladies to-night.

— I don't mind in the least, Miss Morkan.

— But I've a nice partner for you, Mr Bartell D'Arcy, the tenor. I'll get him to sing later on. All Dublin is raving about him.

— Lovely voice, lovely voice! said Aunt Kate.

As the piano had twice begun the prelude to the first figure Mary Jane led her recruits quickly from the room. They had hardly gone when Aunt Julia wandered slowly into the room, looking behind her at something.

— What is the matter, Julia? asked Aunt Kate anxiously. Who is it?

Julia, who was carrying in a column of table-napkins, turned to her sister and said, simply, as if the question had surprised her:

— It's only Freddy, Kate, and Gabriel with him.

In fact right behind her Gabriel could be seen piloting Freddy Malins across the landing. The latter, a young man of about forty, was of Gabriel's size and build, with very round shoulders. His face was fleshy and pallid, touched with colour only at the thick hanging lobes of his ears and at the wide wings of his nose. He had coarse features, a blunt nose, a convex and receding brow, tumid and protruded lips. His heavy-lidded eyes and the disorder of his scanty hair made him look sleepy. He was laughing heartily in a high key at a story which he had been telling Gabriel on the stairs and at the same time rubbing the knuckles of his left fist backwards and forwards into his left eye.

— Good-evening, Freddy, said Aunt Julia.

Freddy Malins bade the Misses Morkan good-evening in what seemed an offhand fashion by reason of the habitual catch in his voice and then, seeing that Mr Browne was grinning at him from the sideboard, crossed the room on rather shaky legs and began to repeat in an undertone the story he had just told to Gabriel.

— He's not so bad, is he? said Aunt Kate to Gabriel.

Gabriel's brows were dark but he raised them quickly and answered:

— O no, hardly noticeable.

— Now, isn't he a terrible fellow! she said. And his poor mother made him take the pledge on New Year's Eve. But come on, Gabriel, into the drawing-room.

Before leaving the room with Gabriel she signalled to Mr Browne by frowning and shaking her forefinger in warning to and fro. Mr Browne nodded in answer and, when she had gone, said to Freddy Malins:

— Now, then, Teddy, I'm going to fill you out a good glass of lemonade just to buck you up.

Freddy Malins, who was nearing the climax of his story, waved the offer aside impatiently but Mr Browne, having first called Freddy Malins' attention to a disarray in his dress, filled out and handed him a full glass of lemonade. Freddy Malins' left hand accepted the glass mechanically, his right hand being engaged in the mechanical readjustment of his dress. Mr Browne, whose face was once more wrinkling with mirth, poured out for himself a glass of whisky while Freddy Malins exploded, before he had well reached the climax of his story, in a kink of high-pitched bronchitic laughter and, setting down his untasted and overflowing glass, began to rub the knuckles of his left fist backwards and forwards into his left eye, repeating words of his last phrase as well as his fit of laughter would allow him.

.   .   .   .

Gabriel could not listen while Mary Jane was playing her Academy piece, full of runs and difficult passages, to the hushed drawing-room. He liked music but the piece she was playing had no melody for him and he doubted whether it had any melody for the other listeners, though they had begged Mary Jane to play something. Four young men, who had come from the refreshment-room to stand in the doorway at the sound of the piano, had gone away quietly in couples after a few minutes. The only persons who seemed to follow the music were Mary Jane herself, her hands racing along the key-board or lifted from it at the pauses like those of a priestess in momentary imprecation, and Aunt Kate standing at her elbow to turn the page.

Gabriel's eyes, irritated by the floor, which glittered with beeswax under the heavy chandelier, wandered to the wall above the piano. A picture of the balcony scene in *Romeo and Juliet* hung there and beside it was a picture of the two murdered princes in the Tower which Aunt Julia had worked in red, blue and brown wools when she was a girl. Probably in the school they had gone to as girls that kind of work had been taught, for one year his mother had worked for him as a birthday present a waistcoat of purple tabinet, with little foxes' heads upon it, lined with brown satin and having round mulberry buttons. It was strange that his mother had had no musical talent though Aunt Kate used to call her the brains carrier of the Morkan family. Both she and Julia had always seemed a little proud of their serious and matronly sister. Her photograph stood before the pierglass. She held an open book on her knees and was pointing out something in it to Constantine who, dressed in a man-o'-war suit, lay at her feet. It was she who had chosen the names for her sons for she was very sensible of the dignity of family life. Thanks to her, Constantine was now senior curate in Balbriggan and, thanks to her, Gabriel himself had taken his degree in the Royal University. A shadow passed over his face as he remembered her sullen opposition to his marriage. Some slighting phrases she had used still rankled in his memory; she had once spoken of Gretta as being country cute and that was not true of Gretta at all. It was Gretta who had nursed her during all her last long illness in their house at Monkstown.

He knew that Mary Jane must be near the end of her piece for she was playing again the opening melody with runs of scales after every bar and while he waited for the end the resentment died down in his heart. The piece ended with a trill of octaves in the treble and a final deep octave in the bass. Great applause greeted Mary Jane as, blushing and rolling up her music nervously, she escaped from the room. The most vigorous clapping came from the four young men in the doorway who had gone away to the refreshment-room at the beginning of the piece but had come back when the piano had stopped.

Lancers were arranged. Gabriel found himself partnered with Miss Ivors. She was a frank-mannered talkative young lady, with a freckled face and prominent brown eyes. She did not wear a low-cut bodice and the large brooch which was fixed in the front of her collar bore on it an Irish device.

When they had taken their places she said abruptly:

— I have a crow to pluck with you.

— With me? said Gabriel.

She nodded her head gravely.

— What is it? asked Gabriel, smiling at her solemn manner.

— Who is G. C.? answered Miss Ivors, turning her eyes upon him.

Gabriel coloured and was about to knit his brows, as if he did not understand, when she said bluntly:

— O, innocent Amy! I have found out that you write for *The Daily Express.*° Now, aren't you ashamed of yourself?

— Why should I be ashamed of myself? asked Gabriel, blinking his eyes and trying to smile.

— Well, I'm ashamed of you, said Miss Ivors frankly. To say you'd write for a rag like that. I didn't think you were a West Briton.°

A look of perplexity appeared on Gabriel's face. It was true that he wrote a literary column every Wednesday in *The Daily Express,* for which he was paid fifteen shillings. But that did not make him a West Briton surely. The books he received for review were almost more welcome than the paltry cheque. He loved to feel the covers and turn over the pages of newly printed books. Nearly every day when his teaching in the college was ended he used to wander down the quays to the second-hand booksellers, to Hickey's on Bachelor's Walk, to Webb's or Massey's on Aston's Quay, or to O'Clohissey's in the by-street. He did not know how to meet her charge. He wanted to say that literature was above politics. But they were friends of many years' standing and their careers had been parallel, first at the University and then as teachers: he could not risk a grandiose phrase with her. He continued blinking his eyes and trying to smile and murmured lamely that he saw nothing political in writing reviews of books.

When their turn to cross had come he was still perplexed and inattentive. Miss Ivors promptly took his hand in a warm grasp and said in a soft friendly tone:

— Of course, I was only joking. Come, we cross now.

When they were together again she spoke of the University question° and Gabriel felt more at ease. A friend of hers had shown her his review of Browning's poems. That was how she had found out the secret: but she liked the review immensely. Then she said suddenly:

— O, Mr Conroy, will you come for an excursion to the Aran Isles°

The Daily Express: A conservative newspaper in Dublin that opposed Irish independence. **a West Briton:** A derogatory term for an Irishman who was not sufficiently nationalist and did not subscribe to all the tenets of the Irish nationalist movement.   **the University question:** Refers to the issue of how to provide a quality university education for Catholics. Until 1871, Trinity College required students to pass Protestant examinations. University College, originally Catholic University, lacked the prestige and rigor of Trinity. **the Aran Isles:** Off Galway on the West Coast, they were regarded as an ideal by the Celtic Renaissance because Irish was spoken and the denizens lived, supposedly, a utopian agrarian life.

this summer? We're going to stay there a whole month. It will be splendid out in the Atlantic. You ought to come. Mr Clancy is coming, and
Mr Kilkelly and Kathleen Kearney. It would be splendid for Gretta too
if she'd come. She's from Connacht,° isn't she?

— Her people are, said Gabriel shortly.

— But you will come, won't you? said Miss Ivors, laying her warm
hand eagerly on his arm.

— The fact is, said Gabriel, I have already arranged to go —

— Go where? asked Miss Ivors.

— Well, you know, every year I go for a cycling tour with some
fellows and so —

— But where? asked Miss Ivors.

— Well, we usually go to France or Belgium or perhaps Germany,
said Gabriel awkwardly.

— And why do you go to France and Belgium, said Miss Ivors, instead of visiting your own land?

— Well, said Gabriel, it's partly to keep in touch with the languages
and partly for a change.

— And haven't you your own language to keep in touch with —
Irish? asked Miss Ivors.

— Well, said Gabriel, if it comes to that, you know, Irish is not my
language.

Their neighbours had turned to listen to the cross-examination. Gabriel glanced right and left nervously and tried to keep his good humour
under the ordeal which was making a blush invade his forehead.

— And haven't you your own land to visit, continued Miss Ivors,
that you know nothing of, your own people, and your own country?

— O, to tell you the truth, retorted Gabriel suddenly, I'm sick of my
own country, sick of it!

— Why? asked Miss Ivors.

Gabriel did not answer for his retort had heated him.

— Why? repeated Miss Ivors.

They had to go visiting together and, as he had not answered her,
Miss Ivors said warmly:

— Of course, you've no answer.

Gabriel tried to cover his agitation by taking part in the dance with
great energy. He avoided her eyes for he had seen a sour expression on
her face. But when they met in the long chain he was surprised to feel

---

Connacht: An area on the West Coast of Ireland.

his hand firmly pressed. She looked at him from under her brows for a moment quizzically until he smiled. Then, just as the chain was about to start again, she stood on tiptoe and whispered into his ear:

— West Briton!

When the lancers were over Gabriel went away to a remote corner of the room where Freddy Malins' mother was sitting. She was a stout feeble old woman with white hair. Her voice had a catch in it like her son's and she stuttered slightly. She had been told that Freddy had come and that he was nearly all right. Gabriel asked her whether she had had a good crossing. She lived with her married daughter in Glasgow and came to Dublin on a visit once a year. She answered placidly that she had had a beautiful crossing and that the captain had been most attentive to her. She spoke also of the beautiful house her daughter kept in Glasgow, and of all the nice friends they had there. While her tongue rambled on Gabriel tried to banish from his mind all memory of the unpleasant incident with Miss Ivors. Of course the girl or woman, or whatever she was, was an enthusiast but there was a time for all things. Perhaps he ought not to have answered her like that. But she had no right to call him a West Briton before people, even in joke. She had tried to make him ridiculous before people, heckling him and staring at him with her rabbit's eyes.

He saw his wife making her way towards him through the waltzing couples. When she reached him she said into his ear:

— Gabriel, Aunt Kate wants to know won't you carve the goose as usual. Miss Daly will carve the ham and I'll do the pudding.

— All right, said Gabriel.

— She's sending in the younger ones first as soon as this waltz is over so that we'll have the table to ourselves.

— Were you dancing? asked Gabriel.

— Of course I was. Didn't you see me? What words had you with Molly Ivors?

— No words. Why? Did she say so?

— Something like that. I'm trying to get that Mr D'Arcy to sing. He's full of conceit, I think.

— There were no words, said Gabriel moodily, only she wanted me to go for a trip to the west of Ireland and I said I wouldn't.

His wife clasped her hands excitedly and gave a little jump.

— O, do go, Gabriel, she cried. I'd love to see Galway again.

— You can go if you like, said Gabriel coldly.

She looked at him for a moment, then turned to Mrs Malins and said:

— There's a nice husband for you, Mrs Malins.

While she was threading her way back across the room Mrs Malins, without adverting to the interruption, went on to tell Gabriel what beautiful places there were in Scotland and beautiful scenery. Her son-in-law brought them every year to the lakes and they used to go fishing. Her son-in-law was a splendid fisher. One day he caught a fish, a beautiful big big fish, and the man in the hotel boiled it for their dinner.

Gabriel hardly heard what she said. Now that supper was coming near he began to think again about his speech and about the quotation. When he saw Freddy Malins coming across the room to visit his mother Gabriel left the chair free for him and retired into the embrasure of the window. The room had already cleared and from the back room came the clatter of plates and knives. Those who still remained in the drawing-room seemed tired of dancing and were conversing quietly in little groups. Gabriel's warm trembling fingers tapped the cold pane of the window. How cool it must be outside! How pleasant it would be to walk out alone, first along by the river and then through the park!° The snow would be lying on the branches of the trees and forming a bright cap on the top of the Wellington Monument.° How much more pleasant it would be there than at the supper-table!

He ran over the headings of his speech: Irish hospitality, sad memories, the Three Graces,° Paris, the quotation from Browning. He repeated to himself a phrase he had written in his review: *One feels that one is listening to a thought-tormented music.* Miss Ivors had praised the review. Was she sincere? Had she really any life of her own behind all her propagandism? There had never been any ill-feeling between them until that night. It unnerved him to think that she would be at the supper-table, looking up at him while he spoke with her critical quizzing eyes. Perhaps she would not be sorry to see him fail in his speech. An idea came into his mind and gave him courage. He would say, alluding to Aunt Kate and Aunt Julia: *Ladies and Gentlemen, the generation which is now on the wane among us may have had its faults but for my part I think it had certain qualities of hospitality, of humour, of humanity,*

---

the park: Phoenix Park, a large park on the western side of Dublin, which was the site where key members of the British government in Ireland were assassinated on May 6, 1882.   Wellington Monument: Although the Duke of Wellington (1769–1852) was born in Ireland, he was an English hero, and his statue was another painful reminder to Dubliners of England's imperial pressure.   the Three Graces: In Greek mythology, the daughters of Zeus and Eurynome: Agalaia (Brilliance), Euphrosyne (Joy), and Thalia (Bloom).

which the new and very serious and hypereducated generation that is growing up around us seems to me to lack. Very good: that was one for Miss Ivors. What did he care that his aunts were only two ignorant old women?

A murmur in the room attracted his attention. Mr Browne was advancing from the door, gallantly escorting Aunt Julia, who leaned upon his arm, smiling and hanging her head. An irregular musketry of applause escorted her also as far as the piano and then, as Mary Jane seated herself on the stool, and Aunt Julia, no longer smiling, half turned so as to pitch her voice fairly into the room, gradually ceased. Gabriel recognised the prelude. It was that of an old song of Aunt Julia's —*Arrayed for the Bridal.*° Her voice, strong and clear in tone, attacked with great spirit the runs which embellish the air and though she sang very rapidly she did not miss even the smallest of the grace notes. To follow the voice, without looking at the singer's face, was to feel and share the excitement of swift and secure flight. Gabriel applauded loudly with all the others at the close of the song and loud applause was borne in from the invisible supper-table. It sounded so genuine that a little colour struggled into Aunt Julia's face as she bent to replace in the music-stand the old leather-bound song-book that had her initials on the cover. Freddy Malins, who had listened with his head perched sideways to hear her better, was still applauding when everyone else had ceased and talking animatedly to his mother who nodded her head gravely and slowly in acquiescence. At last, when he could clap no more, he stood up suddenly and hurried across the room to Aunt Julia whose hand he seized and held in both his hands, shaking it when words failed him or the catch in his voice proved too much for him.

— I was just telling my mother, he said, I never heard you sing so well, never. No, I never heard your voice so good as it is to-night. Now! Would you believe that now? That's the truth. Upon my word and hon-

---

Arrayed for the Bridal: A lyric by George Linley set to music from Vincengo Bellini's opera, *I Puritani* (The Puritans):

Array'd for the bridal, in beauty behold her,
A white wreath entwineth a forehead more fair;
I envy the zephyrs that softly enfold her, enfold her,
And play with the locks of her beautiful hair.
May life to her prove full of sunshine and love, full of love, yes! yes! yes!
Who would not love her
Sweet star of the morning! shining so bright,
Earth's circle adorning, fair creature of light,
Fair creature of light.

honour that's the truth. I never heard your voice sound so fresh and so . . . so clear and fresh, never.

Aunt Julia smiled broadly and murmured something about compliments as she released her hand from his grasp. Mr Browne extended his open hand towards her and said to those who were near him in the manner of a showman introducing a prodigy to an audience:

— Miss Julia Morkan, my latest discovery!

He was laughing very heartily at this himself when Freddy Malins turned to him and said:

— Well, Browne, if you're serious you might make a worse discovery. All I can say is I never heard her sing half so well as long as I am coming here. And that's the honest truth.

— Neither did I, said Mr Browne. I think her voice has greatly improved.

Aunt Julia shrugged her shoulders and said with meek pride:

— Thirty years ago I hadn't a bad voice as voices go.

— I often told Julia, said Aunt Kate emphatically, that she was simply thrown away in that choir. But she never would be said by me.

She turned as if to appeal to the good sense of the others against a refractory child while Aunt Julia gazed in front of her, a vague smile of reminiscence playing on her face.

— No, continued Aunt Kate, she wouldn't be said or led by anyone, slaving there in that choir night and day, night and day. Six o'clock on Christmas morning! And all for what?

— Well, isn't it for the honour of God, Aunt Kate? asked Mary Jane, twisting round on the piano-stool and smiling.

Aunt Kate turned fiercely on her niece and said:

— I know all about the honour of God, Mary Jane, but I think it's not at all honourable for the pope to turn out the women out of the choirs° that have slaved there all their lives and put little whipper-snappers of boys over their heads. I suppose it is for the good of the Church if the pope does it. But it's not just, Mary Jane, and it's not right.

She had worked herself into a passion and would have continued in defence of her sister for it was a sore subject with her but Mary Jane, seeing that all the dancers had come back, intervened pacifically:

— Now, Aunt Kate, you're giving scandal to Mr Browne who is of the other persuasion.

pope to turn out . . . choirs: On November 22, 1903, Pope Pius X in his *Motu Proprio* said that, since church singers have a liturgical office, women had to be excluded and boys would take their parts.

Aunt Kate turned to Mr Browne, who was grinning at this allusion to his religion, and said hastily:

— O, I don't question the pope's being right. I'm only a stupid old woman and I wouldn't presume to do such a thing. But there's such a thing as common everyday politeness and gratitude. And if I were in Julia's place I'd tell that Father Healy straight up to his face . . .

— And besides, Aunt Kate, said Mary Jane, we really are all hungry and when we are hungry we are all very quarrelsome.

— And when we are thirsty we are also quarrelsome, added Mr Browne.

— So that we had better go to supper, said Mary Jane, and finish the discussion afterwards.

On the landing outside the drawing-room Gabriel found his wife and Mary Jane trying to persuade Miss Ivors to stay for supper. But Miss Ivors, who had put on her hat and was buttoning her cloak, would not stay. She did not feel in the least hungry and she had already overstayed her time.

— But only for ten minutes, Molly, said Mrs Conroy. That won't delay you.

— To take a pick itself, said Mary Jane, after all your dancing.

— I really couldn't, said Miss Ivors.

— I am afraid you didn't enjoy yourself at all, said Mary Jane hopelessly.

— Ever so much, I assure you, said Miss Ivors, but you really must let me run off now.

— But how can you get home? asked Mrs Conroy.

— O, it's only two steps up the quay.

Gabriel hesitated a moment and said:

— If you will allow me, Miss Ivors, I'll see you home if you really are obliged to go.

But Miss Ivors broke away from them.

— I won't hear of it, she cried. For goodness sake go in to your suppers and don't mind me. I'm quite well able to take care of myself.

— Well, you're the comical girl, Molly, said Mrs Conroy frankly.

— *Beannacht libh,*° cried Miss Ivors, with a laugh, as she ran down the staircase.

Mary Jane gazed after her, a moody puzzled expression on her face, while Mrs Conroy leaned over the banisters to listen for the hall-door. Gabriel asked himself was he the cause of her abrupt departure. But she

Beannacht libh: Farewell, my blessings go with you.

did not seem to be in ill humour: she had gone away laughing. He stared blankly down the staircase.

At that moment Aunt Kate came toddling out of the supper-room, almost wringing her hands in despair.

— Where is Gabriel? she cried. Where on earth is Gabriel? There's everyone waiting in there, stage to let, and nobody to carve the goose!

— Here I am, Aunt Kate! cried Gabriel, with sudden animation, ready to carve a flock of geese, if necessary.

A fat brown goose lay at one end of the table and at the other end, on a bed of creased paper strewn with sprigs of parsley, lay a great ham, stripped of its outer skin and peppered over with crust crumbs, a neat paper frill round its shin and beside this was a round of spiced beef. Between these rival ends ran parallel lines of side-dishes: two little minsters of jelly, red and yellow; a shallow dish full of blocks of blancmange and red jam, a large green leaf-shaped dish with a stalk-shaped handle, on which lay bunches of purple raisins and peeled almonds, a companion dish on which lay a solid rectangle of Smyrna figs, a dish of custard topped with grated nutmeg, a small bowl full of chocolates and sweets wrapped in gold and silver papers and a glass vase in which stood some tall celery stalks. In the centre of the table there stood, as sentries to a fruit-stand which upheld a pyramid of oranges and American apples, two squat old-fashioned decanters of cut glass, one containing port and the other dark sherry. On the closed square piano a pudding in a huge yellow dish lay in waiting and behind it were three squads of bottles of stout and ale and minerals, drawn up according to the colours of their uniforms, the first two black, with brown and red labels, the third and smallest squad white, with transverse green sashes.

Gabriel took his seat boldly at the head of the table and, having looked to the edge of the carver, plunged his fork firmly into the goose. He felt quite at ease now for he was an expert carver and liked nothing better than to find himself at the head of a well-laden table.

— Miss Furlong, what shall I send you? he asked. A wing or a slice of the breast?

— Just a small slice of the breast.

— Miss Higgins, what for you?

— O, anything at all, Mr Conroy.

While Gabriel and Miss Daly exchanged plates of goose and plates of ham and spiced beef Lily went from guest to guest with a dish of hot floury potatoes wrapped in a white napkin. This was Mary Jane's idea and she had also suggested apple sauce for the goose but Aunt Kate had

said that plain roast goose without apple sauce had always been good
enough for her and she hoped she might never eat worse. Mary Jane
waited on her pupils and saw that they got the best slices and Aunt Kate
and Aunt Julia opened and carried across from the piano bottles of stout
and ale for the gentlemen and bottles of minerals for the ladies. There
was a great deal of confusion and laughter and noise, the noise of orders
and counter-orders, of knives and forks, of corks and glass-stoppers. Gabriel began to carve second helpings as soon as he had finished the first
round without serving himself. Everyone protested loudly so that he
compromised by taking a long draught of stout for he had found the
carving hot work. Mary Jane settled down quietly to her supper but
Aunt Kate and Aunt Julia were still toddling round the table, walking
on each other's heels, getting in each other's way and giving each other
unheeded orders. Mr Browne begged of them to sit down and eat their
suppers and so did Gabriel but they said there was time enough so that,
at last, Freddy Malins stood up and, capturing Aunt Kate, plumped her
down on her chair amid general laughter.

When everyone had been well served Gabriel said, smiling:

— Now, if anyone wants a little more of what vulgar people call
stuffing let him or her speak.

A chorus of voices invited him to begin his own supper and Lily
came forward with three potatoes which she had reserved for him.

— Very well, said Gabriel amiably, as he took another preparatory
draught, kindly forget my existence, ladies and gentlemen, for a few
minutes.

He set to his supper and took no part in the conversation with which
the table covered Lily's removal of the plates. The subject of talk was the
opera company which was then at the Theatre Royal. Mr Bartell D'Arcy,
the tenor, a dark-complexioned young man with a smart moustache,
praised very highly the leading contralto of the company but Miss Furlong thought she had a rather vulgar style of production. Freddy Malins
said there was a negro chieftain singing in the second part of the Gaiety
pantomime who had one of the finest tenor voices he had ever heard.

— Have you heard him? he asked Mr Bartell D'Arcy across the
table.

— No, answered Mr Bartell D'Arcy carelessly.

— Because, Freddy Malins explained, now I'd be curious to hear
your opinion of him. I think he has a grand voice.

— It takes Teddy to find out the really good things, said Mr Browne
familiarly to the table.

— And why couldn't he have a voice too? asked Freddy Malins sharply. Is it because he's only a black?

Nobody answered this question and Mary Jane led the table back to the legitimate opera. One of her pupils had given her a pass for *Mignon.*° Of course it was very fine, she said, but it made her think of poor Georgina Burns. Mr Browne could go back farther still, to the old Italian companies that used to come to Dublin — Tietjens, Ilma de Murzka, Campanini, the great Trebelli, Giuglini, Ravelli, Aramburo.° Those were the days, he said, when there was something like singing to be heard in Dublin. He told too of how the top gallery of the old Royal used to be packed night after night, of how one night an Italian tenor had sung five encores to *Let Me Like a Soldier Fall,* introducing a high C every time, and of how the gallery boys would sometimes in their enthusiasm unyoke the horses from the carriage of some great *prima donna* and pull her themselves through the streets to her hotel. Why did they never play the grand old operas now, he asked, *Dinorah,*° *Lucrezia Borgia?*° Because they could not get the voices to sing them: that was why.

— O, well, said Mr Bartell D'Arcy, I presume there are as good singers to-day as there were then.

— Where are they? asked Mr Browne defiantly.

— In London, Paris, Milan, said Mr Bartell D'Arcy warmly. I suppose Caruso, for example, is quite as good, if not better than any of the men you have mentioned.

— Maybe so, said Mr Browne. But I may tell you I doubt it strongly.

— O, I'd give anything to hear Caruso sing, said Mary Jane.

— For me, said Aunt Kate, who had been picking a bone, there was only one tenor. To please me, I mean. But I suppose none of you ever heard of him.

— Who was he, Miss Morkan? asked Mr Bartell D'Arcy politely.

— His name, said Aunt Kate, was Parkinson. I heard him when he was in his prime and I think he had then the purest tenor voice that was ever put into a man's throat.

— Strange, said Mr Bartell D'Arcy. I never even heard of him.

Mignon: One of the most popular of nineteenth-century French operas (1866) by Ambroise Thomas.   **Tietjens, Ilma de Murzka, Campanini, the great Trebelli, Giuglini, Ravelli, Aramburo:** Famous nineteenth-century singers.   *Dinorah:* Popular name for *Le Pardon de Poërmel* (1859), a French opera in three acts, with music by Giacomo Meyerbeer.   *Lucrezia Borgia:* Italian opera based on Victor Hugo's *Lucrèce Borgia,* music by Gaetano Donizetti. First produced in Dublin in 1852.

— Yes, yes, Miss Morkan is right, said Mr Browne. I remember hearing of old Parkinson but he's too far back for me.

— A beautiful pure sweet mellow English tenor, said Aunt Kate with enthusiasm.

Gabriel having finished, the huge pudding was transferred to the table. The clatter of forks and spoons began again. Gabriel's wife served out spoonfuls of the pudding and passed the plates down the table. Midway down they were held up by Mary Jane, who replenished them with raspberry or orange jelly or with blancmange and jam. The pudding was of Aunt Julia's making and she received praises for it from all quarters. She herself said that it was not quite brown enough.

— Well, I hope, Miss Morkan, said Mr Browne, that I'm brown enough for you because, you know, I'm all brown.

All the gentlemen, except Gabriel, ate some of the pudding out of compliment to Aunt Julia. As Gabriel never ate sweets the celery had been left for him. Freddy Malins also took a stalk of celery and ate it with his pudding. He had been told that celery was a capital thing for the blood and he was just then under doctor's care. Mrs Malins, who had been silent all through the supper, said that her son was going down to Mount Melleray° in a week or so. The table then spoke of Mount Melleray, how bracing the air was down there, how hospitable the monks were and how they never asked for a penny-piece from their guests.

— And do you mean to say, asked Mr Browne incredulously, that a chap can go down there and put up there as if it were a hotel and live on the fat of the land and then come away without paying a farthing?

— O, most people give some donation to the monastery when they leave, said Mary Jane.

— I wish we had an institution like that in our Church, said Mr Browne candidly.

He was astonished to hear that the monks never spoke, got up at two in the morning and slept in their coffins. He asked what they did it for.

— That's the rule of the order, said Aunt Kate firmly.

— Yes, but why? asked Mr Browne.

Aunt Kate repeated that it was the rule, that was all. Mr Browne still seemed not to understand. Freddy Malins explained to him, as best he

---

Mount Melleray: Site of Trappist abbey in which Irish monks presided over a refuge for those needing care; according to Gifford, it was known as a refuge for well-to-do alcoholics.

could, that the monks were trying to make up for the sins committed by all the sinners in the outside world. The explanation was not very clear for Mr Browne grinned and said:

— I like that idea very much but wouldn't a comfortable spring bed do them as well as a coffin?

— The coffin, said Mary Jane, is to remind them of their last end.

As the subject had grown lugubrious it was buried in a silence of the table during which Mrs Malins could be heard saying to her neighbour in an indistinct undertone:

— They are very good men, the monks, very pious men.

The raisins and almonds and figs and apples and oranges and chocolates and sweets were now passed about the table and Aunt Julia invited all the guests to have either port or sherry. At first Mr Bartell D'Arcy refused to take either but one of his neighbours nudged him and whispered something to him upon which he allowed his glass to be filled. Gradually as the last glasses were being filled the conversation ceased. A pause followed, broken only by the noise of the wine and by unsettlings of chairs. The Misses Morkan, all three, looked down at the tablecloth. Someone coughed once or twice and then a few gentlemen patted the table gently as a signal for silence. The silence came and Gabriel pushed back his chair and stood up.

The patting at once grew louder in encouragement and then ceased altogether. Gabriel leaned his ten trembling fingers on the tablecloth and smiled nervously at the company. Meeting a row of upturned faces he raised his eyes to the chandelier. The piano was playing a waltz tune and he could hear the skirts sweeping against the drawing-room door. People, perhaps, were standing in the snow on the quay outside, gazing up at the lighted windows and listening to the waltz music. The air was pure there. In the distance lay the park where the trees were weighted with snow. The Wellington Monument wore a gleaming cap of snow that flashed westward over the white field of Fifteen Acres.°

He began:

— Ladies and Gentlemen.

— It has fallen to my lot this evening, as in years past, to perform a very pleasing task but a task for which I am afraid my poor powers as a speaker are all too inadequate.

— No, no! said Mr Browne.

— But, however that may be, I can only ask you to-night to take the

---

Fifteen Acres: A large open field in Phoenix Park that was the site of British military reviews and maneuvers.

will for the deed and to lend me your attention for a few moments while I endeavour to express to you in words what my feelings are on this occasion.

— Ladies and Gentlemen. It is not the first time that we have gathered together under this hospitable roof, around this hospitable board. It is not the first time that we have been the recipients — or perhaps, I had better say, the victims — of the hospitality of certain good ladies.

He made a circle in the air with his arm and paused. Everyone laughed or smiled at Aunt Kate and Aunt Julia and Mary Jane who all turned crimson with pleasure. Gabriel went on more boldly:

— I feel more strongly with every recurring year that our country has no tradition which does it so much honour and which it should guard so jealously as that of its hospitality. It is a tradition that is unique as far as my experience goes (and I have visited not a few places abroad) among the modern nations. Some would say, perhaps, that with us it is rather a failing than anything to be boasted of. But granted even that, it is, to my mind, a princely failing, and one that I trust will long be cultivated among us. Of one thing, at least, I am sure. As long as this one roof shelters the good ladies aforesaid — and I wish from my heart it may do so for many and many a long year to come — the tradition of genuine warm-hearted courteous Irish hospitality, which our forefathers have handed down to us and which we in turn must hand down to our descendants, is still alive among us.

A hearty murmur of assent ran round the table. It shot through Gabriel's mind that Miss Ivors was not there and that she had gone away discourteously: and he said with confidence in himself:

— Ladies and Gentlemen.

— A new generation is growing up in our midst, a generation actuated by new ideas and new principles. It is serious and enthusiastic for these new ideas and its enthusiasm, even when it is misdirected, is, I believe, in the main sincere. But we are living in a sceptical and, if I may use the phrase, a thought-tormented age: and sometimes I fear that this new generation, educated or hypereducated as it is, will lack those qualities of humanity, of hospitality, of kindly humour which belonged to an older day. Listening to-night to the names of all those great singers of the past it seemed to me, I must confess, that we were living in a less spacious age. Those days might, without exaggeration, be called spacious days: and if they are gone beyond recall let us hope, at least, that in gatherings such as this we shall still speak of them with pride and affection, still cherish in our hearts the memory of those dead and gone great ones whose fame the world will not willingly let die.

— Hear, hear! said Mr Browne loudly.

— But yet, continued Gabriel, his voice falling into a softer inflection, there are always in gatherings such as this sadder thoughts that will recur to our minds: thoughts of the past, of youth, of changes, of absent faces that we miss here to-night. Our path through life is strewn with many such sad memories: and were we to brood upon them always we could not find the heart to go on bravely with our work among the living. We have all of us living duties and living affections which claim, and rightly claim, our strenuous endeavours.

— Therefore, I will not linger on the past. I will not let any gloomy moralising intrude upon us here to-night. Here we are gathered together for a brief moment from the bustle and rush of our everyday routine. We are met here as friends, in the spirit of good-fellowship, as colleagues, also to a certain extent, in the true spirit of *camaraderie*, and as the guests of — what shall I call them? — the Three Graces of the Dublin musical world.

The table burst into applause and laughter at this sally. Aunt Julia vainly asked each of her neighbours in turn to tell her what Gabriel had said.

— He says we are the Three Graces, Aunt Julia, said Mary Jane.

Aunt Julia did not understand but she looked up, smiling, at Gabriel, who continued in the same vein:

— Ladies and Gentlemen.

— I will not attempt to play to-night the part that Paris played on another occasion. I will not attempt to choose between them. The task would be an invidious one and one beyond my poor powers. For when I view them in turn, whether it be our chief hostess herself, whose good heart, whose too good heart, has become a byword with all who know her, or her sister, who seems to be gifted with perennial youth and whose singing must have been a surprise and a revelation to us all tonight, or, last but not least, when I consider our youngest hostess, talented, cheerful, hard-working and the best of nieces, I confess, Ladies and Gentlemen, that I do not know to which of them I should award the prize.

Gabriel glanced down at his aunts and, seeing the large smile on Aunt Julia's face and the tears which had risen to Aunt Kate's eyes, hastened to his close. He raised his glass of port gallantly, while every member of the company fingered a glass expectantly, and said loudly:

— Let us toast them all three together. Let us drink to their health, wealth, long life, happiness and prosperity and may they long continue

to hold the proud and self-won position which they hold in their profession and the position of honour and affection which they hold in our
hearts.

All the guests stood up, glass in hand, and, turning towards the
three seated ladies, sang in unison, with Mr Browne as leader:

> *For they are jolly gay fellows,*
> *For they are jolly gay fellows,*
> *For they are jolly gay fellows,*
> *Which nobody can deny.*

Aunt Kate was making frank use of her handkerchief and even Aunt
Julia seemed moved. Freddy Malins beat time with his pudding-fork
and the singers turned towards one another, as if in melodious confer-
ence, while they sang, with emphasis:

> *Unless he tells a lie,*
> *Unless he tells a lie.*

Then, turning once more towards their hostesses, they sang:

> *For they are jolly gay fellows,*
> *For they are jolly gay fellows,*
> *For they are jolly gay fellows,*
> *Which nobody can deny.*

The acclamation which followed was taken up beyond the door of
the supper-room by many of the other guests and renewed time after
time, Freddy Malins acting as officer with his fork on high.

.   .   .   .

The piercing morning air came into the hall where they were standing so that Aunt Kate said:

— Close the door, somebody. Mrs Malins will get her death of cold.

— Browne is out there, Aunt Kate, said Mary Jane.

— Browne is everywhere, said Aunt Kate, lowering her voice.

Mary Jane laughed at her tone.

— Really, she said archly, he is very attentive.

— He has been laid on here like the gas, said Aunt Kate in the same
tone, all during the Christmas.

She laughed herself this time good-humouredly and then added
quickly:

— But tell him to come in, Mary Jane, and close the door. I hope to goodness he didn't hear me.

At that moment the hall-door was opened and Mr Browne came in from the doorstep, laughing as if his heart would break. He was dressed in a long green overcoat with mock astrakhan cuffs and collar and wore on his head an oval fur cap. He pointed down the snow-covered quay from where the sound of shrill prolonged whistling was borne in.

— Teddy will have all the cabs in Dublin out, he said.

Gabriel advanced from the little pantry behind the office, struggling into his overcoat and, looking round the hall, said:

— Gretta not down yet?

— She's getting on her things, Gabriel, said Aunt Kate.

— Who's playing up there? asked Gabriel.

— Nobody. They're all gone.

— O no, Aunt Kate, said Mary Jane. Bartell D'Arcy and Miss O'Callaghan aren't gone yet.

— Someone is strumming at the piano, anyhow, said Gabriel.

Mary Jane glanced at Gabriel and Mr Browne and said with a shiver:

— It makes me feel cold to look at you two gentlemen muffled up like that. I wouldn't like to face your journey home at this hour.

— I'd like nothing better this minute, said Mr Browne stoutly, than a rattling fine walk in the country or a fast drive with a good spanking goer between the shafts.

— We used to have a very good horse and trap at home, said Aunt Julia sadly.

— The never-to-be-forgotten Johnny, said Mary Jane, laughing.

Aunt Kate and Gabriel laughed too.

— Why, what was wonderful about Johnny? asked Mr Browne.

— The late lamented Patrick Morkan, our grandfather, that is, explained Gabriel, commonly known in his later years as the old gentleman, was a glue-boiler.

— O, now, Gabriel, said Aunt Kate, laughing, he had a starch mill.

— Well, glue or starch, said Gabriel, the old gentleman had a horse by the name of Johnny. And Johnny used to work in the old gentleman's mill, walking round and round in order to drive the mill. That was all very well; but now comes the tragic part about Johnny. One fine day the old gentleman thought he'd like to drive out with the quality to a military review in the park.

— The Lord have mercy on his soul, said Aunt Kate compassionately.

— Amen, said Gabriel. So the old gentleman, as I said, harnessed Johnny and put on his very best tall hat and his very best stock collar and drove out in grand style from his ancestral mansion somewhere near Back Lane, I think.

Everyone laughed, even Mrs Malins, at Gabriel's manner and Aunt Kate said:

— O now, Gabriel, he didn't live in Back Lane, really. Only the mill was there.

— Out from the mansion of his forefathers, continued Gabriel, he drove with Johnny. And everything went on beautifully until Johnny came in sight of King Billy's° statue: and whether he fell in love with the horse King Billy sits on or whether he thought he was back again in the mill, anyhow he began to walk round the statue.

Gabriel paced in a circle round the hall in his goloshes amid the laughter of the others.

— Round and round he went, said Gabriel, and the old gentleman, who was a very pompous old gentleman, was highly indignant. *Go on, sir! What do you mean, sir? Johnny! Johnny! Most extraordinary conduct! Can't understand the horse!*

The peals of laughter which followed Gabriel's imitation of the incident were interrupted by a resounding knock at the hall-door. Mary Jane ran to open it and let in Freddy Malins. Freddy Malins, with his hat well back on his head and his shoulders humped with cold, was puffing and steaming after his exertions.

— I could only get one cab, he said.

— O, we'll find another along the quay, said Gabriel.

— Yes, said Aunt Kate. Better not keep Mrs Malins standing in the draught.

Mrs Malins was helped down the front steps by her son and Mr Browne and, after many manœuvres, hoisted into the cab. Freddy Malins clambered in after her and spent a long time settling her on the seat, Mr Browne helping him with advice. At last she was settled comfortably and Freddy Malins invited Mr Browne into the cab. There was a good deal of confused talk, and then Mr Browne got into the cab. The cabman settled his rug over his knees, and bent down for the address.

King Billy: William of Orange, a Protestant king who won the Battle of the Boyne in 1690 and suppressed the Irish independent movement. The statue of Billy in College Green, like the statue of Lord Nelson in front of the post office, and the Wellington Monument were major irritations to Irish Catholics.

The confusion grew greater and the cabman was directed differently by Freddy Malins and Mr Browne, each of whom had his head out through a window of the cab. The difficulty was to know where to drop Mr Browne along the route and Aunt Kate, Aunt Julia and Mary Jane helped the discussion from the doorstep with cross-directions and contradictions and abundance of laughter. As for Freddy Malins he was speechless with laughter. He popped his head in and out of the window every moment, to the great danger of his hat, and told his mother how the discussion was progressing till at last Mr Browne shouted to the bewildered cabman above the din of everybody's laughter:

— Do you know Trinity College?

— Yes, sir, said the cabman.

— Well, drive bang up against Trinity College gates, said Mr Browne, and then we'll tell you where to go. You understand now?

— Yes, sir, said the cabman.

— Make like a bird for Trinity College.

— Right, sir, cried the cabman.

The horse was whipped up and the cab rattled off along the quay amid a chorus of laughter and adieus.

Gabriel had not gone to the door with the others. He was in a dark part of the hall gazing up the staircase. A woman was standing near the top of the first flight, in the shadow also. He could not see her face but he could see the terracotta and salmonpink panels of her skirt which the shadow made appear black and white. It was his wife. She was leaning on the banisters, listening to something. Gabriel was surprised at her stillness and strained his ear to listen also. But he could hear little save the noise of laughter and dispute on the front steps, a few chords struck on the piano and a few notes of a man's voice singing.

He stood still in the gloom of the hall, trying to catch the air that the voice was singing and gazing up at his wife. There was grace and mystery in her attitude as if she were a symbol of something. He asked himself what is a woman standing on the stairs in the shadow, listening to distant music, a symbol of. If he were a painter he would paint her in that attitude. Her blue felt hat would show off the bronze of her hair against the darkness and the dark panels of her skirt would show off the light ones. *Distant Music* he would call the picture if he were a painter.

The hall-door was closed; and Aunt Kate, Aunt Julia and Mary Jane came down the hall, still laughing.

— Well, isn't Freddy terrible? said Mary Jane. He's really terrible.

Gabriel said nothing but pointed up the stairs towards where his wife was standing. Now that the hall-door was closed the voice and the piano could be heard more clearly. Gabriel held up his hand for them to be silent. The song seemed to be in the old Irish tonality and the singer seemed uncertain both of his words and of his voice. The voice, made plaintive by distance and by the singer's hoarseness, faintly illuminated the cadence of the air with words expressing grief:

> *O, the rain falls on my heavy locks*
> *And the dew wets my skin,*
> *My babe lies cold . . .*°

— O, exclaimed Mary Jane. It's Bartell D'Arcy singing and he wouldn't sing all the night. O, I'll get him to sing a song before he goes.

— O do, Mary Jane, said Aunt Kate.

Mary Jane brushed past the others and ran to the staircase but before she reached it the singing stopped and the piano was closed abruptly.

— O, what a pity! she cried. Is he coming down, Gretta?

Gabriel heard his wife answer yes and saw her come down towards them. A few steps behind her were Mr Bartell D'Arcy and Miss O'Callaghan.

— O, Mr D'Arcy, cried Mary Jane, it's downright mean of you to break off like that when we were all in raptures listening to you.

— I have been at him all the evening, said Miss O'Callaghan, and Mrs Conroy too and he told us he had a dreadful cold and couldn't sing.

O, the rain falls on my heavy locks . . . cold . . . : Part of the refrain from "The Lass of Aughrim," a sad ballad about a young woman from a little village in the west of Ireland not far from Galway. The song relates how she is seduced and later abandoned with her baby in her arms. She visits Lord Gregory, the father-lover, who asks her a series of questions but does not allow her to visit him:

> Oh, Gregory, don't you remember
>   One night on the hill,
> When we swapped rings off each other's hands,
>   Sorely against my will?
> Mine was of the beaten gold,
>   Yours was but black tin.
> The dew wets my yellow locks,
>   The rain wets my skin,
>   The babe's cold in my arms,
>   Oh, Gregory, let me in!
>
> Oh if you be the lass of Aughrim,
>   As I suppose you not to be,
> Come tell me the last token
>   Between you and me.

After the lass is rejected by Lord Gregory, she and her son are drowned.

— O, Mr D'Arcy, said Aunt Kate, now that was a great fib to tell.

— Can't you see that I'm as hoarse as a crow? said Mr D'Arcy roughly.

He went into the pantry hastily and put on his overcoat. The others, taken aback by his rude speech, could find nothing to say. Aunt Kate wrinkled her brows and made signs to the others to drop the subject. Mr D'Arcy stood swathing his neck carefully and frowning.

— It's the weather, said Aunt Julia, after a pause.

— Yes, everybody has colds, said Aunt Kate readily, everybody.

— They say, said Mary Jane, we haven't had snow like it for thirty years; and I read this morning in the newspapers that the snow is general all over Ireland.

— I love the look of snow, said Aunt Julia sadly.

— So do I, said Miss O'Callaghan. I think Christmas is never really Christmas unless we have the snow on the ground.

— But poor Mr D'Arcy doesn't like the snow, said Aunt Kate, smiling.

Mr D'Arcy came from the pantry, fully swathed and buttoned, and in a repentant tone told them the history of his cold. Everyone gave him advice and said it was a great pity and urged him to be very careful of his throat in the night air. Gabriel watched his wife who did not join in the conversation. She was standing right under the dusty fanlight and the flame of the gas lit up the rich bronze of her hair which he had seen her drying at the fire a few days before. She was in the same attitude and seemed unaware of the talk about her. At last she turned towards them and Gabriel saw that there was colour on her cheeks and that her eyes were shining. A sudden tide of joy went leaping out of his heart.

— Mr D'Arcy, she said, what is the name of that song you were singing?

— It's called *The Lass of Aughrim,* said Mr D'Arcy, but I couldn't remember it properly. Why? Do you know it?

— *The Lass of Aughrim,* she repeated. I couldn't think of the name.

— It's a very nice air, said Mary Jane. I'm sorry you were not in voice to-night.

— Now, Mary Jane, said Aunt Kate, don't annoy Mr D'Arcy. I won't have him annoyed.

Seeing that all were ready to start she shepherded them to the door where good-night was said:

— Well, good-night, Aunt Kate, and thanks for the pleasant evening.

— Good-night, Gabriel. Good-night, Gretta!

— Good-night, Aunt Kate, and thanks ever so much. Good-night, Aunt Julia.

— O, good-night, Gretta, I didn't see you.

— Good-night, Mr D'Arcy. Good-night, Miss O'Callaghan.

— Good-night, Miss Morkan.

— Good-night, again.

— Good-night, all. Safe home.

— Good-night. Good-night.

The morning was still dark. A dull yellow light brooded over the houses and the river; and the sky seemed to be descending. It was slushy underfoot; and only streaks and patches of snow lay on the roofs, on the parapets of the quay and on the area railings. The lamps were still burning redly in the murky air and, across the river, the palace of the Four Courts° stood out menacingly against the heavy sky.

She was walking on before him with Mr Bartell D'Arcy, her shoes in a brown parcel tucked under one arm and her hands holding her skirt up from the slush. She had no longer any grace of attitude but Gabriel's eyes were still bright with happiness. The blood went bounding along his veins; and the thoughts went rioting through his brain, proud, joyful, tender, valorous.

She was walking on before him so lightly and so erect that he longed to run after her noiselessly, catch her by the shoulders and say something foolish and affectionate into her ear. She seemed to him so frail that he longed to defend her against something and then to be alone with her. Moments of their secret life together burst like stars upon his memory. A heliotrope envelope was lying beside his breakfast-cup and he was caressing it with his hand. Birds were twittering in the ivy and the sunny web of the curtain was shimmering along the floor: he could not eat for happiness. They were standing on the crowded platform and he was placing a ticket inside the warm palm of her glove. He was standing with her in the cold, looking in through a grated window at a man making bottles in a roaring furnace. It was very cold. Her face, fragrant in the cold air, was quite close to his; and suddenly she called out to the man at the furnace:

— Is the fire hot, sir?

But the man could not hear her with the noise of the furnace. It was just as well. He might have answered rudely.

the palace of the Four Courts: Irish law courts.

A wave of yet more tender joy escaped from his heart and went coursing in warm flood along his arteries. Like the tender fires of stars moments of their life together, that no one knew of or would ever know of, broke upon and illumined his memory. He longed to recall to her those moments, to make her forget the years of their dull existence together and remember only their moments of ecstasy. For the years, he felt, had not quenched his soul or hers. Their children, his writing, her household cares had not quenched all their souls' tender fire. In one letter that he had written to her then he had said: *Why is it that words like these seem to me so dull and cold? Is it because there is no word tender enough to be your name?*

Like distant music these words that he had written years before were borne towards him from the past. He longed to be alone with her. When the others had gone away, when he and she were in their room in the hotel, then they would be alone together. He would call her softly:

— Gretta!

Perhaps she would not hear at once: she would be undressing. Then something in his voice would strike her. She would turn and look at him. . . .

At the corner of Winetavern Street they met a cab. He was glad of its rattling noise as it saved him from conversation. She was looking out of the window and seemed tired. The others spoke only a few words, pointing out some building or street. The horse galloped along wearily under the murky morning sky, dragging his old rattling box after his heels, and Gabriel was again in a cab with her, galloping to catch the boat, galloping to their honeymoon.

As the cab drove across O'Connell Bridge Miss O'Callaghan said:

— They say you never cross O'Connell Bridge without seeing a white horse.

— I see a white man this time, said Gabriel.

— Where? asked Mr Bartell D'Arcy.

Gabriel pointed to the statue,° on which lay patches of snow. Then he nodded familiarly to it and waved his hand.

— Good-night, Dan, he said gaily.

When the cab drew up before the hotel Gabriel jumped out and, in spite of Mr Bartell D'Arcy's protest, paid the driver. He gave the man a shilling over his fare. The man saluted and said:

— A prosperous New Year to you, sir.

---

the statue: A statue of Daniel O'Connell (1775–1847), an Irish patriot for whom the central bridge in Ireland is named.

— The same to you, said Gabriel cordially.

She leaned for a moment on his arm in getting out of the cab and while standing at the curbstone, bidding the others good-night. She leaned lightly on his arm, as lightly as when she had danced with him a few hours before. He had felt proud and happy then, happy that she was his, proud of her grace and wifely carriage. But now, after the kindling again of so many memories, the first touch of her body, musical and strange and perfumed, sent through him a keen pang of lust. Under cover of her silence he pressed her arm closely to his side; and, as they stood at the hotel door, he felt that they had escaped from their lives and duties, escaped from home and friends and run away together with wild and radiant hearts to a new adventure.

An old man was dozing in a great hooded chair in the hall. He lit a candle in the office and went before them to the stairs. They followed him in silence, their feet falling in soft thuds on the thickly carpeted stairs. She mounted the stairs behind the porter, her head bowed in the ascent, her frail shoulders curved as with a burden, her skirt girt tightly about her. He could have flung his arms about her hips and held her still for his arms were trembling with desire to seize her and only the stress of his nails against the palms of his hands held the wild impulse of his body in check. The porter halted on the stairs to settle his guttering candle. They halted too on the steps below him. In the silence Gabriel could hear the falling of the molten wax into the tray and the thumping of his own heart against his ribs.

The porter led them along a corridor and opened a door. Then he set his unstable candle down on a toilet-table and asked at what hour they were to be called in the morning.

— Eight, said Gabriel.

The porter pointed to the tap of the electric-light and began a muttered apology but Gabriel cut him short.

— We don't want any light. We have light enough from the street. And I say, he added, pointing to the candle, you might remove that handsome article, like a good man.

The porter took up his candle again, but slowly for he was surprised by such a novel idea. Then he mumbled good-night and went out. Gabriel shot the lock to.

A ghostly light from the street lamp lay in a long shaft from one window to the door. Gabriel threw his overcoat and hat on a couch and crossed the room towards the window. He looked down into the street in order that his emotion might calm a little. Then he turned and leaned against a chest of drawers with his back to the light. She had taken off her hat and cloak and was standing before a large swinging mirror, un-hooking her waist. Gabriel paused for a few moments, watching her, and then said:

— Gretta!

She turned away from the mirror slowly and walked along the shaft of light towards him. Her face looked so serious and weary that the words would not pass Gabriel's lips. No, it was not the moment yet.

— You looked tired, he said.

— I am a little, she answered.

— You don't feel ill or weak?

— No, tired: that's all.

She went on to the window and stood there, looking out. Gabriel waited again and then, fearing that diffidence was about to conquer him, he said abruptly:

— By the way, Gretta!

— What is it?

— You know that poor fellow Malins? he said quickly.

— Yes. What about him?

— Well, poor fellow, he's a decent sort of chap after all, continued Gabriel in a false voice. He gave me back that sovereign I lent him and I didn't expect it really. It's a pity he wouldn't keep away from that Browne, because he's not a bad fellow at heart.

He was trembling now with annoyance. Why did she seem so abstracted? He did not know how he could begin. Was she annoyed, too, about something? If she would only turn to him or come to him of her own accord! To take her as she was would be brutal. No, he must see some ardour in her eyes first. He longed to be master of her strange mood.

— When did you lend him the pound? she asked, after a pause.

Gabriel strove to restrain himself from breaking out into brutal language about the sottish Malins and his pound. He longed to cry to her from his soul, to crush her body against his, to overmaster her. But he said:

— O, at Christmas, when he opened that little Christmas-card shop in Henry Street.

He was in such a fever of rage and desire that he did not hear her come from the window. She stood before him for an instant, looking at him strangely. Then, suddenly raising herself on tiptoe and resting her hands lightly on his shoulders, she kissed him.

— You are a very generous person, Gabriel, she said.

Gabriel, trembling with delight at her sudden kiss and at the quaint-ness of her phrase, put his hands on her hair and began smoothing it

back, scarcely touching it with his fingers. The washing had made it fine
and brilliant. His heart was brimming over with happiness. Just when he
was wishing for it she had come to him of her own accord. Perhaps her
thoughts had been running with his. Perhaps she had felt the impetuous
desire that was in him and then the yielding mood had come upon her.
Now that she had fallen to him so easily he wondered why he had been
so diffident.

He stood, holding her head between his hands. Then, slipping one
arm swiftly about her body and drawing her towards him, he said softly:

— Gretta dear, what are you thinking about?

She did not answer nor yield wholly to his arm. He said again, softly:

— Tell me what it is, Gretta. I think I know what is the matter. Do
I know?

She did not answer at once. Then she said in an outburst of tears:

— O, I am thinking about that song, *The Lass of Aughrim*.

She broke loose from him and ran to the bed and, throwing her
arms across the bed-rail, hid her face. Gabriel stood stock-still for a moment in astonishment and then followed her. As he passed in the way of
the cheval-glass he caught sight of himself in full length, his broad, well-
filled shirt-front, the face whose expression always puzzled him when he
saw it in a mirror and his glimmering gilt-rimmed eyeglasses. He halted
a few paces from her and said:

— What about the song? Why does that make you cry?

She raised her head from her arms and dried her eyes with the back
of her hand like a child. A kinder note than he had intended went into
his voice.

— Why, Gretta? he asked.

— I am thinking about a person long ago who used to sing that
song.

— And who was the person long ago? asked Gabriel, smiling.

— It was a person I used to know in Galway when I was living with
my grandmother, she said.

The smile passed away from Gabriel's face. A dull anger began to
gather again at the back of his mind and the dull fires of his lust began
to glow angrily in his veins.

— Someone you were in love with? he asked ironically.

— It was a young boy I used to know, she answered, named Michael Furey. He used to sing that song, *The Lass of Aughrim*. He was
very delicate.

Gabriel was silent. He did not wish her to think that he was interested in this delicate boy.

— I can see him so plainly, she said after a moment. Such eyes as he had: big dark eyes! And such an expression in them — an expression!

— O then, you were in love with him? said Gabriel.

— I used to go out walking with him, she said, when I was in Galway.

A thought flew across Gabriel's mind.

— Perhaps that was why you wanted to go to Galway with that Ivors girl? he said coldly.

She looked at him and asked in surprise:

— What for?

Her eyes made Gabriel feel awkward. He shrugged his shoulders and said:

— How do I know? To see him perhaps.

She looked away from him along the shaft of light towards the window in silence.

— He is dead, she said at length. He died when he was only seventeen. Isn't it a terrible thing to die so young as that?

— What was he? asked Gabriel, still ironically.

— He was in the gasworks,° she said.

Gabriel felt humiliated by the failure of his irony and by the evocation of this figure from the dead, a boy in the gasworks. While he had been full of memories of their secret life together, full of tenderness and joy and desire, she had been comparing him in her mind with another. A shameful consciousness of his own person assailed him. He saw himself as a ludicrous figure, acting as a pennyboy for his aunts, a nervous well-meaning sentimentalist, orating to vulgarians and idealising his own clownish lusts, the pitiable fatuous fellow he had caught a glimpse of in the mirror. Instinctively he turned his back more to the light lest she might see the shame that burned upon his forehead.

He tried to keep up his tone of cold interrogation but his voice when he spoke was humble and indifferent.

— I suppose you were in love with this Michael Furey, Gretta, he said.

— I was great with him at that time, she said.

Her voice was veiled and sad. Gabriel, feeling now how vain it would be to try to lead her whither he had purposed, caressed one of her hands and said, also sadly:

— And what did he die of so young, Gretta? Consumption, was it?

---

the gasworks: A plant for manufacturing coal gas.

— I think he died for me, she answered.

A vague terror seized Gabriel at this answer as if, at that hour when he had hoped to triumph, some impalpable and vindictive being was coming against him, gathering forces against him in its vague world. But he shook himself free of it with an effort of reason and continued to caress her hand. He did not question her again for he felt that she would tell him of herself. Her hand was warm and moist: it did not respond to his touch but he continued to caress it just as he had caressed her first letter to him that spring morning.

— It was in the winter, she said, about the beginning of the winter when I was going to leave my grandmother's and come up here to the convent. And he was ill at the time in his lodgings in Galway and wouldn't be let out and his people in Oughterard° were written to. He was in decline, they said, or something like that. I never knew rightly.

She paused for a moment and sighed.

— Poor fellow, she said. He was very fond of me and he was such a gentle boy. We used to go out together, walking, you know, Gabriel, like the way they do in the country. He was going to study singing only for his health. He had a very good voice, poor Michael Furey.

— Well; and then? asked Gabriel.

— And then when it came to the time for me to leave Galway and come up to the convent he was much worse and I wouldn't be let see him so I wrote a letter saying I was going up to Dublin and would be back in the summer and hoping he would be better then.

She paused for a moment to get her voice under control and then went on:

— Then the night before I left I was in my grandmother's house in Nuns' Island,° packing up, and I heard gravel thrown up against the window. The window was so wet I couldn't see so I ran downstairs as I was and slipped out the back into the garden and there was the poor fellow at the end of the garden, shivering.

—And did you not tell him to go back? asked Gabriel.

—I implored of him to go home at once and told him he would get his death in the rain. But he said he did not want to live. I can see his eyes as well as well! He was standing at the end of the wall where there was a tree.

—And did he go home? asked Gabriel.

—Yes, he went home. And when I was only a week in the convent

---

Oughterard: A village near Galway in the west of Ireland.   **Nuns' Island:** A section of Galway, named after Convent of the Poor Clares.

he died and he was buried in Oughterard where his people came from. O, the day I heard that, that he was dead!

She stopped, choking with sobs, and, overcome by emotion, flung herself face downward on the bed, sobbing in the quilt. Gabriel held her hand for a moment longer, irresolutely, and then, shy of intruding on her grief, let it fall gently and walked quietly to the window.

She was fast asleep.

Gabriel, leaning on his elbow, looked for a few moments un-resentfully on her tangled hair and half-open mouth, listening to her deep-drawn breath. So she had had that romance in her life: a man had died for her sake. It hardly pained him now to think how poor a part he, her husband, had played in her life. He watched her while she slept as though he and she had never lived together as man and wife. His curi-ous eyes rested long upon her face and on her hair: and, as he thought of what she must have been then, in that time of her first girlish beauty, a strange friendly pity for her entered his soul. He did not like to say even to himself that her face was no longer beautiful but he knew that it was no longer the face for which Michael Furey had braved death.

Perhaps she had not told him all the story. His eyes moved to the chair over which she had thrown some of her clothes. A petticoat string dangled to the floor. One boot stood upright, its limp upper fallen down: the fellow of it lay upon its side. He wondered at his riot of emo-tions of an hour before. From what had it proceeded? From his aunt's supper, from his own foolish speech, from the wine and dancing, the merry-making when saying good-night in the hall, the pleasure of the walk along the river in the snow. Poor Aunt Julia! She, too, would soon be a shade with the shade of Patrick Morkan and his horse. He had caught that haggard look upon her face for a moment when she was singing *Arrayed for the Bridal*. Soon, perhaps, he would be sitting in that same drawing-room, dressed in black, his silk hat on his knees. The blinds would be drawn down and Aunt Kate would be sitting beside him, crying and blowing her nose and telling him how Julia had died. He would cast about in his mind for some words that might console her, and would find only lame and useless ones. Yes, yes: that would happen very soon.

The air of the room chilled his shoulders. He stretched himself cau-tiously along under the sheets and lay down beside his wife. One by one they were all becoming shades. Better pass boldly into that other world, in the full glory of some passion, than fade and wither dismally with age. He thought of how she who lay beside him had locked in her heart for so many years that image of her lover's eyes when he had told her that he did not wish to live.

Generous tears filled Gabriel's eyes. He had never felt like that himself towards any woman but he knew that such a feeling must be love. The tears gathered more thickly in his eyes and in the partial darkness he imagined he saw the form of a young man standing under a dripping tree. Other forms were near. His soul had approached that region where dwell the vast hosts of the dead. He was conscious of, but could not apprehend, their wayward and flickering existence. His own identity was fading out into a grey impalpable world: the solid world itself which these dead had one time reared and lived in was dissolving and dwindling.

A few light taps upon the pane made him turn to the window. It had begun to snow again. He watched sleepily the flakes, silver and dark, falling obliquely against the lamplight. The time had come for him to set out on his journey westward. Yes, the newspapers were right: snow was general all over Ireland. It was falling on every part of the dark central plain, on the treeless hills, falling softly upon the Bog of Allen° and, farther westward, softly falling into the dark mutinous Shannon° waves. It was falling, too, upon every part of the lonely churchyard on the hill where Michael Furey lay buried. It lay thickly drifted on the crooked crosses and headstones, on the spears of the little gate, on the barren thorns. His soul swooned slowly as he heard the snow falling faintly through the universe and faintly falling, like the descent of their last end, upon all the living and the dead.

Bog of Allen: An extensive bog southwest of Dublin.   **Shannon:** Estuary of the River Shannon, on the southwest coast of Ireland.

PART TWO

"The Dead":
A Case Study in
Contemporary Criticism

A Critical History of
"The Dead"

I

"The Dead," composed in 1907, was the last story Joyce completed for his collection *Dubliners*. Joyce had planned the story in Rome in 1906–07, but it was completed while he was living in Trieste. Prior to adding "The Dead," Joyce wrote to Grant Richards, a London publisher, on May 5, 1906:

> My intention was to write a chapter of the moral history of my country and I chose Dublin for the scene because that city seemed to me the centre of paralysis. I have tried to present it to the indifferent public under four of its aspects: childhood, adolescence, maturity and public life. The stories are arranged in this order. I have written it for the most part in a style of scrupulous meanness and with the conviction that he is a very bold man who dares to alter in the presentment, still more to deform, whatever he has seen and heard.[1]

If in a sense the major character of *Dubliners*, including "The Dead," is the city of Dublin, the major antagonists are the British presence in Ireland and the Roman Catholic church in which Joyce was educated. He

[1]Richard Ellmann, ed., *The Letters of James Joyce*, vol. 2 (New York: Viking, 1966) 132.

wrote to Nora in August 1904: "My mind rejects the whole present social order and Christianity — home, the recognized virtues, classes of life, and religious doctrines."[2] In *Ulysses,* the semi-autobiographical Stephen Dedalus says, "I am a servant of two masters . . . an English and Italian . . . the imperial British state . . . and the holy Roman Catholic and apostolic church" (171).

Joyce struggled for nine years to get his book published after it was first accepted by Grant Richards in early 1906 before he wrote "The Dead," the fifteenth and last story. Asking if he might submit it originally as a collection of twelve stories, he wrote Richards:

> I do not think that any writer has yet presented Dublin to the world. It has been a capital of Europe for thousands of years; it is supposed to be the second city of the British Empire and it is nearly three times as big as Venice. Moreover, on account of many circumstances which I cannot detail here, the expression "Dubliner" seems to me to have some meaning and I doubt whether the same can be said for such words as "Londoner" and "Parisian" both of which have been used by writers as titles. (*Letters* 2:122)

In "Gabriel and Michael: The Conclusion of 'The Dead' " Florence L. Walzl explains the structure of *Dubliners* in 1906 prior to the addition of "The Dead":

> The 1905 version was highly symmetrical, consisting of an opening triad of stories of individual children ("The Sisters," "An Encounter," and "Araby"), a quartet of stories dealing with youthful men and women ("Eveline," "After the Race," "Two Gallants," and "The Boarding House"), another quartet picturing mature characters ("A Little Cloud," "Counterparts," "Clay," and "A Painful Case"), and a final triad dealing with public groups in public situations ("Ivy Day in the Committee Room," "A Mother," and "Grace"). The first and final triads obviously balance individuals and groups, and all the stories in the middle quartets are arranged in pairs contrasting sex, age, and social type or status. Also, the characterizations have a patterning that is unusual in short story collections. Though the protagonist of each story is a different character, all — children or adults — are variants of a basic type, a central everyman figure. Since each main character is older in the first eleven tales, a life cycle is presented. This chronological structure is matched to a thematic one of hemiplegia. The result is a

[2]Richard Ellmann, *James Joyce,* 1984 ed. (New York: Oxford UP, 1959; new and rev. 1984) 165.

progression in which children are depicted as disillusioned, youths as frustrated or trapped, men and women as passive and non-productive, and social groups as completely static. The central image of the book is a creeping paralysis that ends in a dead society.[3]

But "The Dead" extended the implications of moral and spiritual paralysis to the urban, bourgeoisie Dublin culture, even as it offered the possibility of love as an escape from that condition.

Even before "The Dead" was added in 1907, Richards's objections to certain passages as obscene drastically delayed publication. In particular, Richards objected to the story "Two Gallants," a passage in "Counterparts," and the word "bloody":

> Personally I prefer the word "bloody" in the places in which it occurs to any word you could substitute for it since it is, as you say, the right word; on the other hand a publisher has to be influenced by other considerations. Personally I have no objection to the other stories we have discussed, although I may say that in their present form they would damage their publisher. (274–75)

Joyce and Richards could not agree on changes, and in 1909 he entered into a publishing agreement with Messrs Maunsel, an Irish publisher, but that agreement got bogged down in a debate about a passage referring to Edward VII in "Ivy Day in the Committee Room." Later Messrs Maunsel wished him to omit "An Encounter," with its homosexual overtones; certain passages in "Two Gallants"; "The Boarding House"; and "A Painful Case"; and all references to names of businesses in Dublin. Eventually the book was printed according to Messrs Maunsel's stipulations; but when Joyce and the publisher couldn't come to an agreement about terms, all the copies were burned. Joyce retained the printed proof, which he submitted to Richards who finally published it in 1914.

II

Important to *Dubliners* and "The Dead" in particular is Joyce's concept of epiphany. In *Stephen Hero,* Joyce's earlier version of *A Portrait of the Artist as a Young Man,* Joyce defines the concept of epiphany:

[3]Florence L. Walzl, "Gabriel and Michael: The Conclusion of 'The Dead,' " *James Joyce Quarterly* 4 (1966): 17–31; see esp. 18.

By an epiphany he meant a sudden spiritual manifestation, whether in the vulgarity of speech or of gesture or in a memorable phase of the mind itself. . . . The three things requisite for beauty are, integrity, a wholeness, symmetry and radiance. . . . That is the first quality of beauty: it is declared in a simple sudden synthesis of the faculty which apprehends. What then? Analysis then. The mind considers the object in whole and in part, in relation to itself and to other objects, examines the balance of its parts, contemplates the form of the object, traverses every cranny of the structure. So the mind receives the impression of the symmetry of the object. The mind recognises that the object is in the strict sense of the word, a *thing*, a definitely constituted entity. You see? . . . Now for the third quality. . . . First we recognise that the object is *one* integral thing, then we recognise that it is an organised composite structure, a *thing* in fact: finally, when the relation of the parts is exquisite, when the parts are adjusted to the special point, we recognise that it is *that* thing which it is. Its soul, its whatness, leaps to us from the vestment of its appearance. The soul of the commonest object, the structure of which is so adjusted, seems to us radiant. The object achieves its epiphany.[4]

This concept comes from the manifestation of Christ to the gentiles in the person of the Magi or Wise Men, a manifestation celebrated by the Feast of the Epiphany. In the Greek drama, it refers to the moment when a god appears and imposes order on a chaotic or turbulent situation. While some critics have emphasized only the character's moment of awareness within the text, Joyce expected the reader to have her or his own revelatory moment of awareness that went beyond the character's and to see the plight of the central character from a larger and often ironic perspective.

In many stories, including "The Dead," the reader's epiphany is different from the character's epiphany; indeed, the reader's epiphany is an *awareness* of the limitations of the character's epiphany. Thus we understand that the retrospective narrator of "Araby" is reverting to the very Catholic epistemology that inscribed his conscience with guilt and anxiety: "Gazing up into the darkness I saw myself as a creature driven and derided by vanity; and my eyes burned with anguish and anger" (*Dubliners* 35) and we understand that in "Eveline" Eveline's epiphany is a catatonic moment and really no epiphany at all: "He rushed beyond the barrier and called to her to follow. He was shouted at to go on but

---

[4]Chester G. Anderson, ed., *A Portrait of the Artist as a Young Man: Text, Criticism, and Notes* (New York: Viking, 1968) 288–89.

he still called to her. She set her white face to him, passive, like a helpless animal. Her eyes gave him no sign of love or farewell or recognition" (41).

In "The Dead" Gabriel, after becoming *aware* of his limitations as a lover and public figure, lapses out of his paralytic self-consciousness to become part of the reality of being. In a sense, his epiphany is a necessary prelude to his suspension of ego and will. But the reader is aware that Joyce is performing the suspension of consciousness and moving beyond Gabriel's awareness to imply the value of human love, particularly between a man and a woman (a theme that is central to his later *Ulysses*). And Gabriel's moment of transcendence ironically joins him to all the actual dead, including Michael Furey, who have lived passionately, and all those living dead in the *Dubliners* who, like himself, have been constrained by Dublin's social and political milieu, including a debilitating Catholic education, the British presence in Ireland, and the Irish capacity for self-delusion.

III

"The Dead" has been read both as the last story of a closely integrated collection entitled *Dubliners* and as a separate story in its own right. Undoubtedly stimulated by *Ulysses* and the publication of Joyce's schema by Stuart Gilbert in his 1930 study *James Joyce's Ulysses: A Study* — which Joyce influenced — Richard Levin and Charles Shattuck in "First Flight to Ithaca"[5] stress parallels to the *Odyssey*. In 1931 Edmund Wilson in his chapter on James Joyce in *Axel's Castle* spoke of *Dubliners* as "a strong work of naturalistic fiction." Brewster Ghiselin's innovative 1956 essay argued convincingly for the unity of *Dubliners*:

> When the outlines of the symbolic pattern have been grasped, the whole unifying development will be discernible as a sequence of events in a moral drama, an action of the human spirit struggling for survival under peculiar conditions of deprivation, enclosed and disabled by a degenerate environment that provides none of the primary necessities of spiritual life. So understood, *Dubliners* will be seen for what it is, in effect, both a group of short stories and a novel, the separate histories of its protagonists composing one essential history, that of the soul of a people which has confused and

[5]Richard Levin and Charles Shattuck, "First Flight to Ithaca," *Two Decades of Criticism*, ed. Seon Givens (New York: Vanguard, 1948, 1963) 47–94.

weakened its relation to the source of spiritual life and cannot restore it.[6]

Also attentive to the unity of *Dubliners,* in 1969 Edward Brandabur
wrote of the relationship of the first three stories to what follows: "In
the first three stories of *Dubliners,* Joyce adumbrates the character of his
book as an evaluation of motive. 'The Sisters,' 'An Encounter,' 'Araby,'
all portray specific quests by sensitive young Dubliners who stand off
from a perverse environment with a degree of disengagement resem-
bling that of Joyce himself."[7]

The interpretive history of a text tells us as much about the values of
the critics at a particular time as it does about the text, and a major text
like "The Dead" becomes a way of seeing how critical fashions change
and contend. In the 1940–60 period, formalists like Allen Tate and
Kenneth Burke read "The Dead" in terms of its patterns of language
and internal structures, while under the influence of Richard Ellmann's
monumental biography *James Joyce,* published in 1959 and revised in
1982, historical and biographical scholars focused on Joyce's life and
the world in which he lived.

New Criticism, dominant in the 1950s and 1960s, saw a literary
work as an autonomous object — a "well-wrought urn" — and rejected
information about the author's life as biographical fallacy. In *The House
of Fiction,* a much used and admired anthology, Allen Tate writes a classic New Critical essay that praised "The Dead" as an example of a work
that used showing rather than telling: "All . . . we see is dramatized; it is
all made active. Nothing is given us from the externally omniscient
point of view."[8] New Critics believed that the unity and meaning of a
work are discovered by a close reading of its image patterns and that the
more a novel employed the aesthetic of consistent, dramatized point of
view — the aesthetic of Henry James — the better the work. In the formalist mode of the New Critics that values showing rather than telling,
Tate writes:

> In fact, from the beginning to the end of the story we are never
> told anything; we are shown everything. We are not told, for ex-
> ample, that the *milieu* of the story is the provincial, middle-class,

[6]Brewster Ghiselin, "The Unities of Joyce's *Dubliners,*" *Accent* 16 (1956) 75–88 and
196–213; see esp. 76.
[7]Robert Scholes and A. Walton Litz, eds., *James Joyce, Dubliners: Text, Criticism,
and Notes* (New York: Viking, 1968) 333.
[8]Allen Tate and Caroline Gordon, *The House of Fiction* (New York: Scribner's, 1950)
280.

"cultivated" society of Dublin at the turn of the century; we are not told that Gabriel represents its emotional sterility (as contrasted with the "peasant" richness of his wife Gretta), its complacency, its devotion to genteel culture, its sentimental evasion of "reality." All this we see dramatized; it is all made active.[9]

Many of the formalist critics of "The Dead" writing in the 1950s and 1960s — including Tate, Ghiselin, and Walzl — stressed the symbolic aspects of the text.

Aristotelian critics were more concerned with the evolving *agon* as it enacted the tale's values and the structure of effects and tended to be somewhat less interested in symbolism. Working in an Aristotelian mode, Kenneth Burke focuses on the effects of the text and its progress as a tripartite structure of effects as it moves from beginning to middle to end:

> In the first of its three parts, the keynote is expectancy, which is amplified by many appropriate details: talk of preparations, arrivals, introductions, apprehensions, while fittingly the section ends on an unfinished story. . . .
> The second stage, dealing with the party at its height, could be analysed almost as a catalogue of superficial socialities, each in its way slightly false or misfit.
> . . . But the third section concerns initiation into a mystery. It is to take us beyond the realm of realism, as so conceived, into the realm of *ideality*.[10]

Burke's focus is on what he calls significant form.

C. C. Loomis, in an important March 1960 *PMLA* essay entitled "Structure and Sympathy in 'The Dead'" builds on Burke's work on the structure of "The Dead." Writing in the formalist mode of the 1950s and 1960s, and using the vocabulary that values a dialogue between the particular and the general, he concludes,

> "The Dead" follows a logical pattern; we move from the general to the particular, then to a final universal. We see Gabriel's world generally; then we focus down to the particular, and from the combination of the general and particular we are given a universal symbol in the vision itself.
> The logic of "The Dead," however, is not the logic of mere in-

---

[9]Tate and Gordon 405.
[10]Kenneth Burke, *Perspectives by Incongruity*, ed. Stanley Edgar Hyman and Barbara Karmiller (Bloomington: Indiana UP, 1954) 145–47.

tellect; it is the logic which exists on a plane where intellectual perception and emotional intuition, form and content, blend.[11]

Any survey of Joyce criticism must acknowledge the eclectic criticism of Hugh Kenner. Beginning with *Dublin's Joyce* (1956) and including *Joyce's Voices* (1978), Hugh Kenner has contributed to our understanding of Joyce. Kenner finds in the latter part of *Dubliners* a "multiplication of spectres, of choices negated, passions unexplored, opportunities missed, aspects of the self denied" (*Dublin's Joyce* 480). Kenner coined what he called his "Uncle Charles principle" to argue that "the narrative idiom need not be the narrator's" (*Joyce's Voices* 18). When Joyce wants his narrator to show us how a character thinks or feels, his description of a character modifies the voice that is describing that character. Thus, the narrator would want us to see that it is Lily, not the narrator, who would use the word "literally" when "figuratively" is the proper word in the first sentence of "The Dead": "Lily, the caretaker's daughter, was literally run off her feet."

In part because *Ulysses* depends on what T. S. Eliot calls "the mythic method" to give a "shape and significance to the immense panorama of futility and anarchy which is contemporary history," critics have sought to discover structuring patterns of allusions in "The Dead."[12] Northrop Frye's influence in the late 1950s and 1960s was another stimulus to the search for recurring archetypes; his *Anatomy of Criticism* appeared in 1967. Florence L. Walzl's 1966 essay on the conclusion shows how, as the final story of *Dubliners,* "The Dead" is a crystallization of preceding themes and a story in its own right:

> In contrast to the stern role of the archangel Michael, Gabriel is a messenger angel associated with God's beneficence. In the Old Testament he is the angel sent to Daniel to interpret two great visions of salvation, one of them a Messianic prophecy.
> . . . The recollections of Christ's passion in the spears and thorns are reminders that sacrifice of self is the condition of revival. The judgment that Michael brings is a salvation, and Gabriel's swoon is a symbolic death from which he will rise revivified. Gabriel is rightly named: he is a figure of annunciation and new life. (29–30)

---

[11]C. C. Loomis, Jr., "Structure and Sympathy in Joyce's 'The Dead,' " *PMLA* 35 (1960): 149–51; see esp. 151.

[12]T. S. Eliot, "*Ulysses,* Order, and Myth," *Dial* 75 (1923): 480–83; rpt. as "Myth and Literary Classicism" in *The Modern Tradition: Backgrounds of Modern Literature,* ed. Richard Ellmann and Charles Feidelson, Jr. (New York: Oxford UP, 1965) 675–81.

Written at a time when ambiguity — a kind of charged ambiguity that allowed for contradictory readings — was a value, Walzl's essay argues for a reading that stresses *both* Gabriel's acceptance of his material conditions *and* his spiritual redemption: "*Dubliners* as a whole work suggests that Ireland betrays its children. 'The Dead' in this symbolic identification seems to imply that the Dubliner betrays Ireland. This is only one of the ambiguities that 'The Dead' offers" (27). In 1981 Donald T. Torchiana argued that Gabriel's life closely parallels that of St. Patrick and that at the end, unlike St. Patrick who converted the Irish, he undergoes a conversion by the Irish.[13]

IV

Richard Ellmann develops the crucial relationship between Joyce's life and work:

> In Gretta's old sweetheart, in Gabriel's letter, in the book reviews and the discussion of them, as well as in the physical image of Gabriel with hair parted in the middle and rimmed glasses, Joyce drew directly upon his own life. . . . Gabriel's quarrels with his mother also suggest John Joyce's quarrels with his mother, who never accepted her son's marriage to a woman of lower station.[14]

One of the great literary biographies of our time, Ellmann's study shows conclusively how Joyce's art draws upon his own experience growing up in Ireland. That we need to know about the author to know the work is often called expressionist criticism, a criticism that seeks to establish that the work is a psychic and moral gesture of the author's own emotional life. Relating the artist's life to his work is only one method and one that has often been called into question in the last several decades by both New Criticism and deconstruction. However, Joyce himself argued for the centrality of this approach in the crucial "Scylla and Charybdis" chapter of *Ulysses* where he and Stephen Dedalus read Shakespeare in expressionistic terms. Joyce believed that the writer of genius — such as Shakespeare or *himself* (Joyce did not suffer from paroxysms of false modesty) — "found in the world without as actual what was in his world within as possible" (*Ulysses* 9.1041–42) and that "his errors were volitional and the portals of discovery." It is worth noting that Joyce

[13]Donald T. Torchiana, "The Ending of 'The Dead': I Follow St. Patric," *James Joyce Quarterly* 18 (1981): 123–32.
[14]Ellmann 247.

wrote at a time when such an expressionistic approach was more in vogue. Indeed, contemporary Irish writers, and in particular Yeats who was a towering figure when Joyce reached maturity in 1898–1904, drew upon a wide range of personal and cultural references.

Of "The Dead" Ellmann writes:

> Although the story dealt mainly with three generations of his family in Dublin, it drew also upon an incident in Galway in 1903. There Michael ("Sonny") Bodkin courted Nora Barnacle; but he contracted tuberculosis and had to be confined to bed. Shortly afterwards Nora resolved to go to Dublin, and Bodkin stole out of his sickroom, in spite of the rainy weather, to sing to her under an apple tree and bid her good-by. In Dublin Nora soon learned that Bodkin was dead, and when she met Joyce she was first attracted to him, as she told a sister, because he resembled Sonny Bodkin.[15]

Certainly Joyce's wonder at and passion for Nora, a simple country girl who was socially beneath the pretensions of the Joyce family, find their way into the portrait of Gretta and into her relationship with Gabriel. Joyce's unjustified and irrational jealousy of possible rivals for Nora is repeated in the text. When Joyce wrote "The Dead" Gabriel, a high school teacher and writer of minor reviews, was the kind of bourgeois figure Joyce feared becoming. Of the ending, Ellmann writes,

> From a biographical point of view, these final pages compose one of Joyce's several tributes to his wife's artless integrity. Nora Barnacle, in spite of her defects of education, was independent, unselfconscious, instinctively right. Gabriel acknowledges the same coherence in his own wife, and he recognizes in the west of Ireland, in Michael Furey, a passion he has himself always lacked.[16]

Brenda Maddox's important *Nora: The Real Life of Molly Bloom* also offers insight on the relationship between the fictional Gretta and the actual Nora:

> If Nora did go direct from her late grandmother's house to the Presentation Convent, it means that the events upon which Joyce drew for the background of his most famous short story, "The Dead," took place just before her thirteenth birthday. The details of her life in that year fit the story well. . . .
>   The proximity of Michael Feeney's death in February to that of Nora's grandmother on New Year's Day and the occasion of

[15]Ellmann 243.
[16]Ellmann 249.

her leaving her grandmother's home make Feeney a closer model for the fictional Michael Furey than Nora's later admirer, Michael Bodkin, who has been widely cast in the part. . . .

In all likelihood, Joyce fused Nora's memories of her two last friends.[17]

Over the past fifty years, literary criticism has oscillated between the poles of formalism (close scrutiny of the text as an independent imagined ontology) and contextualism (placing a work in the context of cultural, historical, biographical, and socioeconomical contexts). Recently, as deconstructive formalism has receded, more emphasis has been placed on historical and literary contexts. Because of Ellmann's work, the emphasis on the world in which Joyce lived was never neglected as much as the world of many other modernists. Important studies stressing cultural contexts include Donald T. Torchiana's *Backgrounds for Joyce's "Dubliners"* (1986). R. B. Kershner has put "The Dead" in the context of popular culture in *Joyce, Bakhtin, and Popular Culture* (1989). For example, Kershner points out a parallel between Bret Harte's *Gabriel Conroy* (1871) and the three operas invoked by Mary Jane and Mr. Browne, *Mignon, Dinorah*, and *Lucrezia Borgia*, and reminds us that they

> turn upon the figure of the passionate, unrecognized woman whose love is not reciprocated; in all three death threatens as a result of the young man's failure to recognize the woman and her passion. . . . The main force of the operatic intertexts, like that of Harte's novel, is to suggest that there is a fundamental sexual reversal in "The Dead"; once Gabriel learns to speak as Woman, the intertextual tensions are resolved, though perhaps at the price of "the descent of their last end, upon all the living and the dead."[18]

The movement away from pure formalism has been stimulated by the rediscovery of the work of the Russian critic M. M. Bakhtin. Bakhtin argues that a text is a contending field where diverse ways of telling to which the author was exposed interact; this interaction or dialogism is called *heteroglossia:*

> Thus at any given moment of its historical existence, language is heteroglot from top to bottom: it represents the co-existence of socio-ideological contradictions between the present and the past,

[17]Brenda Maddox, *Nora: The Real Life of Molly Bloom* (Boston: Houghton, 1988) 16–17.

[18]R. B. Kershner, *Joyce, Bakhtin, and Popular Literature: Chronicles of Disorder* (Chapel Hill and London: U of North Carolina P, 1989) 150.

between differing epochs of the past, between different socio-
ideological groups in the present, between tendencies, schools, circles and so forth, all given a bodily form. These "languages" of
heteroglossia intersect each other in a variety of ways, forming
new socially typifying "languages."

Each of these "languages" of heteroglossia requires a method-
ology very different from the others; each is grounded in a completely different principle for marking differences and for establishing units (for some this principle is functional, in others it is the
principle of theme and content, in yet others it is, properly speaking, a socio-dialectological principle). Therefore languages do not
exclude each other, but rather intersect with each other in many
different ways. . . .

. . . All languages of heteroglossia, whatever the principle underlying them and making each unique, are specific points of view
on the world, forms for conceptualizing the world in words, specific world views, each characterized by its own objects, meanings
and values. As such they all may be juxtaposed to one another,
mutually supplement one another, contradict one another and be
interrelated dialogically. As such they encounter one another and
co-exist in the consciousness of real people — first and foremost,
in the creative consciousness of people who write novels. As such,
these languages live a real life, they struggle and evolve in an environment of social heteroglossia. Therefore they are all able to
enter into the unitary plane of the novel, which can unite in itself
parodic stylizations of generic languages, various forms of stylizations and illustrations of professional and period-bound languages,
the languages of particular generations, of social dialects and others
(as occurs, for example, in the English comic novel). They may all
be drawn in by the novelist for the orchestration of his themes
and for the refracted (indirect) expression of his intentions and
values.[19]

In "The Dead" we see multiple kinds of discourse in a dialogue in
which they struggle for position and interaction; remnants of Gabriel's
Catholic education; his university education, including Elizabethan language; the language of Irish music; performative, non-syntactical language; the language of fastidious manners as well as the language of
passion; the language of nineteenth-century literary materialism and its
opposite, aestheticism; the discourse of Irish nationalism and the Celtic
Renaissance, including the Celtic language itself; and the language of

[19]M. M. Bakhtin, *The Dialogic Imagination,* ed. Michael Holquist, trans. Caryl Emerson and Michael Holquist (Austin: U of Texas P, 1981) 291–92.

desire and sexuality. Kershner's work also shows the importance of
Bakhtin and his theory of heteroglossia. According to Bakhtin, novels
are not monologic, but dialogic in that they contain a dialogue among
diverse styles. According to Kershner,

> On the one hand Gabriel's experience is shaped by the series of
> outwardly manifest dialogical encounters with others, culminating
> in his dialogue with his wife; on the other, his perceptions are in-
> creasingly dominated by an internal dialogue between his everyday
> inner monologue and the disturbing, unwonted inner voice that
> calls him lyrically to the outdoors, to the snow, to the west, and to
> the dead. (139–40)

As Kershner explains,

> For Bakhtin, both written and spoken language and inner mono-
> logue are made up of a great variety of conflicting variants —
> "languages" of officialdom, vernaculars, occupational jargons,
> technical, literary, and subliterary languages, all polyphonically re-
> sounding. (15)

In a recent interesting essay, which combines Bakhtinian aspects
with the Aristotelian focus on how narration persuades readers, "Distant Music: Sound and the Dialogics of Satire in 'The Dead,' "[20] Bruce
Avery argues that while "most critics argue that the story creates a perspective that invites some kind of judgment of Gabriel, one that the
narrator makes and seeks to implicate the reader in: either Gabriel
achieves transcendence or he does not," he also argues that "we need to
look at Gabriel and the narrator differently, because the narrator does
not implicate us in a judgment of Gabriel for the simple reason that by
the end of 'The Dead,' he is unable to make any judgment of his own
for fear that in so doing he would invite the same fate for himself"
(473). At the ending, the narrator shifts attention:

> Whereas before the narrator's discourse concentrated on its dia-
> logue with the discourse of Gabriel and the other characters, tak-
> ing for granted, as it were, its position relative to the listeners,
> now it has entered a new dialogue, this time attentive to its dis-
> tance from the *listener*. Having constructed a discourse which says
> that the petty elitism of Gabriel results in both self-deception and
> isolation from everyone else, including Gretta, the narrator has

[20]Bruce Avery, "Distant Music: Sound and the Dialogics of Satire in 'The Dead,' "
James Joyce Quarterly 28.2 (1991): 473–83.

aligned himself and his listener (or reader) with a specific conceptual horizon — one which condemns elitism. . . .

. . . We are left pondering whether perhaps, in these final pages of "The Dead," Joyce heard in the echoes of his "moral history" a voice too much like his own sounding too much like the voice of judgment — too much, in fact, like Gabriel. Perhaps then he began to see and hear Dublin in a way that would stir him to write the more compassionate history he would come to call *Ulysses*. (Avery 481–82)

With the development of women's studies in the past decade, Joyce's view of women and heterosexual relationships has come in for considerable reevaluation. As Richard Brown has pointed out, "the story of Gabriel Conroy seems tailor-made for feminist interpretation. Gabriel's evening consists of a succession of significant encounters with women."[21] In an insightful study, "Joyce and Lacan: 'The Woman' as a Symptom of 'Masculinity' in 'The Dead,' " Garry Leonard applies the theories of the French psychoanalyst Jacques Lacan — theories that have become increasingly influential in literary studies in the past decade — to "The Dead." Lacan has argued that for males, women are a function of their phallic sexuality, and women are reinvented by males to fill an absence they experience in their consciousness. Of the ending of "The Dead" Leonard writes,

> Gabriel believes the time has come for him to set out on his journey westward: away from the Dublin / fictional self that he thought he knew, towards the Galway / want-in-being that he has refused to acknowledge. He must read the censored chapters of his history, the ones that refute the unity of his subjective consciousness and are therefore not consciously known. Joyce ends "The Dead" with Gabriel adrift between the "lumber room" of the unconscious and subjective consciousness: his fictional unity, what a woman is a symbol of, cannot, for the moment, be found.[22]

Important feminist studies include the collection *Women in Joyce,* edited by Suzette Henke and Elaine Unkeless (1982) and Bonnie Kime Scott's *Joyce and Feminism* (1984). An example of recent feminist criticism is Ruth Bauerle's "Date Rape, Mate Rape: A Liturgical Interpretation of 'The Dead,' " *New Alliances in Joyce Studies,* edited by Bonnie

[21]Richard Brown, *James Joyce and Sexuality* (Cambridge: Cambridge UP, 1985) 92.
[22]Garry Leonard, "Joyce and Lacan: 'The Woman' as a Symptom of 'Masculinity' in 'The Dead,' " *James Joyce Quarterly* 28.2 (1991): 451–72.

Kime Scott (113–25), which examines biographical evidence, including the relationship between Joyce's father and mother. She sees Gabriel as betrayer, seducer, and even rapist. Stressing the role of women in "The Dead," Kershner writes, "The paradox of 'The Dead' — that within a society in which women are disempowered there should arise an opposing imaginative scenario in which women are omnipotent — is wholly parallel to the original paradox of courtly love to which Lacan points in an analysis of the phenomenon's historical rise" (147).

In recent years, critics have been more aware of the continuity of Joyce's major works — *Dubliners, A Portrait of the Artist as a Young Man, Ulysses,* and *Finnegans Wake* — and of how *Dubliners* anticipates these later, more experimental texts. Recent work on "The Dead" has reflected the theoretical explosion of the past two decades. Indeed, recent critics stressed the text as an example of theoretical models. Colin MacCabe's work demonstrates the influence of deconstruction: "Language introduces us to an existence which can never be satisfied, for, as a condition of our speech, something is always missing."[23] MacCabe makes the further point that "in Joyce's text the division between signifier and signified becomes an area in which the reader is in (and at) play — producing meaning through his or her own activity."[24]

In *Joyce Between Freud and Jung* (1980) and a subsequent study of Joyce and Lacan, *The Veil of Signs: Joyce, Lacan, and Perception* (1991), Sheldon Brivic has written compellingly of the importance of seeing Joyce in the context of twentieth-century psychology. Suzette A. Henke in "James Joyce and Women: The Matriarchal Muse,"[25] was among the first to discuss the possibilities of Lacan for Joyce studies.

V

Much of the criticism has focused on the ending. The debate is whether Gabriel can escape the sterile and paralyzed world of Dublin or whether he remains locked in his narcissistic prize. One can locate two basic strands of the first argument, the dominant one that Gabriel achieves heroic transcendence and achieves a new level of self-knowl-

---

[23]Colin MacCabe, *James Joyce and the Revolution of the Word* (New York: Harper, 1979) 2.
[24]MacCabe 2.
[25]Suzette A. Henke, "James Joyce and Women: The Matriarchal Muse," *Work-in-Progress: Joyce Centenary Essays,* ed. Richard Peterson, Alan M. Cohn, and Edmund L. Epstein (Carbondale: Southern Illinois UP, 1983) 117–31.

edge as he transcends his material circumstances. A somewhat different version of the argument that Gabriel escapes his confining world is that he moves to a more authentic awareness of his material existence rather than to an epiphanic revelation. In an influential study, *A Reader's Guide to James Joyce,* William York Tindall focuses upon symbolic patterns of imagery and speaks of Gabriel's "enlargement" and moral expansion: "Gabriel, facing reality at last, goes westward to encounter life and death."[26] Ellmann focuses on the westward journey to "the place where life had been lived simply and passionately" (249). But on occasion even a humanistic critic demurs from either version of this optimistic reading; Charles Peake, in *James Joyce: The Citizen and the Artist,* believes that Gabriel's "swooning surrender" is not a "vision of reconciliation."[27] And Edward Brandabur argues that "Gabriel anticipates the paralysis which will befall him. . . . Throughout the story, personal encounters disturb his poise until he finally gives in to the annihilation he has not only anticipated but invited."[28] Phillip Herring argues that "Isolated by education, temperament, and egotism, Conroy is defeated by forces that conspire against him, and by his ultimate awareness of inadequacy as a man."[29]

Vincent P. Pecora stresses uncertainty in "The Dead." Contrary to most prior criticism, in " 'The Dead' and the Generosity of the Word," Pecora argues that

> In fact, however, Gabriel in no way overcomes or transcends the conditions of his existence. Rather, he merely recapitulates them unconsciously in this self-pitying fantasy. . . . Moreover, he appears completely assured of the sincerity of his gesture. That is, Gabriel has reproduced in himself, like his vision of Michael Furey, the most fundamental structuring device for heroism, generosity, self-knowledge, and spiritual transcendence in his culture: the story of Christ. . . . If Gabriel fools himself, if in the very process that we accept as self-discovery he only reimplicates himself blindly in the cultural conditions he longs to transcend, then we may simply be doing the same thing, in our reading, in our lives. And if it is the Christlike "hero" who is "the bloodiest imposter of all,"

[26] William York Tindall, *A Reader's Guide to James Joyce* (New York: Farrar, 1959) 46.

[27] Charles Peake, *James Joyce: The Citizen and the Artist* (Stanford: Stanford UP, 1977) 53.

[28] Edward Brandabur, *A Scrupulous Meanness: A Study of James Joyce's Early Work* (Chicago: U of Illinois P, 1971) 116.

[29] Phillip F. Herring, *Joyce's Uncertainty Principle* (Princeton: Princeton UP, 1987) 71.

then we are forced to question one of the most deeply embedded institutions of his entire culture — and ours. Gabriel may see "mystical" union with all humanity as the only possible escape from the real humiliation of his Dublin life. The question remains, Must we escape with him?[30]

Pecora's work is also symptomatic of placing readings in the context of the intellectual tradition of modernism:

> My reading of "The Dead" is grounded in Nietzsche's response to Schopenhauer's "ascetic ideal" and the Christian tradition as simultaneously powerful negations and unconscious preservations of suffering existence (see esp. third essay in *On the Genealogy of Morals,* "What Is the Meaning of Ascetic Ideals" 97–163). (243–44)

Pecora identifies himself with what he calls "Joseph Buttigieg's antihumanist reappraisal of Joyce's work, with lenses provided by Nietzsche."[31] His is an example of a deconstructive reading which, rather than confine itself to the text, traces an elaborate pattern of intertextual relations that establish a rhetorical argument in opposition to the usually construed reading of the central *agon.*

John Paul Riquelme has written an excellent response to Pecora in "Joyce's 'The Dead': The Dissolution of the Self and the Police."[32] Riquelme takes issue with Pecora's view that "the self in 'The Dead' is dissolved into exhaustion and incoherence." He believes that Pecora attributes thoughts to Gabriel that might be more adequately assigned to the narrator:

> The death signaled in Joyce's story by the dissolving of the self and by the intensified use of free indirect style tends to reverse rather than to reinforce some conventional attitudes. As the vehicle for communicating and transferring the reversal to the reader, free indirect style is central to the effect that "The Dead" has on the living. (Riquelme 489)

Influenced by the work of Stephen Greenblatt — especially his *Renaissance Self-Fashioning: From More to Shakespeare* — the New Historians have emphasized the micropolitical implications of texts and have

---

[30]Vincent P. Pecora, " 'The Dead' and the Generosity of the Word," *PMLA* 101:2 (1986): 243.

[31]See Joseph Buttigieg, "The Struggle against Meta (Phantasma)-physics: Nietzsche, Joyce and the 'Excess of History,' " *Boundary* 2.10 (1981): 187–204.

[32]J. P. Riquelme, "Joyce's 'The Dead': The Dissolution of the Self and the Police," *Style* 25.3 (1991): 489–505.

stressed how texts both reveal and conceal hidden power relations among socioeconomic groups and genders. New historicism and its critical companion, cultural criticism, focus on the suppressive and repressive role of the church; the relationship between rural Ireland and Dublin; and the debate between Joyce's view that Ireland should be a European country and Yeats's view that it should be a separate Celtic country. In this mode Gabriel is a dominating male in a sexist exploitive society, and the culture of Dublin is examined in terms of failed capitalism. Thus Riquelme contends that "Gabriel has the disposable income and the time to purchase goods and engage in activities intended to promote health, fitness, and longevity. He participates in cultural mythology about improving and prolonging life that includes a denial of death" (489). As I argue in my essay in this volume, Gabriel's fortunes in his own mind are interconnected with his fears about the economic fortunes of his extended family: the three spinsters who run the music school and who are hosting an annual party, a party that is really an advertisement.

VI

Critics have differed over the meaning of the snow. David Daiches argued in *The Novel and the Modern World* (1939) that the snow represents "Gabriel's new sense of identity with the world, of the breakdown of the circle of his egoism."[33] For Allen Tate, snow stands for "Gabriel's escape from his ego in a larger world of humanity" (409). He argues for the centrality of the snow imagery:

> The snow is the story. . . . At the beginning, the snow is the cold and even hostile force of nature, humanly indifferent, enclosing the warm conviviality of the Misses Morkan's party. But just as the human action in which Gabriel is involved develops in the pattern of the plot of Reversal, his situation at the end being the opposite of its beginning, so the snow reverses its meaning, in a kind of rhetorical dialectic: from naturalistic *coldness* it develops into a symbol of warmth, of expanded consciousness; it stands for Gabriel's escape from his own ego into the larger world of humanity, including "all the living and the dead." (282)

For Kenneth Burke the snow is a mythic image by which he transcends Gabriel's conditional and materialistic world: "We return to the

[33]David Daiches, *The Novel and the Modern World* (Chicago: U of Chicago P, 1939) 99.

topic of snow, which becomes the *mythic image,* in the world of conditions, standing for the transcendence above the conditioned" (150).
For William York Tindall it represents life and death. In his *The Literary
Symbol,*[34] he discusses how the story occurs during Christmas season, "a
season of birth and of the year's death" (225). Snow thaws to become
water, a traditional image of life, suggesting life and hope despite its
death-like whiteness and coldness. Gabriel's vision of the falling snow
becomes, for Tindall, "an acceptance of death as a part of life" (227).
Somewhat in agreement with Tindall, Richard Ellmann believes that the
snow represents "mutuality" between the dead and the living, "a sense
of their connection with each other, a sense that none has his being
alone" (251), and he stresses that "The snow does not stand alone in
the story. It is part of the complex imagery that includes heat and cold
air, fire, and rain, as well as snow" (251). By contrast, Charles Peake
contends that snow represents "Dublin as a moribund city" and argues
that it is an image for "a people who have allowed their lives to be an-
nexed by the dead" (53). For Hugh Kenner, Gabriel's desire to be alone
in the snow is a longing for death indicated by the fact that he "pursues
the 'wayward and flickering existence' of the dead."[35]

VII

To conclude: "The Dead" is among the most read short novels in
English. It has wide appeal to students because it dramatizes emotions
that most of us share: love, hope, passion, insecurity, jealousy, a sense
that our lives are not turning out as we wish, and a fear that our dreams
will end in failure and compromise. For high school and college students, Gabriel is an example of a man who has compromised in both his
career and personal aspirations. "The Dead" has brought pleasure and
insight to generations of readers, and it has provided food for critical
speculation and hermeneutical exercises. Its multiple perspectives, dense
linguistic texture, and complex unity remind us that "The Dead" was
written as Picasso was experimenting with his great study of sexuality,
Les Demoiselles d'Avignon (1907) and remind us, too, that Thomas
Mann would soon write *Death in Venice* (1912), his tale of debilitating
repression. That each critical approach finds a rich source in "The

---

[34]William York Tindall, *The Literary Symbol* (New York: Columbia UP, 1955)
224–28.
    [35]Hugh Kenner, *Dublin's Joyce,* (1956; Boston: Beacon, 1962) 68.

Dead" is testimony to its complexity, subtlety, and appeal as a human story.

Daniel R. Schwarz

WORKS CITED

Anderson, Chester G., ed. *A Portrait of the Artist as a Young Man: Text, Criticism, and Notes.* New York: Viking, 1968.

Avery, Bruce. "Distant Music: Sound and the Dialogics of Satire in 'The Dead.' " *James Joyce Quarterly* 28.2 (1991): 473–83.

Bakhtin, M. M. *The Dialogic Imagination.* Ed. Michael Holquist. Trans. Caryl Emerson and Michael Holquist. Austin: U of Texas P, 1981.

Bauerle, Ruth. "Date Rape, Mate Rape: A Liturgical Interpretation of 'The Dead.' " *New Alliances in Joyce Studies.* Ed. Bonnie Kime Scott. Newark: U of Delaware P, 1988. 113–25.

Brandabur, Edward. *A Scrupulous Meanness: A Study of James Joyce's Early Work.* Chicago: U of Illinois P, 1971.

Brivic, Sheldon. *Joyce Between Freud and Jung.* New York: Kennickat, 1980.

———. *The Veil of Signs: Joyce, Lacan, and Perception.* Urbana: U of Illinois P, 1991.

Brown, Richard. *James Joyce and Sexuality.* Cambridge: Cambridge UP, 1985.

Burke, Kenneth. *Perspectives by Incongruity.* Ed. Stanley Edgar Hyman and Barbara Karmiller. Bloomington: Indiana UP, 1954.

Buttigieg, Joseph. "The Struggle against Meta (Phantasma)-physics: Nietzsche, Joyce and the 'Excess of History.' " *Boundary* 2.10 (1981): 187–204.

Daiches, David. *The Novel and the Modern World.* Chicago: U of Chicago P, 1939.

Eliot, T. S. "*Ulysses,* Order, and Myth." *Dial* 75 (1923): 480–83. Rpt. as "Myth and Literary Criticism." *The Modern Tradition: Backgrounds of Modern Literature.* Ed. Richard Ellmann and Charles Feidelson, Jr. New York: Oxford UP, 1965.

Ellmann, Richard. *James Joyce.* Rev. ed. New York: Oxford UP, 1984.

Ellmann, Richard, ed. *The Letters of James Joyce.* 3 vols. New York: Viking, 1966.

Frye, Northrup. *Anatomy of Criticism: Four Essays*. Princeton: Princeton UP, 1957.

Ghiselin, Brewster. "The Unities of Joyce's *Dubliners*." *Accent* 16 (1956): 15–88, 196–213.

Gilbert, Stuart. *James Joyce's Ulysses: A Study*. Rev. ed. New York: Random, 1955.

Greenblatt, Stephen Jay. *Renaissance Self-Fashioning: From More to Shakespeare*. Chicago: U of Chicago P, 1980.

Henke, Suzette A. "James Joyce and Women: The Matriarchal Muse," *Work-in-Progress: Joyce Centenary Essays*. Ed. Richard Peterson, Alan M. Cohn, and Edmund L. Epstein. Carbondale: Southern Illinois UP, 1983. 117–31.

Henke, Suzette, and Elaine Unkeless, eds. *Women in Joyce*. Urbana: U of Illinois P, 1982.

Herring, Phillip F. *Joyce's Uncertainty Principle*. Princeton: Princeton UP, 1987.

Joyce, James. *Dubliners: Text, Criticism, and Notes*. Ed. Robert Scholes and A. Walton Litz. New York: Viking, 1968.

Kenner, Hugh. *Dublin's Joyce*. 1956. Boston: Beacon, 1962.

———. *Joyce's Voices*. Berkeley: U of California P, 1978.

———. "Molly's Masterstroke." *Fifty Years: Ulysses*. Ed. Thomas Staley. Bloomington: Indiana UP, 1974.

———. *The Stoic Comedians: Flaubert, Joyce, and Beckett*. Berkeley: U of California P, 1962.

———. *Ulysses*. London: Allen, 1980.

Kershner, R. B. *Joyce, Bakhtin, and Popular Literature: Chronicles of Disorder*. Chapel Hill and London: U of North Carolina P, 1989.

Leonard, Garry. "Joyce and Lacan: 'The Woman' as a Symptom of 'Masculinity' in 'The Dead.' " *James Joyce Quarterly* 28.2 (1991): 451–72.

Levin, Richard, and Charles Shattuck. "First Flight to Ithaca." *Two Decades of Criticism*. Ed. Seon Givens. 1948. New York: Vanguard, 1963. 47–94.

Loomis, C. C., Jr. "Structure and Sympathy in Joyce's 'The Dead.' " *PMLA* 35 (1960): 149–51.

MacCabe, Colin. *James Joyce and the Revolution of the Word*. New York: Harper, 1979.

Maddox, Brenda. *Nora: The Real Life of Molly Bloom*. Boston: Houghton, 1988.

Peake, Charles. *James Joyce: The Citizen and the Artist*. Stanford: Stanford UP, 1977.

Pecora, Vincent P. " 'The Dead' and the Generosity of the Word."
PMLA 101.2 (1986): 233–45.

Riquelme, J. P. "Joyce's 'The Dead': The Dissolution of the Self and
the Police." *Style* 25.3 (1991): 489–505.

Scott, Bonnie Kime. *Joyce and Feminism*. Bloomington: Indiana UP,
1984.

Tate, Alan, and Caroline Gordon. *The House of Fiction*. New York:
Scribner's, 1950.

Tindall, William York. *The Literary Symbol*. New York: Columbia UP,
1955.

———. *A Reader's Guide to James Joyce*. New York: Farrar, 1959.

Torchiana, Donald T. *Backgrounds for Joyce's "Dubliners."* Boston:
Allen, 1986.

———. "The Ending of 'The Dead': I Follow St. Patric." *James Joyce
Quarterly* 18 (1981): 123–32.

Walzl, Florence L. "Gabriel and Michael: The Conclusion of 'The
Dead.' " *James Joyce Quarterly* 4 (1966): 17–31.

Wilson, Edmund. *Axel's Castle: A Study in the Imaginative Literature
of 1870–1930*. New York: Scribner's, 1931.

Psychoanalytic Criticism
and
"The Dead"

WHAT IS PSYCHOANALYTIC CRITICISM?

It seems natural to think about literature in terms of dreams. Like dreams, literary works are fictions, inventions of the mind that, although based on reality, are by definition not literally true. Like a literary work, a dream may have some truth to tell, but, like a literary work, it may need to be interpreted before that truth can be grasped. Many works of literature contain dreams and reveal important aspects of character through dreams.

There are other reasons why it seems natural to make an analogy between dreams and novels. We can live vicariously through romantic fictions, much as we can through daydreams. Terrifying novels and nightmares affect us in much the same way, plunging us into an atmosphere that continues to cling, even after the last chapter has been read — or the alarm clock has sounded. Thus it is not surprising to hear someone say in class that Mary Shelley's *Frankenstein* is a nightmarish tale. Nor are we likely to be surprised by the claim of Frederick Karl, Joseph Conrad's biographer, that *Heart of Darkness* is characterized by the same kind of distortion, condensation, and displacement that Sigmund Freud described in his *Interpretation of Dreams* (1900).

Karl, who invokes Conrad's text and psychoanalytic theory in the same breath, is a Freudian literary critic. But what about the reader who simply compares *Frankenstein* to a nightmare, or Emily Brontë's *Wuthering Heights* to a dream? Is such a reader a Freudian as well? Is he or she, too, a psychoanalytic critic?

To some extent the answer to both questions has to be yes. We are all Freudians, really, whether or not we have read a single work by the famous Austrian psychoanalyst. At one time or another, most of us have referred to ego, libido, complexes, unconscious desires, and sexual repression. The premises of Freud's thought have changed the way the Western world thinks about itself. Psychoanalytic criticism has influenced the teachers our teachers studied with, the works of scholarship and criticism they read, and the critical and creative writers *we* read as well.

What Freud did was develop a language that described, a model that explained, a theory that encompassed human psychology. Many of the elements of psychology he sought to describe and explain are present in the literary works of various ages and cultures, from Sophocles' *Oedipus Rex* to Shakespeare's *Hamlet* to works being written in our own day. When the great novel of the twenty-first century is written, many of these same elements of psychology will probably inform its discourse as well. If, by understanding human psychology according to Freud, we can appreciate literature on a new level, then we should acquaint ourselves with his insights.

Freud's theories are either directly or indirectly concerned with the nature of the unconscious mind. Freud didn't invent the notion of the unconscious; others before him had suggested that even the supposedly "sane" human mind was conscious and rational only at times, and even then at possibly only one level. But Freud went further, suggesting that the powers motivating men and women are *mainly* and *normally* unconscious.

Freud, then, powerfully developed an old idea: that the human mind is essentially dual in nature. He called the predominantly passional, irrational, unknown, and unconscious part of the psyche the *id,* or "it." The *ego,* or "I," was his term for the predominantly rational, logical, orderly, conscious part. Another aspect of the psyche, which he called the *superego,* is really a projection of the ego. The superego almost seems to be outside of the self, making moral judgments, telling us to make sacrifices for good causes even though self-sacrifice may not be quite logical or rational. And, in a sense, the superego *is* "outside," since much of what it tells us to do or think we have learned from our parents, our schools, or our religious institutions.

What the ego and superego tell us *not* to do or think is repressed, forced into the unconscious mind. One of Freud's most important contributions to the study of the psyche, the theory of repression, goes something like this: much of what lies in the unconscious mind has been put there by consciousness, which acts as a censor, driving underground unconscious or conscious thoughts or instincts that it deems unacceptable. Censored materials often involve infantile sexual desires, Freud postulated. Repressed to an unconscious state, they emerge only in disguised forms: in dreams, in language (so-called Freudian slips), in creative activity that may produce art (including literature), and in neurotic behavior.

According to Freud, all of us have repressed wishes and fears; we all have dreams in which repressed feelings and memories emerge disguised, and thus we are all potential candidates for dream analysis. One of the unconscious desires most commonly repressed is the childhood wish to displace the parent of our own sex and take his or her place in the affections of the parent of the opposite sex. This desire really involves a number of different but related wishes and fears. (A boy — and it should be remarked in passing that Freud here concerns himself mainly with the male — may fear that his father will castrate him, and he may wish that his mother would return to nursing him.) Freud referred to the whole complex of feelings by the word "oedipal," naming the complex after the Greek tragic hero Oedipus, who unwittingly killed his father and married his mother.

Why are oedipal wishes and fears repressed by the conscious side of the mind? And what happens to them after they have been censored? As Roy P. Basler puts it in *Sex, Symbolism, and Psychology in Literature* (1975), "from the beginning of recorded history such wishes have been restrained by the most powerful religious and social taboos, and as a result have come to be regarded as 'unnatural,' " even though "Freud found that such wishes are more or less characteristic of normal human development":

> In dreams, particularly, Freud found ample evidence that such wishes persisted. . . . Hence he conceived that natural urges, when identified as "wrong," may be repressed but not obliterated. . . .
> In the unconscious, these urges take on symbolic garb, regarded as nonsense by the waking mind that does not recognize their significance. (14)

Freud's belief in the significance of dreams, of course, was no more original than his belief that there is an unconscious side to the psyche.

Again, it was the extent to which he developed a theory of how dreams work — and the extent to which that theory helped him, by analogy, to understand far more than just dreams — that made him unusual, important, and influential beyond the perimeters of medical schools and psychiatrists' offices.

The psychoanalytic approach to literature not only rests on the theories of Freud; it may even be said to have *begun* with Freud, who was interested in writers, especially those who relied heavily on symbols. Such writers regularly cloak or mystify ideas in figures that make sense only when interpreted, much as the unconscious mind of a neurotic disguises secret thoughts in dream stories or bizarre actions that need to be interpreted by an analyst. Freud's interest in literary artists led him to make some unfortunate generalizations about creativity; for example, in the twenty-third lecture in *Introductory Lectures on Psycho-Analysis* (1922), he defined the artist as "one urged on by instinctive needs that are too clamorous" (314). But it also led him to write creative literary criticism of his own, including an influential essay on "The Relation of a Poet to Daydreaming" (1908) and "The Uncanny" (1919), a provocative psychoanalytic reading of E. T. A. Hoffmann's supernatural tale "The Sandman."

Freud's application of psychoanalytic theory to literature quickly caught on. In 1909, only a year after Freud had published "The Relation of a Poet to Daydreaming," the psychoanalyst Otto Rank published *The Myth of the Birth of the Hero*. In that work, Rank subscribes to the notion that the artist turns a powerful, secret wish into a literary fantasy, and he uses Freud's notion about the "oedipal" complex to explain why the popular stories of so many heroes in literature are so similar. A year after Rank had published his psychoanalytic account of heroic texts, Ernest Jones, Freud's student and eventual biographer, turned his attention to a tragic text: Shakespeare's *Hamlet*. In an essay first published in the *American Journal of Psychology*, Jones, like Rank, makes use of the oedipal concept: he suggests that Hamlet is a victim of strong feelings toward his mother, the queen.

Between 1909 and 1949 numerous other critics decided that psychological and psychoanalytic theory could assist in the understanding of literature. I. A. Richards, Kenneth Burke, and Edmund Wilson were among the most influential to become interested in the new approach. Not all of the early critics were committed to the approach; neither were all of them Freudians. Some followed Alfred Adler, who believed that writers wrote out of inferiority complexes, and others applied the ideas of Carl Gustav Jung, who had broken with Freud over Freud's emphasis on sex and who had developed a theory of the *collective* unconscious. According to Jungian theory, a great work of literature is not a disguised expression of its author's personal, repressed wishes; rather, it is a manifestation of desires once held by the whole human race but now repressed because of the advent of civilization.

It is important to point out that among those who relied on Freud's models were a number of critics who were poets and novelists as well. Conrad Aiken wrote a Freudian study of American literature, and poets such as Robert Graves and W. H. Auden applied Freudian insights when writing critical prose. William Faulkner, Henry James, James Joyce, D. H. Lawrence, Marcel Proust, and Toni Morrison are only a few of the novelists who have either written criticism influenced by Freud or who have written novels that conceive of character, conflict, and creative writing itself in Freudian terms. The poet H. D. (Hilda Doolittle) was actually a patient of Freud's and provided an account of her analysis in her book *Tribute to Freud*. By giving Freudian theory credibility among students of literature that only they could bestow, such writers helped to endow earlier psychoanalytic criticism with a largely Freudian orientation that has only begun to be challenged in the last two decades.

The willingness, even eagerness, of writers to use Freudian models in producing literature and criticism of their own consummated a relationship that, to Freud and other pioneering psychoanalytic theorists, had seemed fated from the beginning; after all, therapy involves the close analysis of language. Renè Wellek and Austin Warren included "psychological" criticism as one of the five "extrinsic" approaches to literature described in their influential book, *Theory of Literature* (1942). Psychological criticism, they suggest, typically attempts to do at least one of the following: provide a psychological study of an individual writer; explore the nature of the creative process; generalize about "types and laws present within works of literature"; or theorize about the psychological "effects of literature upon its readers" (81). Entire books on psychoanalytic criticism even began to appear, such as Frederick J. Hoffman's *Freudianism and the Literary Mind* (1945).

Probably because of Freud's characterization of the creative mind as "clamorous" if not ill, psychoanalytic criticism written before 1950 tended to psychoanalyze the individual author. Poems were read as fantasies that allowed authors to indulge repressed wishes, to protect themselves from deep-seated anxieties, or both. A perfect example of author analysis would be Marie Bonaparte's 1933 study of Edgar Allan Poe. Bonaparte found Poe to be so fixated on his mother that his repressed longing emerges in his stories in images such as the white spot on a black cat's breast, said to represent mother's milk.

A later generation of psychoanalytic critics often paused to analyze the characters in novels and plays before proceeding to their authors. But not for long, since characters, both evil and good, tended to be seen by these critics as the author's potential selves, or projections of various repressed aspects of his or her psyche. For instance, in *A Psychoanalytic Study of the Double in Literature* (1970), Robert Rogers begins with the view that human beings are double or multiple in nature. Using this assumption, along with the psychoanalytic concept of "dissociation" (best known by its result, the dual or multiple personality), Rogers concludes that writers reveal instinctual or repressed selves in their books, often without realizing that they have done so.

In the view of critics attempting to arrive at more psychological insights into an author than biographical materials can provide, a work of literature is a fantasy or a dream — or at least so analogous to daydream or dream that Freudian analysis can help explain the nature of the mind that produced it. The author's purpose in writing is to gratify secretly some forbidden wish, in particular an infantile wish or desire that has been repressed into the unconscious mind. To discover what the wish is, the psychoanalytic critic employs many of the terms and procedures developed by Freud to analyze dreams.

The literal surface of a work is sometimes spoken of as its "manifest content" and treated as a "manifest dream" or "dream story" would be treated by a Freudian analyst. Just as the analyst tries to figure out the "dream thought" behind the dream story — that is, the latent or hidden content of the manifest dream — so the psychoanalytic literary critic tries to expose the latent, underlying content of a work. Freud used the words *condensation* and *displacement* to explain two of the mental processes whereby the mind disguises its wishes and fears in dream stories. In condensation several thoughts or persons may be condensed into a single manifestation or image in a dream story; in displacement, an anxiety, a wish, or a person may be displaced onto the image of another, with which or whom it is loosely connected through a string of associations that only an analyst can untangle. Psychoanalytic critics treat metaphors as if they were dream condensations; they treat metonyms — figures of speech based on extremely loose, arbitrary associations — as if they were dream displacements. Thus figurative literary language in general is treated as something that evolves as the writer's conscious mind resists what the unconscious tells it to picture or describe. A symbol is, in Daniel Weiss's words, "a meaningful concealment of truth as the truth promises to emerge as some frightening or forbidden idea" (20).

In a 1970 article entitled "The 'Unconscious' of Literature," Norman Holland, a literary critic trained in psychoanalysis, succinctly sums up the attitudes held by critics who would psychoanalyze authors, but without quite saying that it is the *author* that is being analyzed by the psychoanalytic critic. "When one looks at a poem psychoanalytically," he writes, "one considers it as though it were a dream or as though some ideal patient [were speaking] from the couch in iambic pentameter." One "looks for the general level or levels of fantasy associated with the language. By level I mean the familiar stages of childhood development — oral [when desires for nourishment and infantile sexual desires overlap], anal [when infants receive their primary pleasure from defecation], urethral [when urinary functions are the locus of sexual pleasure], phallic [when the penis or, in girls, some penis substitute is of primary interest], oedipal." Holland continues by analyzing not Robert Frost but Frost's poem "Mending Wall" as a specifically oral fantasy that is not unique to its author. "Mending Wall" is "about breaking down the wall which marks the separated or individuated self so as to return to a state of closeness to some Other" — including and perhaps essentially the nursing mother ("Unconscious" 136, 139).

While not denying the idea that the unconscious plays a role in creativity, psychoanalytic critics such as Holland began to focus more on the ways in which authors create works that appeal to *our* repressed wishes and fantasies. Consequently, they shifted their focus away from the psyche of the author and toward the psychology of the reader and the text. Holland's theories, which have concerned themselves more with the reader than with the text, have helped to establish another school of critical theory: reader-response criticism. Elizabeth Wright explains Holland's brand of modern psychoanalytic criticism in this way: "What draws us as readers to a text is the secret expression of what we desire to hear, much as we protest we do not. The disguise must be good enough to fool the censor into thinking that the text is respectable, but bad enough to allow the unconscious to glimpse the unrespectable" (117).

Holland is one of dozens of critics who has revised Freud significantly in the process of revitalizing psychoanalytic criticism. Another such critic is R. D. Laing, whose controversial and often poetical writings about personality, repression, masks, and the double or "schizoid" self have (re)blurred the boundary between creative writing and psychoanalytic discourse. Yet another is D. W. Winnicott, an "object relations" theorist who has had a significant impact on literary criticism. Critics influenced by Winnicott and his school have questioned the tendency to see reader/text as an either/or construct; instead, they have seen reader and text (or audience and play) in terms of a *relationship* taking place in what Winnicott calls a "transitional" or "potential space" — space in which binary terms like real and illusory, objective and subjective, have little or no meaning.

Psychoanalytic theorists influenced by Winnicott see the transitional or potential reader/text (or audience/play) space as being *like* the space entered into by psychoanalyst and patient. More important, they also see it as being similar to the space between mother and infant: a space characterized by trust in which categorizing terms such as *knowing* and *feeling* mix and merge and have little meaning apart from one another.

Whereas Freud saw the mother-son relationship in terms of the son and his repressed oedipal complex (and saw the analyst-patient relationship in terms of the patient and the repressed "truth" that the analyst could scientifically extract), object-relations analysts see both relationships as *dyadic* — that is, as being dynamic in both directions. Consequently, they don't depersonalize analysis or their analyses. It is hardly surprising, therefore, that contemporary literary critics who apply object-relations theory to the texts they discuss don't depersonalize critics or categorize their interpretations as "truthful," at least, not in any objective or scientific sense. In the view of such critics, interpretations are made of language — itself a transitional object — and are themselves the mediating terms or transitional objects of a relationship.

Like critics of the Winnicottian School, the French structuralist theorist Jacques Lacan focuses on language and language-related issues. He treats the unconscious *as* a language and, consequently, views the dream not as Freud did (that is, as a form and symptom of repression) but rather as a form of discourse. Thus we may study dreams psychoanalytically in order to learn about literature, even as we may study literature in order to learn more about the unconscious. In Lacan's seminar on Poe's "The Purloined Letter," a pattern of repetition like that used by psychoanalysts in their analyses is used to arrive at a reading of the story. According to Wright, "the new psychoanalytic structural approach to literature" employs "analogies from psychoanalysis . . . to explain the workings of the text as distinct from the workings of a particular author's, character's, or even reader's mind" (125).

Lacan, however, did far more than extend Freud's theory of dreams, literature, and the interpretation of both. More significantly, he took Freud's whole theory of psyche and gender and added to it a crucial third term — that of language. In the process, he both used and significantly developed Freud's ideas about the oedipal stage and complex.

Lacan points out that the pre-oedipal stage, in which the child at first does not even recognize its independence from its mother, is also a pre*verbal* stage, one in which the child communicates without the medium of language, or — if we insist on calling the child's communications a language — in a language that can only be called *literal*. ("Coos," certainly, cannot be said to be figurative or symbolic.) Then, while still in the pre-oedipal stage, the child enters the *mirror* stage.

During the mirror period, the child comes to view itself and its mother, later other people as well, *as* independent selves. This is the stage in which the child is first able to fear the aggressions of another, to desire what is recognizably beyond the self (initially the mother), and, finally, to want to compete with another for the same, desired object. This is also the stage at which the child first becomes able to feel sympathy with another being who is being hurt by a third, to cry when another cries. All of these developments, of course, involve projecting beyond the self and, by extension, constructing one's own self (or "ego" or "I") as others view one — that is, as *another*. Such constructions, according to Lacan, are just that: constructs, products, artifacts — fictions of coherence that in fact hide what Lacan calls the "absence" or "lack" of being.

The mirror stage, which Lacan also refers to as the *imaginary* stage, is fairly quickly succeeded by the oedipal stage. As in Freud, this stage begins when the child, having come to view itself as self and the father and mother as separate selves, perceives gender and gender differences between its parents and between itself and one of its parents. For boys, gender awareness involves another, more powerful recognition, for the recognition of the father's phallus as the mark of his difference from the mother involves, at the same time, the recognition that his older and more powerful father is also his rival. That, in turn, leads to the understanding that what once seemed wholly his and even indistinguishable from himself is in fact someone else's: something properly desired only at a distance and in the form of socially acceptable *substitutes*.

The fact that the oedipal stage roughly coincides with the entry of the child into language is extremely important for Lacan. For the linguistic order is essentially a figurative or "Symbolic order"; words are not the things they stand for but are, rather, stand-ins or substitutes for those things. Hence boys, who in the most critical period of their development have had to submit to what Lacan calls the "Law of the Father" — a law that prohibits direct desire for and communicative intimacy with what has been the boy's whole world — enter more easily into the realm of language and the Symbolic order than do girls, who have never really had to renounce that which once seemed continuous with the self: the mother. The gap that has been opened up for boys, which includes the gap between signs and what they substitute — the gap marked by the phallus and encoded with the boy's sense of his maleness — has not opened up for girls, or has not opened up in the same way, to the same degree.

For Lacan, the father need not be present to trigger the oedipal stage; nor does his phallus have to be seen to catalyze the boy's (easier) transition into the Symbolic order. Rather, Lacan argues, a child's recognition of its gender is intricately tied up with a growing recognition of the system of names and naming, part of the larger system of substitutions we call language. A child has little doubt about who its mother is, but who is its father, and how would one know? The father's claim rests on the mother's *word* that he is in fact the father; the father's relationship to the child is thus established through language and a system of marriage and kinship — names — that in turn is basic to rules of everything from property to law. The name of the father *(nom du père,* which in French sounds like *non du père)* involves, in a sense, nothing of the father — nothing, that is, except his word or name.

Lacan's development of Freud has had several important results. First, his sexist-seeming association of maleness with the Symbolic order, together with his claim that women cannot therefore enter easily into the order, has prompted feminists not to reject his theory out of hand but, rather, to look more closely at the relation between language and gender, language and women's inequality. Some feminists have gone so far as to suggest that the social and political relationships between male and female will not be fundamentally altered until language itself has been radically changed. (That change might begin dialectically, with the development of some kind of "feminine language" grounded in the presymbolic, literal-to-imaginary, communication between mother and child.)

Second, Lacan's theory has proved of interest to deconstructors and other poststructuralists, in part because it holds that the ego (which in

Freud's view is as necessary as it is natural) is a product or construct. The ego-artifact, produced during the mirror stage, *seems* at once unified, consistent, and organized around a determinate center. But the unified self, or ego, is a fiction, according to Lacan. The yoking together of fragments and destructively dissimilar elements takes its psychic toll, and it is the job of the Lacanian psychoanalyst to "deconstruct," as it were, the ego, to show its continuities to be contradictions as well.

In the essay that follows, Daniel R. Schwarz distinguishes his approach to literature from that of Freudian psychoanalytic critics. He refers to his approach as "psychological," although he goes on to define psychological criticism in a way that Freudians could live with: "A psychological approach" to literature, he maintains, "discusses the relationship between author and characters and seeks to understand how the author's creative imagination transfers, sublimates, displaces, and represses as it produces a work of art." It also sees character as a means by which "the reader's psyche is shaped by the author."

Schwarz's focus is thus generally on character and, in particular, on the character of Gabriel. He contends that the reader's relationship with a character such as Gabriel is a function of at least two things: the structure of the text, which changes and shapes the reader's psychology, and the individual psychologies of readers that, because they are different, respond in different ways to the same patterns of language.

Whether Joyce's manipulations of language (and our initial responses to those manipulations) are conscious or unconscious seems hardly to matter to Schwarz. What does matter is this: upon re-viewing "The Dead" from the vantage point of psychological criticism, the reader notices "patterns of language beneath the surface and understands the verbal play as if the text were a patient recalling more than she/he realizes." For example, we may be struck with the fact that Joyce's text is like a dream in which a single desire or anxiety is multiplied and represented in a number of dream images or characters. And if we reread the text, we are likely to be struck by the fact that Joyce has created "a word world in which phrases that are applied to other people actually define Gabriel." What we are told about Julia — that she "did not know where she was or where she was going" — is equally true of Gabriel.

It might seem, at first, that psychological criticism as practiced by Schwarz is a kind of throwback to early versions of psychoanalytic criticism in which character analysis was the order of the day. A closer look, however, will show that Schwarz's critical discourse is informed by the work of a number of post-Freudian critics. His analysis of Gabriel makes use of R. D. Laing's account of the process whereby certain individuals become "threatened with the possibility of becoming no more than a thing in the world of the other, without any life for oneself." Schwarz depends as well on Jacques Lacan's discussion of the painter's gaze in analyzing Gabriel's self-regarding self-detachment.

As a result of these and other contemporary moves, Schwarz goes far beyond old-fashioned character analysis, as well as beyond the kind of author analysis in which characters are viewed as symptoms of their authors' repressed wishes and fears. (This is true notwithstanding Schwarz's belief that Joyce's characters "were means by which he explored and defined his identity" and that "Gabriel expresses Joyce's fear of betrayal — sexual, political, and personal.")

Schwarz even goes beyond the kind of reader-oriented psychoanalytic criticism practiced by Norman Holland and his followers, for although he is interested in individual, even idiosyncratic responses (that is, the guilty response of a bookish, academic reader to the overly fastidious, "paralytically self-conscious" character of Gabriel), he is even more interested in the broader contexts within which the psyches of readers are located — and within which readers make sense of texts. For instance, he argues that "the psychological aspect of 'The Dead' needs to be understood in terms of [the] economic and class issues . . . which shape Gabriel's psychic responses" (that is, his sense of social and cultural superiority). Additionally, whereas Schwarz sees Gabriel as a particular representation of Joyce's psyche, he also sees him in terms of his similarity to characters such as Thomas Mann's Aschenbach, T. S. Eliot's Prufrock, and Joseph Conrad's Kurtz; thus, the psychology of a single character participates in a larger, collective psychology of modernism. Lest we think, however, that only modernist texts have shaped the psychological conditions within which Joyce wrote and we read, Schwarz argues that "a psychological criticism may also address how characters iterate and depart from mythic prototypes" such as Paris and the Three Graces.

The result of Schwarz's rich psychological reading is an awareness, on our part, of the richness *of* psychological reading. For, in his words, "as we read we respond in multiple ways," recognizing the potential validity of each response even "in the face of the claims of the other."

Ross C Murfin

PSYCHOANALYTIC CRITICISM: A SELECTED BIBLIOGRAPHY

Some Short Introductions to Psychological and Psychoanalytic Criticism

Holland, Norman. "The 'Unconscious' of Literature." *Contemporary Criticism*. Ed. Norman Bradbury and David Palmer. Stratford-upon-Avon Series 12. New York: St. Martin's, 1970. 131–54.

Natoli, Joseph, and Frederik L. Rusch, comps. *Psychocriticism: An Annotated Bibliography*. Westport: Greenwood, 1984.

Scott, Wilbur. *Five Approaches to Literary Criticism*. London: Collier-Macmillan, 1962. See the essays by Burke and Gorer as well as Scott's introduction to the section "The Psychological Approach: Literature in the Light of Psychological Theory."

Wellek, René, and Austin Warren. *Theory of Literature*. New York: Harcourt, 1942. See the chapter "Literature and Psychology" in pt. 3, "The Extrinsic Approach to the Study of Literature."

Wright, Elizabeth. "Modern Psychoanalytic Criticism." *Modern Literary Theory: A Comparative Introduction*. Ed. Ann Jefferson and David Robey. Totowa, NJ: Barnes, 1982. 113–33.

Freud, Lacan, and Their Influence

Basler, Roy P. *Sex, Symbolism, and Psychology in Literature*. New York: Octagon, 1975. See especially 13–19.

Clément, Catherine. *The Lives and Legends of Jacques Lacan*. Trans. Arthur Goldhammer. New York: Columbia UP, 1983.

Freud, Sigmund. *Introductory Lectures on Psycho-Analysis*. Trans. Joan Riviere. London: Allen, 1922.

Gallop, Jane. *Reading Lacan*. Ithaca: Cornell UP, 1985.

Hoffman, Frederick J. *Freudianism and the Literary Mind*. Baton Rouge: Louisiana State UP, 1945.

Hogan, Patrick Colm, and Lalita Pandit, eds. *Lacan and Criticism: Essays and Dialogue on Language, Structure, and the Unconscious*. Athens: U of Georgia P, 1990.

Kazin, Alfred. "Freud and His Consequences." *Contemporaries*. Boston: Little, 1962. 351–93.

Lacan, Jacques. *Écrits: A Selection*. Trans. Alan Sheridan. New York: Norton, 1977.

———. *Feminine Sexuality: Lacan and the école freudienne*. Ed. Juliet

Mitchell and Jacqueline Rose. Trans. Rose. New York: Norton, 1982.

————. *The Four Fundamental Concepts of Psychoanalysis.* Trans. Alan Sheridan. London: Penguin, 1980.

Macey, David. *Lacan in Contexts.* New York: Verso, 1988.

Meisel, Perry, ed. *Freud: A Collection of Critical Essays.* Englewood Cliffs: Prentice, 1981.

Muller, John P., and William J. Richardson. *Lacan and Language: A Reader's Guide to "Écrits."* New York: International UP, 1982.

Porter, Laurence M. *"The Interpretation of Dreams": Freud's Theories Revisited.* Twayne's Masterwork Studies Series. Boston: G. K. Hall, 1986.

Ragland Sullivan, Ellie. *Jacques Lacan and the Philosophy of Psychoanalysis.* Champaign: U of Illinois P, 1986.

Ragland Sullivan, Ellie, and Mark Bracher, eds. *Lacan and the Subject of Language.* New York: Routledge, 1991.

Reppen, Joseph, and Maurice Charney. *The Psychoanalytic Study of Literature.* Hillsdale: Analytic, 1985.

Schneiderman, Stuart. *Jacques Lacan: The Death of an Intellectual Hero.* Cambridge: Harvard UP, 1983.

————. *Returning to Freud: Clinical Psychoanalysis in the School of Lacan.* New Haven: Yale UP, 1980.

Selden, Raman. *A Reader's Guide to Contemporary Literary Theory.* 2nd ed. Lexington: U of Kentucky P, 1989. See "Jacques Lacan: Language and the Unconscious."

Trilling, Lionel. "Art and Neurosis." *The Liberal Imagination.* New York: Scribner's, 1950. 160–80.

Wilden, Anthony. "Lacan and the Discourse of the Other." In Lacan, *Speech and Language in Psychoanalysis.* Trans. Wilden. Baltimore: Johns Hopkins UP, 1981. (Published as *The Language of the Self* in 1968.) 159–311.

Psychoanalysis, Feminism, and Literature

Chodorow, Nancy. *The Reproduction of Mothering: Psychoanalysis and the Sociology of Gender.* Berkeley: U of California P, 1978.

Gallop, Jane. *The Daughter's Seduction: Feminism and Psychoanalysis.* Ithaca: Cornell UP, 1982.

Garner, Shirley Nelson, Claire Kahane, and Madelon Sprengnether. *The (M)other Tongue: Essays in Feminist Psychoanalytic Interpretation.* Ithaca: Cornell UP, 1985.

Irigaray, Luce. *This Sex Which Is Not One.* Trans. Catherine Porter. Ithaca: Cornell UP, 1985.

————. *The Speculum of the Other Woman.* Trans. Gillian C. Gill. Ithaca: Cornell UP, 1985.

Jacobus, Mary. "Is There a Woman in This Text?" *New Literary History* 14 (1982): 117–41.

Kristeva, Julia. *The Kristeva Reader.* Ed. Toril Moi. New York: Columbia UP, 1986. See especially the selection from *Revolution in Poetic Language,* 89–136.

Mitchell, Juliet. *Psychoanalysis and Feminism.* New York: Random House, 1974.

Mitchell, Juliet, and Jacqueline Rose, "Introduction I" and "Introduction II." Lacan, *Feminine Sexuality: Jacques Lacan and the école freudienne.* New York: Norton, 1985. 1–26, 27–57.

Sprengnether, Madelon. *The Spectral Mother: Freud, Feminism, and Psychoanalysis.* Ithaca: Cornell UP, 1990.

Psychological and Psychoanalytic
Studies of Literature

Bettelheim, Bruno. *The Uses of Enchantment: The Meaning and Importance of Fairy Tales.* New York: Knopf, 1976. Although this book is about fairy tales instead of literary works written for publication, it offers model Freudian readings of well-known stories.

Crews, Frederick C. *Out of My System: Psychoanalysis, Ideology, and Critical Method.* New York: Oxford UP, 1975.

————. *Relations of Literary Study.* New York: MLA, 1967. See the chapter "Literature and Psychology."

Diehl, Joanne Feit. "Re-Reading *The Letter:* Hawthorne, the Fetish, and the (Family) Romance." *Nathaniel Hawthorne, The Scarlet Letter.* Ed. Ross C Murfin. Case Studies in Contemporary Criticism Series. Ed. Ross C Murfin. Boston: Bedford–St. Martin's, 1991. 235–51.

Hallman, Ralph. *Psychology of Literature: A Study of Alienation and Tragedy.* New York: Philosophical Library, 1961.

Hartman, Geoffrey, ed. *Psychoanalysis and the Question of the Text.* Baltimore: Johns Hopkins UP, 1978. See especially the essays by Hartman, Johnson, Nelson, and Schwartz.

Hertz, Neil. *The End of the Line: Essays on Psychoanalysis and the Sublime.* New York: Columbia UP, 1985.

Holland, Norman N. *Dynamics of Literary Response.* New York: Oxford UP, 1968.

———. *Poems in Persons: An Introduction to the Psychoanalysis of Literature*. New York: Norton, 1973.

Kris, Ernest. *Psychoanalytic Explorations in Art*. New York: International, 1952.

Lucas, F. L. *Literature and Psychology*. London: Cassell, 1951.

Natoli, Joseph, ed. *Psychological Perspectives on Literature: Freudian Dissidents and Non-Freudians: A Casebook*. Hamden: Archon Books–Shoe String, 1984.

Phillips, William, ed. *Art and Psychoanalysis*. New York: Columbia UP, 1977.

Rogers, Robert. *A Psychoanalytic Study of the Double in Literature*. Detroit: Wayne State UP, 1970.

Skura, Meredith. *The Literary Use of the Psychoanalytic Process*. New Haven: Yale UP, 1981.

Strelka, Joseph P. *Literary Criticism and Psychology*. University Park: Pennsylvania State UP, 1976. See especially the essays by Lerner and Peckham.

Weiss, Daniel. *The Critic Agonistes: Psychology, Myth, and the Art of Fiction*. Ed. Eric Solomon and Stephen Arkin. Seattle: U of Washington P, 1985.

Lacanian Psychoanalytic Studies of Literature

Collings, David. "The Monster and the Imaginary Mother: A Lacanian Reading of *Frankenstein*." *Mary Shelley, Frankenstein*. Ed. Johanna M. Smith. Case Studies in Contemporary Criticism Series. Ed. Ross C Murfin. Boston: Bedford–St. Martin's, 1992. 245–58.

Davis, Robert Con, ed. *The Fictional Father: Lacanian Readings of the Text*. Amherst: U of Massachusetts P, 1981.

———. "Lacan and Narration." *Modern Language Notes* 5 (1983): 843–1063.

Felman, Shoshana, ed. *Literature and Psychoanalysis: The Question of Reading: Otherwise*. Baltimore: Johns Hopkins UP, 1982.

———, ed. *Jacques Lacan and the Adventure of Insight: Psychoanalysis in Contemporary Culture*. Cambridge, MA: Harvard UP, 1987.

Froula, Christine. "When Eve Reads Milton: Undoing the Canonical Economy." *Canons*. Ed. Robert von Hallberg. Chicago: U of Chicago P, 1984. 149–75.

Homans, Margaret. *Bearing the Word: Language and Female Experience in Nineteenth-Century Women's Writing*. Chicago: U of Chicago P, 1986.

Muller, John P., and William J. Richardson, eds. *The Purloined Poe: Lacan, Derrida, and Psychoanalytic Reading.* Baltimore: Johns Hopkins UP, 1988. Includes Lacan's seminar on Poe's "The Purloined Letter."

Psychoanalytic Approaches to Joyce

Anderson, Chester G. "Baby Tuckoo: Joyce's 'Features of Infancy,' " *Approaches to Joyce's "Portrait": Ten Essays.* Ed. Thomas F. Staley and Bernard Benstock. Pittsburgh: U of Pittsburgh P, 1976. 135–69.

Boheemen, Christine van. *The Novel as Family Romance: Language, Gender, and Authority from Fielding to Joyce.* Ithaca: Cornell UP, 1987, passim.

Brivic, Sheldon. *Joyce the Creator.* Madison and London: U of Wisconsin P, 1985.

———. *Joyce Between Freud and Jung.* Port Washington, NY, and London: Kennikat P, 1980.

———. *The Veil of Signs: Joyce, Lacan, and Perception.* Champaign: U of Illinois P, 1991.

Fenichel, Robert. "A Portrait of the Artist as a Young Orphan." *Literature and Psychology* 9 (Spring 1959): 19–22.

Henke, Suzette. *James Joyce and the Politics of Desire.* New York: Routledge, 1990.

Hoffman, Frederick C. "Infroyce." *Freudianism and the Literary Mind.* Baton Rouge: Louisiana State UP, 1945.

James Joyce Quarterly 13 (Spring 1976). "Joyce and Modern Psychology" issue.

James Joyce Quarterly 29 (Fall 1991). "Joyce Between Genders: Lacanian Views" issue.

Kimball, Jean. "Freud, Leonardo, and Joyce: The Dimensions of a Childhood Memory." *The Seventh of Joyce.* Ed. Bernard Benstock. Bloomington: Indiana UP, 1982. 57–73.

Leonard, Garry. "Joyce and Lacan: 'The Woman' as a Symptom of 'Masculinity' in 'The Dead.' " *James Joyce Quarterly* 28 (Winter 1991): 451–72.

O'Brien, Darcy. "Some Psychological Determinants of Joyce's View of Love and Sex." *New Light on Joyce from the Dublin Symposium.* Ed. Fritz Senn. Bloomington: Indiana UP, 1970. 137–55.

Rea, Joanne E. "Joyce's 'Beastly' Bitch Motif: Sadic Castration Threat and Separation Anxiety." *Journal of Evolutionary Psychology* 7 (Mar. 1986): 28–33.

Shechner, Mark. *Joyce in Nighttown: A Psychoanalytic Inquiry into "Ulysses."* Berkeley: U of California P, 1974.

Wasson, Richard. "Stephen Dedalus and the Imagery of Sight: A Psychological Approach." *Literature and Psychology* 15 (Fall 1965): 195–209.

A PSYCHOANALYTIC PERSPECTIVE

DANIEL R. SCHWARZ

Gabriel Conroy's Psyche: Character as Concept in Joyce's "The Dead"

I prefer to call my approach psychological rather than psychoanalytical. Implying a Freudian paradigm, psychoanalytic criticism is a subdivision of psychological criticism. To be sure, Freudian perspectives have informed the criticism of twentieth-century art. "The Dead" dramatizes a dialogue between Gabriel's consciousness and unconsciousness, or, in Freudian terms, among his sexual desire (id) and his sense of responsibility (superego) and ego. And a Freudian criticism stresses that a literary work expresses the author's repressed impulses, while the reader finds in a literary work an outlet for fantasies and a place to unconsciously and consciously explore psychic conflicts.

But I wish to be more eclectic and pluralistic in my use of a psychological approach. A psychological approach inquires into the motives and behavior of the characters and of the author, but it need not quote elaborately from psychoanalytic theory. It is attentive to the findings of those who have studied the human psyche, but is not rigorously defined by any one model. I shall explore issues of awareness, motivation, and feeling as they pertain to characters in the imaginary world created by the author, the author's act of creation, and the reader's response. A psychological approach discusses the relationship between author and characters, and seeks to understand how the author's creative imagination transfers, sublimates, displaces, and represses as it produces a work of art.

My essay will examine Gabriel Conroy's character as the unifying concept of "The Dead." In demonstrating the possibilities of psychological criticism, I shall include discussions of author, reader, and characters within the imaginary world presented by the text. Being eclectic and pluralistic, my method will include aspects of Freudian, Jungian, and Lacanian perspectives. In Part One I will briefly discuss the relation between Joyce's psyche and Gabriel's before examining in Part Two Gabriel's paralytic self-consciousness in detail. In the third section, I shall place Gabriel's psyche in a cultural and historical context. Finally, I shall pull together biographical, formal, and cultural aspects in a sustained reading of the conclusion of "The Dead." Because this is the volume's first critical essay, I shall present readings of major passages to provide a reference point for ensuing discussions in the subsequent four essays.

I. Joyce and Gabriel

A psychological criticism needs to consider issues that undermine traditional shibboleths about the separation of life and text. For Joyce uses his life as a source and believed that the universal genius (himself) "found," as Stephen says of Shakespeare in the "Scylla and Charybdis" section of *Ulysses*, "in the world without as actual what was in his world within as possible." Joyce created characters who were metaphors for himself, who were the means by which he explored and defined his identity. Joyce's fiction draws upon the actual — the life he lived — and, influenced by Wilde's *The Decay of Lying*, he creates masques for what he fears to become. Isn't Gabriel a metaphor for one facet of Joyce, just as Stephen Dedalus and Bloom are metaphors for other facets?

Wearing glasses, hair parted in the middle, Gabriel resembles Joyce. And his appearance, like his character, is a version of what Joyce feared becoming: bourgeois, conventional, a writer of reviews who supported himself teaching. Ellmann has reminded us of other important ways in which Gabriel resembles Joyce.

> In Gretta's old sweetheart, in Gabriel's letter, in the book reviews and the discussion of them, as well as in the physical image of Gabriel with hair parted in the middle and rimmed glasses, Joyce drew directly upon his own life. . . .
> Gabriel's quarrels with his mother also suggest John Joyce's quarrels with his mother, who never accepted her son's marriage to a woman of lower station.[1]

---

[1] Ellsworth Mason and Richard Ellmann, eds., *The Critical Writings of James Joyce* (New York: Viking, 1959) 228.

There is no doubt that Gabriel saw Gretta, like Joyce saw Nora Barnacle, as an alternative to the petty, insular Dublin social rituals.

We should think of Gabriel as a function of Joyce's self-critique.
Gabriel is middle-class, conventional, neurotic, married to a woman of
greater passion than himself, a writer of minor reviews for a newspaper
(a conservative newspaper, *The Daily Express* which was opposed to
Irish independence), and a secondary school teacher. He represented a
life that Joyce in 1907 could see himself leading had he not left Ireland
or had he failed as a writer and had to return to Ireland. Another way of
putting it is to say that Gabriel was that bourgeois nightmare which in
part took Joyce away from Ireland. Indeed, does not Gabriel have the
same kind of alternating sympathy and irony toward himself, whom he
often regards as strangely detached, the object of his own gaze, a kind
of painting he regards in the same way he gazes at his wife on the stairs
— as Joyce does to himself? Like Stephen Dedalus and Joyce himself,
Gabriel tries unsuccessfully to maintain a stance of iconoclastic aloof-
ness. Gabriel expresses Joyce's fear of betrayal — sexual, political, and
personal. His tone toward Gabriel oscillates among sympathy, empathy,
and grimly ironic disdain. Joyce is bitter toward a culture which, in his
view, creates the kind of sexually dysfunctional adults that we see in
Dubliners; from the acorn of the boy in "Araby" grows the tree of James
Duffy in "A Painful Case." *Dubliners* thinly disguises Joyce's anger at a
culture he feels is paralyzed by Catholic dogma, British exploitation, its
own proponents for self-delusion, alcoholism, and Irish hyperbole and
blarney. Indeed, "The Dead" enacts some of Joyce's own discomfort
with Yeats and the Irish Renaissance — including a need to separate
himself from Yeats as an artistic father-figure — and what he felt was a
misplaced effort to align Ireland with Celtic culture and away from
Western culture.

Our reading will depend on whether we see "The Dead" as the last
of a sequence of stories about the "moral history" of Ireland written in,
what Joyce calls, "a style of scrupulous meanness" (*Dubliners* 269) or as
an independent story of Gabriel's self-delusion and troubled relationship with Gretta. To a reader of the preceding stories of *Dubliners,* Gabriel is the result of a sequence of acculturation that has been developed
carefully about why contemporary Dublin is morally sterile, and Gabriel
is a somewhat more benign and pitiful figure because we see him in the
context of the claustrophobic world in which he was raised, and we understand that the young boy in the first three stories — "The Sisters,"
"An Encounter," and "Araby" — is a metonymy for both Joyce *and*
Gabriel as very young men.

II. Gabriel's Paralytic Self-Consciousness

At the opening of "The Dead," we watch Gabriel from an ironic distance as he behaves clumsily toward Lily and we respond with a complex set of emotions — sympathy, judgment, impatience — to his failure to connect fully with other people. As he vacillates uncomfortably from self-diminishment to self-aggrandizement, as we realize that his social clumsiness relates to an emptiness within, does not the ironic distance narrow, at least for many readers and particularly for rereaders whose responses are likely to be even less visual? Can we look at this paralytically self-conscious man from a steep and icy peak? Gabriel's own narrative of failure begins with Lily's retort:

> He was still discomposed by the girl's bitter and sudden retort.
> . . . He *would* only make himself ridiculous by quoting poetry to
> them which they could not understand. They *would* think that he
> was airing his superior education. He would fail with them just as
> he had failed with the girl in the pantry. He had taken up a wrong
> tone. His whole speech was a mistake from first to last, an utter
> failure. (24, emphasis added)[2]

Gabriel's sense of superior education, debilitating self-consciousness, and emotional dwarfism not only reflects his creator, but speaks to a characteristic paralytic self-consciousness of modernism. More than that, it reflects Joyce's fear that education isolates us from our focus; it also speaks to our doubts that education anesthetizes us to feelings. When we reread the paragraph and see the words "discomposed," "undecided," "feared," "make himself ridiculous," we see Gabriel as if he were a part of a code that prepares for his later failure — or his perceptions of that failure. Gradually we realize that Gabriel is almost pathologically tense and nervous; twice our attention is called to his trembling fingers and his nervous laughter; his anxiety and desire to escape seem disproportionate unless he suffers from claustrophobia.

Pompous, pedantic, and patronizing, Gabriel vacillates between self-diminishment and self-aggrandizement, between seeing himself as a Lilliputian and a Brobdingnagian. As the above paragraph indicates, when Lily distances his efforts to charm and to be fatherly with what he takes as a rebuke, he responds with characteristic lack of proportion. When threatened, he characteristically finds refuge in self-importance

---

[2]Page references refer to the text of "The Dead" in this volume.

and, in this case, begins to look at his speech. While thinking of his audience, he searches for a psychic oasis in which he can slake the thirst of his insecurities:

> It had cast a gloom over him which he tried to dispel. . . . He was undecided about the lines from Robert Browning for he feared they would be above the heads of his hearers. Some quotation that they could recognise from Shakespeare or from the Melodies would be better. The indelicate clacking of the men's heels and the shuffling of their soles reminded him that their grade of culture differed from his. (24)

While Gabriel seems to be an established teacher and enthusiastic bibliophile, he lacks a coherent self. He takes his identity from his social position; his appearance, his dandified appearance — "patent-leather shoes," waistcoat to cover his "plump body," "glossy black hair . . . parted in the middle and brushed in a long curve behind his ears," "gilt rims of glasses," "goloshes" — reinforces this. While he seems to see himself as the center of the party and to feed on the attention he receives, he continually allows minor events to marginalize him and deprive him of his self-worth. In truth, his need to control is equal to his need to be loved. His fixation on the health of his intimates demonstrates his need to *improve* and *correct* and ultimately live through others; he insists that his wife wear galoshes, has his son wearing shades at night and lifting dumbbells, and has his daughter eating "stirabout." Gabriel loves *by controlling*.

Because of his pomposity and patronization, Gabriel is reduced to a bundle of quirks and tics. We see a man stripped of his pretensions as the evening progresses. He "laugh[s] nervously" when Gretta gently rebukes him for his smothering solicitude (25). Gabriel mistakes solicitude for love. Thinking of his speech after Lily's rebuke, he not only reduces Lily to "the girl in the pantry," but shows that his purported self-esteem is a sham.

Among other things, the psychological aspect of "The Dead" needs to be understood in terms of economic and class issues, class distinctions that shape Gabriel's psychic responses. While the aunts dress plainly and live in a rental house, their students are from the "better-class families." He is conscious that Gretta is a country girl from Connacht and that he has married beneath him. He feels that the guests come from a "grade of culture beneath him." From this we infer that by going to a university and becoming a teacher, Gabriel has raised himself and is extremely proud of this. Note how uncomfortable Mary Jane, his cousin (and perhaps a little younger than he) is with herself.

The reason for the annual party is that it is a way for his aunts, Julia and Kate, and their niece, Mary Jane, to advertise their music school. Indeed, the protagonist of *Ulysses,* Leopold Bloom, advertising salesman, might have imagined it. Lacking social security and sufficient old age pensions, the music lesson business provides a means of support for the women. If their economic provision disappeared, hyperconscientious Gabriel, as the oldest surviving male relative, would feel that he was responsible for their support. That is why he thinks of himself as a pennyboy for his aunt. A pennyboy is both a boy who runs errands for a penny and the monkey that shakes a cup for an organ grinder — a street or arcade figure — who was what we now call a street musician. Gabriel has a desperate need to be needed, and we realize that *he* is a family caretaker of a kind; he has been reduced to that role and *relishes* that role. Like Lily and her father he performs tasks for his aunts' party. Kate says to Gretta: "I always feel easier in my mind when he's here" (26).

In a sense, Gabriel's orphaned cousin Mary Jane is the delegated provider for the family in that she has taken on the task of supporting the aunts and, not so incidentally, herself. For Mary Jane gives the piano lessons on which the older women live. We need to be aware of the position of the women; Lily and, presumably, Gretta, and Gabriel's servant girl do not go to school; Gretta apparently does not work. Perhaps the party is short of women because, except for pupils and an independent woman like Miss Ivors, single women are less likely, in contrast to men like Freddy Malins and Mr. Browne, to go to such parties alone, in part because, as the rest of *Dubliners* shows, many women have caretaker roles of one kind or another. We recall other women in prior stories of *Dubliners* — Eveline in the story of that name, Maria in "Clay," and the sisters in the opening story of that name — who seemed to sacrifice their own lives for relatives.

Ironically, once Gabriel carves the goose and sits down to eat, he does not converse. Rereading, we realize that until the conversation in the hotel with Gretta — a conversation in which he reveals his awkwardness in achieving intimacy — he has not really listened and responded or expressed his feelings in conversation. He is a man of words without the ability to communicate; he is frustrated in expressing himself; he would say — if he had self-knowledge — with Eliot's Prufrock: "It is impossible to say just what I mean!" ("The Love Song of J. Alfred

Prufrock"). His language reveals a pedestrian mind, full of banalities. Indeed, he lives in clichés: "Here I am as right as the mail" is how he announces his arrival, or when he declares of galoshes: "everyone wears them on the continent" (26). The quintessence of his self-created identity is his public after-dinner speech:

> — Let us toast them all three together. Let us drink to their health, wealth, long life, happiness and prosperity and may they long continue to hold the proud and self-won position which they hold in their profession and the position of honour and affection which they hold in our hearts. (107–108)

The chorus led by Mr. Browne stands and sings "For they are jolly gay fellows, / Which nobody can deny. / Unless he tells a lie," and, we realize, telling a lie is what Gabriel has been doing since he does not believe what he says at all.

Gabriel allows himself to become a function of the perceptions of others, to be drained of his self-hood and deprived of his ego. Lacking a coherent identity, Gabriel can chameleonically (like Conrad's Kurtz) get himself to believe in anything because finally he believes in nothing. (And this crisis of belief — after Christianity no longer provides emotional bulwarks — is a subject of modernism and a cause, too.) Gabriel's crisis of identity recalls that of Eliot's Prufrock and the captain-narrator in Conrad's "The Secret Sharer," other characters in modern literature who are defined by anxious, self-doubting thoughts about how others regard them. Conrad's captain himself is a stranger and outsider and begins to become depersonalized by the appearance of Leggatt, whom he regards as a second self, until he cannot distinguish between self and other. Like Prufrock and Conrad's captain, Gabriel is fixated on the approval of others. As with those characters, the integrity of Gabriel's personality is threatened by a disbelief in the authenticity of self. As the existential psychologist R. D. Laing puts it in *The Divided Self*:

> If one experiences the other as a free agent, one is open to the possibility of experiencing oneself as an *object* of his experience and thereby of feeling one's own subjectivity drained away. One is threatened with the possibility of becoming no more than a thing in the world of the other, without any life for oneself, without any being for oneself. . . . One may find oneself enlivened and the sense of one's own being enhanced by the other, or one may experience the other as deadening and impoverishing.[3]

---

[3]R. D. Laing, *The Divided Self: An Existential Study in Sanity and Madness* (Baltimore: Penguin Books, 1965), 4.

Gabriel is a divided self, regarding his sexuality as something that belongs to another. Confused about the difference between love and lust, he rebukes himself for feeling lust when he is sexually aroused. Are not the terms of the modernist crisis directly related to Laing's description of schizoid conditions? The modernists fear that we will become what others in our culture expect us to be; even if we strive for our own way, we may return to the beaten path of acculturation, the verbal symptom of which may be cliché. What is Gabriel's failure? In part, it is simply a sense that he is not good enough, the self-accusation that permeates the fiction of the era from Hardy's Jude and Sue in *Jude the Obscure* to Conrad's Jim in *Lord Jim* to Woolf's Lily Briscoe in *To the Lighthouse*. Like those characters, Gabriel is paralytically self-conscious. Isn't part of Gabriel always standing to one side watching his behavior? He thinks he is being watched and talked about more than he is. He has trouble reaching a decision. He is at once a self-absorbed narcissist and someone who thinks he is always the object of the gazes of others.

Like Eliot's Prufrock or Gerontion, Gabriel embodies the world about which he complains:

> [W]e are living in a sceptical and, if I may use the phrase, a thought-tormented age: and sometimes I fear that this new generation, educated or hypereducated as it is, will lack those qualities of humanity, of hospitality, of kindly humour which belonged to an older day. . . . I must confess, that we were living in a less spacious age. Those days might, without exaggeration, be called spacious days: and if they are gone beyond recall let us hope, at least, that in gatherings such as this we shall still speak of them with pride and affection, still cherish in our hearts the memory of those dead and gone great ones whose fame the world will not willingly let die. (43)

His fastidiousness, pretension, and pomposity are mirrored in his circumlocutious speech, including the use of the first person pronoun — "If I may use," "I fear," "I must confess" — to make minute, hesitant, and verbose distinctions. Gabriel finds his refuge in his own fantasies. As with Prufrock, his separation from instinctive behavior renders the comparison between past figures and himself as ironic. Gabriel's ego is not adequately negotiating between the demands of his superego and his id. His ego is embedded in a welter of temporary refuges and disguises, and his speech puts him in the same new generation he so critically patronizes. He cannot have a conversation without replaying it in his mind; it is as if his ego were separated from his libido and his passions. He is the living embodiment of mind-consciousness — of creeping mentalism — that Joyce's contemporary and rival D. H. Lawrence spent his life fighting. His speech is a disguised autobiography in which he unwittingly becomes the object of his own text: "[W]e could not find the heart to go on bravely with our work among the living. We have all of us living duties and living affections which claim, and rightly claim, our strenuous endeavours" (44). Do we not as rereaders hear the shadow of the dead in his repetition of "living" three times in two lines? Unwittingly, Gabriel's genre is elegy. To a rereader his speech, full of clichés and bromides, resonates with irony at his expense. He is caught in a verbal labyrinth of his own making. Put another way, his words are a mirror of his own psyche, and he has not been able to move beyond himself.[4]

Gabriel has problems with women: Lily, his mother, Miss Ivors, and, of course, Gretta. Both Gretta and Miss Ivors are more comfortable with themselves than Gabriel and more integrated than he is; they have a healthy self-regard and positive egotism. But Gabriel is made uncomfortable by their very coherence. Women become mirrors by which he sees himself; they penetrate his fantasy of self-importance, and intrude *other*, difference, libido, shadows. When he thinks of Miss Ivors as one of the *"serious and hypereducated generation"* (35), we realize that it is the epithet "serious" he had used for his mother (his aunts "seemed a little proud of their serious and matronly sister" [30]). "A shadow passed over his face as he remembered her sullen opposition to his marriage" (30). These recurring shadows and shades are the visual metaphors both for inevitable death and the obsessions, memories, fixations that enclose him in a coffin of his own making — a coffin which he, like the monks, rests in.

Gabriel finds refuge in manners, fastidious behavior, small social distinctions, and a nostalgic and idealized view of the past, and some of this

---

[4]"The lyrical form is in fact the simplest verbal vesture of an instant of emotion, a rhythmical cry such as ages ago cheered on the man who pulled at the oar or dragged stones up a slope. He who utters it is more conscious of the instant of emotion than of himself as feeling emotion. The simplest epical form is seen emerging out of lyrical literature when the artist prolongs and broods upon himself as the centre of an epical event and this form progresses till the centre of emotional gravity is equidistant from the artist himself and from others. The narrative is no longer purely personal. . . . The dramatic form is reached when the vitality which has flowed and eddied round each person fills every person with such vital force that he or she assumes a proper and intangible esthetic life. The personality of the artist, at first a cry or a cadence or a mood and then a fluid and lambent narrative, finally refines itself out of existence, impersonalises itself, so to speak. The esthetic image in the dramatic form is life purified in and reprojected from the human imagination" (James Joyce, *Portrait of the Artist as a Young Man,* ed. R. B. Kershner [Boston: Bedford–St. Martin's, 1993] 186–87).

comes from his memory of his mother. Gabriel has something of an oedipal complex. His eye is drawn to a family photograph containing his mother, a photograph in which "she held an open book on her knees and was pointing out something in it to Constantine who, dressed in a man-o'-war suit, lay at her feet. It was she who had chosen the names for her sons for she was very sensible of the dignity of family life" (30). He has been acculturized by his mother's snobbery. He is haunted by her picture in the family photograph — as Stephen Dedalus will be haunted by the ghost of his mother and Bloom by the ghost of his father. He worries about his mother's dismissal of Gretta as "country cute" (30); isn't Gabriel, like his mother, "very sensible of the dignity of family life" (30)? He knows Gretta's standards of value are not those of his family, but he was drawn to her as a younger man, when he loved passionately enough to overcome his mother's objection. When Miss Ivors scolds him and tells him that "I'm ashamed of you," it is as if his mother were scolding him, as if Miss Ivors were his mother. Mother and mother church may have a role in his harsh judgment of his own sexual arousal; for after Gretta rejects his advances, he thinks of "his own clownish lusts" and alludes to the Cain story: "he turned his back more to the light lest she might see the *shame* that burned upon his forehead" (56, emphasis added).

Gabriel is haunted by memories of the past. Isn't his speech finally an elegy for himself? The irony at Gabriel's expense includes his pompous, self-serving speech in which he uses the rhetoric of revenge to get back at Miss Ivors. Gabriel savors small pretensions and lives in a simplified world he has created — a world with, on one hand, rigid assumptions about marriage and courtship, and, on the other, fears about how Gretta regards him despite his self-importance. He has wrapped himself in an envelope of defensiveness and allusion. Note his snobbery when she tells him about Michael, "*What* was he?" he asks (56, emphasis added).

Gabriel needs to be the center of attention, the object of the gazes of others. He is *realized* by the knowledge that he is part of the perception of others, and seeks fulfillment and completion in the opinion of others. Yet, paradoxically, he is uncomfortable with himself and dislikes being the focus; as if he were claustrophobic, he longs to be outside, elsewhere and beyond: "How cool it must be outside! How pleasant it would be to walk out alone, first along by the river and then through the park! The snow would be lying on the branches of the trees and forming a bright cap on the top of the Wellington Monument. How much more pleasant it would be there than at the supper-table!" (34).

Because he is uncomfortable he continually imagines another world — a kind of psychic utopia — outside. For he desperately needs to be else-where. Insecure and anxious, he creates a reductive version of another place, a kind of imaginative journey away from the pain he feels. When he is anxious he engages in repression and transference; he feels others looking at him. Directly before his speech, he nervously sees others looking at him: "People, perhaps, were standing in the snow on the quay outside, gazing up at the lighted windows and listening to the waltz music. The air was pure there. In the distance lay the park where the trees were weighted with snow. The Wellington Monument wore a gleaming cap of snow that flashed westward over the white field of Fif-teen Acres" (42). We should notice how, in anticipation of the perform-ative ending, Joyce shows that for Gabriel the snow becomes an image of escape and distance and the west is associated with the primitive and spontaneous.

III. "Distant Music": Gabriel's Psyche Amidst Cultural and Historical Contexts

Gabriel always sees himself as other. We must also understand that Gabriel has aspects of paranoia — the domestic kind that haunts all of our insecurities — in his sense that he is always being watched, weighed, regarded, put to a test, and found wanting. Sometimes the division between his public presence and his private, insecure self is so great that he perceives as if he were traumatized or at least depressed. He is reactive rather than active and occasionally behaves as if he were anesthetized. Of course, we understand that the one who is always watching Gabriel *is* Gabriel. In the tiny world of his aunts' party, he is the dominant male who knows how to carve a goose, cope with a drunk guest, give a speech. But he is as fragmented as his hodgepodge of knowledge. He needs to differentiate himself from others and to pa-tronize others. Gabriel suffers from hyperacuity of perception, and the narrator uses modes of hyperacuity to invite the reader to measure him. Ironically, Gabriel sees *himself* as if he were a painting, an object, or a text requiring another to bring him to life. We might recall Lacan's in-sight about the painter's gaze:

> The painter gives something to the person who must stand in front of his painting which, in part, at least, of the painting, might be summed up thus — *You want to see? Well, take a look at this!* He gives something for the eye to feed on, but he invites the per-son to whom this picture is presented to lay down his gaze there

as one lays down one's weapons. This is the pacifying, Apollonian effect of painting. Something is given not so much to the gaze as to the eye, something that involves the abandonment, the *laying down,* of the gaze.[5]

Indeed, Gabriel has the same kind of alternating sympathy and irony toward himself whom he often regards as strangely detached, the object of his own gaze, a kind of painting he regards in the same way he gazes at his wife on the stairs. His watching her laughing at him for making her wear galoshes anticipates the later view of her as a painting: his "admiring and happy eyes had been wandering from her dress to her face and hair" (25).

The Lacanian perspective, like the Freudian and Laing perspectives, is important, in part because it stresses the need to be aware of the place of women in the text. We realize that Lacan's words apply to the way he watches himself, and that it is this division between himself as subject and as object which is at the heart of his problem. As Garry Leonard writes:

> In the most fundamental sense, Lacan divides the subject in two. The speaking subject he calls *je* or "I." The object-like stable sense of subjectivity, what we might call an ideal sense of identity, Lacan designates as the *moi* or me. . . . The *je* tries to bring about, through other subjects, the messages that the *moi* requires in order to believe in its existence. . . . One cannot become aware of the perpetual failure of language to join the *moi* and *je* into a unified whole without also becoming aware of the fact that masculine subjectivity is a cultural construct that only appears to exist between the two.[6]

But isn't the disjunction between the *moi* and *je* a cultural construct for *both* genders and thus also true of the feminine subjectivity of Miss Ivors, Lily, and Gretta? Who — except Gabriel who oscillates between too much and too little of that quality — has self-awareness in "The Dead"?

When he sees Gretta as a painting, Gabriel is a captive of his visual imagination, which is ironic because he wears spectacles and has difficulty seeing.

> He stood still in the gloom of the hall, trying to catch the air that the voice was singing and gazing up at his wife. There was grace

[5]Jacques Lacan, *The Four Fundamental Concepts of Psycho-Analysis,* ed. Jacques-Alain Miller, trans. Alan Sheridan (New York: Norton, 1981).

[6]Garry Leonard, "Joyce and Lacan: The 'Woman' as a Symptom of 'Masculinity' in 'The Dead,' " *James Joyce Quarterly* 28.2 (1991): 451, 460.

and mystery in her attitude as if she were a symbol of something. He asked himself what is a woman standing on the stairs in the shadow, listening to distant music, a symbol of. If he were a painter he would paint her in that attitude. Her blue felt hat would show off the bronze of her hair against the darkness and the dark panels of her skirt would show off the light ones. *Distant Music* he would call the picture if he were a painter. (48)

Earlier, Gabriel notices the *painting* over the piano of the death scenes in *Romeo and Juliet* and one of the murdered princes; notice how these are not Irish pictures that Miss Ivors — or followers of the Celtic Renaissance — would approve of. It is indicative of Gabriel's attachment to western Europe that he travels to the continent, cites the continental precedent for galoshes, thinks of Browning and Shakespeare, and alludes to Paris and the Golden Apple. When Gabriel declares to Miss Ivors that he is sick of his own country, we may think of Stephen telling Bloom in "Eumaeus," "Since we can't change the country, let's change the subject." That the west of Ireland is associated with the primitive and sexual recalls the association of sexuality with primitivism — with the Orient or with the South Sea Islands — in the paintings of Gauguin or Matisse or the writings of Stevenson and Conrad.

In turn-of-the-century modernist texts, dance becomes an image of the Dionysian and libidinous. We might think of Aschenbach's dream of a Dionysian, orgiastic dance featuring a version of his beloved Tadzio in Mann's *Death in Venice* (1912). Dance became a sanctioned expression of the libido; it enabled participants to express sexuality in forms ranging from passion to flirtation within permissible activities. Diaghilev was in Paris, and Isadora Duncan performed in 1909. One might say that Gabriel does a pirouette around an arabesque of uncertainty. After Gretta falls asleep at the hotel, he thinks of how the "riot of emotions" — his sexual desire — had derived "[f]rom his aunts' supper, from his own foolish speech, from the wine and dancing, the merrymaking when saying good-night in the hall, the pleasure of the walk along the river in the snow" (58). The place of dance — waltzes, quadrilles, and lancers — in this 1907 text is significant if we think of Matisse's great painting *Dance* (1910) and its sequel *Music* (1911), which showed the importance of dance and music to turn-of-the-century culture. Does not the dispute between Miss Ivors and Gabriel while they are dancing recall the broken circle of Matisse's *Dance,* where we realize that the individual dancers are dancing partly alone, some clockwise and some counterclockwise, in their own private space? Under the influence of Walter Pater, music was thought by many turn-of-the-century artists to be the highest form of art and the one toward which other arts should strive, but it is diluted in "The Dead" by Mary Jane's Academy piano piece, which can only be followed by Mary Jane and Aunt Kate. Most of the best music seems to be in the past, except for Bartell D'Arcy, a theme reinforced by much of *Dubliners*, especially "A Mother." Indeed, we might think of the anaesthetized, isolated musicians of Matisse's *Music*. Among other things, we might note that "The Dead" is about the inability of other arts to revivify Gabriel's life; neither music, nor dance, nor painting do the trick.

A psychological criticism may also address how characters iterate and depart from mythic prototypes. (Joyce would have known Fraser's *The Golden Bough*.) What Eliot wrote of *Ulysses* is also applicable to "The Dead"; Joyce's references to myth, he contended, are "a way of controlling, of ordering, of giving shape and significance to the immense panorama of futility and anarchy which is contemporary history."[7] The allusive technique of "The Dead" anticipates *Ulysses*. After calling his Aunt Kate, Aunt Julia, and Mary Jane "The Three Graces," he says, "I will not attempt to play to-night the part that Paris played on another occasion. I will not attempt to choose between them" (44). We as rereaders realize that it is not Gabriel but Gretta who is the Paris figure choosing between men — and, at least in Gabriel's mind, it is *he* who has not been chosen. Indeed, Paris does not award the Golden Apple among the Three Graces, but among Athena, Aphrodite, and Hera. (The Three Graces were Aylaia [splendor], Euphrosyne [mirth], and Thalia [good cheer].) The judgment of Paris inspired the *Iliad* and the *Odyssey*, but what will Gabriel inspire? He is mocked by his own allusions which weave a circumference of irony around him. Isn't there a bathetic irony in his comparing himself with Paris and his aunts and cousin with "The Three Graces"? Moreover, Paris's abduction of Helen began the Trojan war, and Gabriel is a kind of mock Paris who took Gretta from the west of Ireland.

Gabriel aesthetizes his experience as if he were locked into a set of perceptions from which he can't escape; Gabriel perceives in set scenes. Similarly, the narrator creates a perceptual epistemology that emphasizes the breakdown of narrative and development of Gabriel's sense of self. The dinner is described as if it were a still life, and may have been

---

[7] "*Ulysses*, Order, and Myth," *Dial* 75 (1923): 480–83; rpt. as "Myth and Literary Classicism" in *The Modern Tradition: Backgrounds of Modern Literature*, ed. Richard Ellmann and Charles Feidelson, Jr. (New York: Oxford UP, 1965) 675–81.

influenced by Joyce's awareness of that form in post-impressionistic paintings that he saw in Paris, including those of Cézanne:

> A fat brown goose lay at one end of the table and at the other end, on a bed of creased paper strewn with sprigs of parsley, lay a great ham, stripped of its outer skin and peppered over with crust crumbs, a neat paper frill round its shin and beside this was a round of spiced beef. Between these rival ends ran parallel lines of side-dishes: two little minsters of jelly, red and yellow; a shallow dish full of blocks of blancmange and red jam, a large green leaf-shaped dish with a stalk-shaped handle, on which lay bunches of purple raisins and peeled almonds, a companion dish on which lay a solid rectangle of Smyrna figs, a dish of custard topped with grated nutmeg, a small bowl full of chocolates and sweets wrapped in gold and silver papers and a glass vase in which stood some tall celery stalks. In the centre of the table there stood, as sentries to a fruit-stand which upheld a pyramid of oranges and American apples, two squat old-fashioned decanters of cut glass, one containing port and the other dark sherry. On the closed square piano a pudding in a huge yellow dish lay in waiting and behind it were three squads of bottles of stout and ale and minerals, drawn up according to the colours of their uniforms, the first two black, with brown and red labels, the third and smallest squad white, with transverse green sashes. (38)

The striking juxtaposition of this unfolding presentation of *plenty* — superficial plenty — coming within the context of spiritual and physical want not only in "The Dead" but in preceding stories like "A Painful Case," "Ivy Day in the Committee Room," "A Mother," and "Grace" emphasizes the *limits* of life in Dublin. It is as if Joyce were stressing the voyeuristic at the expense of intimacy and making the visual focus on voyeurism, as opposed to the touch of physical intimacy, a theme as a way of showing how Gabriel has displaced his feelings onto a world of material stuff. Seen from this perspective, is not the tale's last paragraph a conclusion to a narrative of landscapes and a hint that Gabriel still has a way to go before he becomes a flexible, responsive adult — like Bloom?

A psychological criticism notices patterns of language beneath the surface and understands the verbal play as if the text were a patient recalling more than she/he realizes. Joyce deftly creates a verbal texture that immerses the reader's mind in death and mortality until the reader is shaped to see an inevitability about death; it is almost as if the verbal texture were subliminally supporting the plot. Within the text there are continual references to death: Gabriel speaks of how his wife "takes three mortal hours" and the aunts respond that "she must be perished alive" (23). The monks "slept in their coffins"; the "subject" of the monks "had grown lugubrious" and "was buried in a silence" (42). Later we are told that Mrs. Malins "will get her death of cold" (45). The pictures on the wall above the piano of the murdered princes and of the balcony scene in *Romeo and Juliet* suggest death as well as the frustration of love and hope. Words like "gloom" and "shadows" become almost ghosts invisibly stalking the text. When Gabriel gazes at his wife listening to Bartell D'Arcy's singing, he is in "the gloom of the hall" and we recall the gloom he felt after Lily's retort, a gloom that left him wanting to be outside the room in which the waltzing was taking place.

In a sense, Joyce invites the reader to join him as one of those who are emotionally and spiritually alive, and one way that the reader feels enlivened is by seeing more perspicaciously than the characters in the tale entitled "The Dead." Rereading, we realize that Joyce creates a word world in which phrases that are applied to other people actually define Gabriel. Thus, it is not only Julia but Gabriel, too, "who did not know where she was or where she was going" (24). When Gabriel refuses to acknowledge that he should be ashamed of himself for writing for *The Daily Express,* the very iteration of "ashamed" three times in the context of his conversation creates an association in our minds between Gabriel and ashamed that is fulfilled when we are later told: "A shameful consciousness of his own person assailed him" (56). Note, too, the passivity of his stance in his sense of being assailed; it is as if things happen to him that he can't control, as when he feels at the moment when he expected to triumph in his affection for Gretta "some impalpable and vindictive being was coming against him" (57). While Gabriel's paralytic self-consciousness is a poignant echo of Hamlet, another figure caught up in a rotting, alcoholic culture and drawn to his mother, Michael Furey is posing perhaps as the ghost of Hamlet's father.

IV. Gabriel's Transformation

While Gabriel's irony fails when he learns of Michael and his passionate love for Gretta, Joyce's narrator's irony does not. Can we be sure that Gretta is any more reliable than Gabriel? Ironically, Gretta has taken seriously Gabriel's advice in his speech to "cherish in our hearts the memory of those dead" which "the world will not willingly let die" (43). Perhaps in her imagination she creates the passionate, heroic lover. This is the kind of legend that has informed the whole story. And

Gabriel, as Vincent P. Pecora has written, then reinvents himself as a heroic figure with abundant generosity:

> To avoid being further humiliated by others, Gabriel must of course humiliate himself. In the name of Michael Furey, his legendary hero and personal saint, Gabriel sacrifices himself to the past, and to the dead, more profoundly than any of his compatriots does. Moreover, he appears completely assured of the sincerity of his gesture. That is, Gabriel has reproduced in himself, like his vision of Michael Furey, the most fundamental structuring device for heroism, generosity, self-knowledge, and spiritual transcendence in his culture: the story of Christ. . . . If Gabriel fools himself, if in the very process that we accept as self-discovery he only reimplicates himself blindly in the cultural conditions he longs to transcend, then we may simply be doing the same thing, in our reading, in our lives.[8]

That Gretta's memories of Michael are evoked by associations and provoked by a song, *The Lass of Aughrim,* recalls Freud's free association as well as Proust's. It is necessary to know that Gretta is responding to a song which tells of a seduced and abandoned young woman standing in the rain with her baby in her arms who is rejected in an attempt to see her former lover; the lover asks her a series of questions but does not let the young woman in to see him. For Gabriel, Gretta's associations become ironically Gabriel's reality; this is part of the vulnerability of his insecurity. Joyce shows how the interior space of the mind can become hell to those who lack religious faith; indeed, raised as an orthodox Catholic and a former novitiate, Joyce disbelieves as only a former believer can. Gabriel's hell is his obsessions, fixations, memories, insecurities, and dimly acknowledged needs. But throughout he is aware of aging and mortality. He knows his wife's face is "no longer the face for which Michael Furey had braved death" (58). As much as the dead, they are the shades and shadows which resist him. Indeed, in speaking so much of death and the dead, Gabriel creates a subtext that undermines the conclusion's positive implications and makes us aware of how he is reformulating and recirculating the elegiac and nostalgic mode that stresses the past.

That Gabriel cannot respond to Gretta as a sexual equal, that he is awkward and displaces his desire and cannot separate lust from passion is Joyce's way of castigating the Catholic church for producing dysfunc-

---

[8]Vincent P. Pecora, " 'The Dead' and the Generosity of the Word," *PMLA* 101.2 (1986): 243.

tional Irish males. (In Joyce's rural Ireland, as opposed to Dublin, both men and women seem to be less deflected from desire by the church: think of Gretta and Michael, and the woman who seduced Davin in *Portrait*, and, of course, Nora.) Because, Joyce implies, of his Irish Catholic upbringing, Gabriel cannot speak the language of desire: "To take her as she was would be brutal. No, he must see some ardour in her eyes first. He longed to be master of her strange mood. . . . He longed to cry to her from his soul, to crush her body against his, to overmaster her" (54). Yet Gabriel's need to master and control is an extension of his own problems as well as an instance of his culturally produced responses. Indeed, lacking a coherent self, Gabriel is a weather vane, affected by both cultural practices and the most recent conversations. Because of his awkwardness in sexual and passionate matters, he seeks refuge in Elizabethan language: "Gabriel, feeling now how vain it would be to try to lead her whither he had purposed" (56).

Yet one should also think about Gretta's behavior and motives. Why does she not realize that her words will hurt Gabriel and that this hyperconscious, insecure, anxious, and guilt-ridden man — her husband — will be upset and troubled? Is she not somewhat insensitive and inconsiderate to her husband? Should she not know that Gabriel, educated in a Catholic epistemology that regards premarital sex as a sin, will respond almost as if he were a victim of adultery? Even if she had been passionately in love, even if (which is hardly supported by the text) she and Michael had been lovers, does that discredit their marriage? His response to her revelation shows the degree to which he has suffered acculturation and recalls — in a kind of pentimento that makes us aware of how the boy in the early stories is the spiritual father of the man Gabriel — the final retrospective comment of the boy in "Araby" who thinks he has sinned because of his puppy love: "Gazing up into the darkness I saw myself as a creature driven and derided by vanity; and my eyes burned with anguish and anger" (*Dubliners* 35). Isn't it part of Gabriel's immaturity that he regards this relationship that took place before he met Gretta as a rejection? Joyce's criticism is directed at an Irish moral education, which includes a Catholic epistemology that teaches that the bride must be an innocent and a virgin. Part of the story's irony is that Gabriel, who would reject Irish superstition and be more enlightened, is locked into the system of values that he would reject.

Poignantly, Gabriel does not believe in his own intellect or passion. It is in the last section that Gabriel descends into hell. While the box-like hotel room recalls a coffin, the Charon-like clerk who takes them to their room upstairs as if he were rowing them across the river Lethe recalls other journeys to hell and death, including Mann's *Death in Venice,* and anticipates the "Hades" section in *Ulysses.*[9] That Gabriel has no coherent identity is underlined when he imagines himself approaching the region of the dead: "His own identity was fading out into a grey impalpable world: the solid world itself which these dead had one time reared and lived in was dissolving and dwindling" (59). In the face of disappointment, he, like snow, melts, and his ego dissolves. Note how he intuits something threatening when Gretta refers to the song to which she has been listening, *The Lass of Aughrim:* "As he passed in the way of the cheval-glass he caught sight of himself in full length, his broad, well-filled shirt-front, the face whose expression always puzzled him when he saw it in a mirror and his glimmering gilt-rimmed eyeglasses" (55). His gaze reflexively catches himself, as it does so often throughout the text. He is both subject and object in the mirror; we recall Wilde's *The Picture of Dorian Gray,* which Joyce surely would have had in mind, where Dorian's superego is transferred to the portrait which ages as a reflection of his dissipated life style, even while he apparently retains his youthful appearance.

After Gretta tells him about the boy of her past, he thinks that he has been rejected.

> Gabriel felt humiliated by the failure of his irony and by the evocation of this figure from the dead, a boy in the gasworks. While he had been full of memories of their secret life together, full of tenderness and joy and desire, she had been comparing him in her mind with another. A shameful consciousness of his own person assailed him. He saw himself as a ludicrous figure, acting as a pennyboy for his aunts, a nervous well-meaning sentimentalist, orating to vulgarians and idealising his own clownish lusts, the pitiable fatuous fellow he had caught a glimpse of in the mirror. Instinctively he turned his back more to the light lest she might see the shame that burned upon his forehead. (56; to the 1916 reader, the term "secret life" was a term that implied one's sexual life.)

When we look at this passage we should respond pluralistically to Gabriel's psychological drama in terms of other characters, of Joyce's doubts and fears, and of his narrator's elegizing a culture that now lacks coherence. We should see, too, Gabriel as an instance of *fin de siècle*

---

[9]Walzl notes, "The box-like hotel room, the removal of a candle, the darkness, the chill, and the bed on which Gretta lies, all build the impression of a vault where the dead rest frozen on their biers." Qtd. in *Dubliners: Text, Criticism, and Notes,* 433.

intellectual isolation, which looks forward to that theme in *Portrait* and in *Ulysses*.

The man of words is deprived of words. Finally he realizes that he had always spoken in clichés and abstractions, and that he speaks in words that are culturally inscribed. After he hears of Gretta's love for Michael — and the emperor's new clothes are once again stripped from his vulnerable vanity — he thinks of how he will be speaking at Aunt Julia's funeral:

> Soon, perhaps, he would be sitting in that same drawing-room, dressed in black, his silk hat on his knees. The blinds would be drawn down and Aunt Kate would be sitting beside him, crying and blowing her nose and telling him how Julia had died. He would cast about in his mind for some words that might console her, and would find only lame and useless ones. Yes, yes: that would happen very soon. (58)

Again he imagines himself playing a part. Readers of *Ulysses* will recall how *yes*, iterated by Bloom and affirmed by Molly, is a crucial word linking the two estranged lovers throughout June 16, 1904. In the above passage, Joyce might have expected Irish readers to hear the echo of a line from *Arrayed for the Bridal:* "May life to her prove full of sunshine and love, full of love, yes! yes! yes!!"

As we read we respond in multiple ways, including our awareness of how each of these aspects alternately becomes more dominant and then recedes in the face of the claims of the other. Does not the ending of "The Dead" make this clear? For as the last protagonist in a series of stories about moral paralysis in Ireland, Gabriel's paralytic self-consciousness and his inability to connect with Gretta give him significance as a representative of the failure of will, breakdown of family, and sexual inadequacy that, along with (and perhaps as a result of) Catholicism and English imperialism, are paralyzing Ireland. But as a particularized figure who has realized his limitations as a lover and a man and feels generosity to his wife, Gabriel is interesting and significant because he has the potential for growth and transformation. Thus Gabriel's transformation at the end of "The Dead" is a personal one — one that does not free the rest of the Dublin residents from moral and spiritual paralysis but is a moment of hope rendered as a performance in which the reader participates:

> Generous tears filled Gabriel's eyes. He had never felt like that himself towards any woman but he knew that such a feeling must be love. The tears gathered more thickly in his eyes and in the

partial darkness he imagined he saw the form of a young man standing under a dripping tree. Other forms were near. His soul had approached that region where dwell the vast hosts of the dead. He was conscious of, but could not apprehend, their wayward and flickering existence. His own identity was fading out into a grey impalpable world: the solid world itself which these dead had one time reared and lived in was dissolving and dwindling.

A few light taps upon the pane made him turn to the window. It had begun to snow again. He watched sleepily the flakes, silver and dark, falling obliquely against the lamplight. The time had come for him to set out on his journey westward. Yes, the newspapers were right: snow was general all over Ireland. It was falling on every part of the dark central plain, on the treeless hills, falling softly upon the Bog of Allen and, farther westward, softly falling into the dark mutinous Shannon waves. It was falling, too, upon every part of the lonely churchyard on the hill where Michael Furey lay buried. It lay thickly drifted on the crooked crosses and headstones, on the spears of the little gate, on the barren thorns. His soul swooned slowly as he heard the snow falling faintly through the universe and faintly falling, like the descent of their last end, upon all the living and the dead. (59)

What is performed is the suspension of rational and linear thought. While, as we know from John Huston's film of "The Dead," the passage can be visualized, does it not enact a state of being that finally transcends the visual, a state when the soul, as Yeats puts it in "Sailing to Byzantium," "clap[s] its hands and sing[s]"? It is Gabriel's reward — just as the vision of Rudy is Bloom's reward — for loving Gretta, for understanding that passion is itself a value ("Better pass boldly into that other world, in the full glory of some passion, than fade and wither dismally with age"). Discursively, the last sentence makes little sense. One cannot hear snow falling and the antecedent of "their" is indeterminate (snowflakes? all the dead? Gretta and Michael? Gretta, Michael, and himself? all the past and future dead?). Gabriel's move outside the enclosure of his ego is enabled/performed by the phonics and reversals of the passage, particularly the last sentence. The passage's meaning derives from its place in a process; it contrasts with the mimesis of the preceding pages of the story and with Gabriel's paralytic self-consciousness, rationality, and literalism.

The ending is discourse not story; yet as discourse it shows us what Gabriel needs and lacks: song, lyricism, metaphoricity, escape from time into non-rational, passionate states of being, a loosening of the bonds of self-consciousness. Gabriel's dissolution of his ego is a positive move because he can surrender to the lyrical moment, a time when the soul claps hands and sings. In a sense, at this moment he joins the dance of life, or thinks he does.[10] It is a moment of rare serenity — visual, tonal, emotional serenity — a moment which resists (perhaps resents?) the critic's rational efforts to order it because it is allegorical and asyntactical. Even while acknowledging the brilliance of Huston's visualization, do we not feel that it encroaches on our interior experience, on our private admiration of the scene and reduces our rich, polyauditory response to Gabriel's interior life and Joyce's rendering of it to a sequence of visual images? Isn't that often the problem when we see our intimate reading experience transformed into a film?

What is absent is as important as what is present in responding to character. The snow imagery focuses our attention on a world outside Gabriel — a natural world where generations live and die and survive their sense of self-importance; we recall that snow has the potential to become ice (death) and water (life). Obviously, as ice it also suggests the emotional sterility of a world reduced to social gestures, empty talk, and loveless relationships — a world where a tiny pathetic "I" cannot connect to others to form a loving, passionate, tender couple; a world that does not even give the feeling he so desperately needs that he is part of a social mosaic. We can never be sure whether Gretta is waiting for Gabriel in the way that Molly is waiting for Bloom, because we see less of Gabriel's dignity and integrity and we know more of Gabriel's selfishness and narrow-mindedness. Perhaps we do not quite sympathize with Gabriel's sense of isolation and disappointment as we do with Bloom's because of the latter's generous concern for others — such as Paddy Dignam's family and Mrs. Purefoy.

Note how the mimetic code inserts itself when basic emotions of love and death are the subject. We respond powerfully to descriptions of Gabriel's transformation and use psychological grammar to understand that transformation, including his realization that conscience and self-consciousness are not the full parameters of living, that the love shared by Michael and Gretta contained passion, intensity, love, and intimacy that go beyond concern with whether Gretta wears goloshes. We might therefore speak of the precedence of subjects and note how our

---

[10]In *Portrait*, we recall Stephen dreams that he no longer exists: "How strange to think of him passing out of existence in such a way, not by death but by fading out in the sun or being lost or forgotten somewhere in the universe" (89). And in "Hades" Bloom descends into his own hell which includes the fear that he will no longer exist, but Bloom — far more emphatically than Gabriel — returns because of his resilience and coherence, because his ego negotiates effectively between his id and superego.

aesthetic sense itself is more likely to be pushed aside and relegated to the back burner when we are engaged by issues that matter to our human feelings — notably, issues of the human psyche. And we might say that most of us will be engaged mainly by the representation of emotions that interest us. Indeed, in speaking of the precedence of subject, should we not acknowledge that a culture's ever-changing preference and interest in certain themes and problems help create and recreate its canon?

WORKS CITED

Eliot, T. S. "*Ulysses,* Order, and Myth," *Dial* 75 (1923): 480–83. Rpt. as "Myth and Literary Classicism." *The Modern Tradition: Backgrounds of Modern Literature.* Ed. Richard Ellmann and Charles Feidelson, Jr. New York: Oxford UP, 1965. 675–81.

Joyce, James. *Dubliners: Text, Criticism, and Notes.* Ed. Robert Scholes and A. Walton Litz. New York: Viking, 1968.

———. *A Portrait of the Artist as a Young Man.* Ed. R. B. Kershner. Boston: Bedford–St. Martin's, 1993.

Lacan, Jacques. *The Four Fundamental Concepts of Psycho-Analysis.* Ed. Jacques-Alain Miller. Trans. Alan Sheridan. New York: Norton, 1981.

Laing, R. D. *The Divided Self: An Existential Study in Sanity and Madness.* Baltimore: Penguin, 1965.

Leonard, Garry. "Joyce and Lacan: The 'Woman' as a Symptom of 'Masculinity' in 'The Dead.' " *James Joyce Quarterly* 28.2 (1991): 451–72.

Mason, Ellsworth, and Richard Ellmann, eds. *The Critical Writings of James Joyce.* New York: Viking, 1959.

Pecora, Vincent P. " 'The Dead' and the Generosity of the Word." *PMLA* 101.2 (1986): 233–45.

Reader-Response Criticism
and
"The Dead"

WHAT IS READER-RESPONSE CRITICISM?

Students are routinely asked in English courses for their reactions to texts they are reading. Sometimes there are so many different reactions that we may wonder whether everyone has read the same text. And some students respond so idiosyncratically to what they read that we say their responses are "totally off the wall."

Reader-response critics are interested in the variety of our responses. Reader-response criticism raises theoretical questions about whether our responses to a work are the same as its meanings, whether a work can have as many meanings as we have responses to it, and whether some responses are more valid than, or superior to, others. It asks us to pose the following questions: What have we internalized that helps us determine what is and what isn't "off the wall"? In other words, what is the wall, and what standards help us to define it?

Reader-response criticism also provides models that are useful in answering such questions. Adena Rosmarin has suggested that a work can be likened to an incomplete work of sculpture: to see it fully, we *must* complete it imaginatively, taking care to do so in a way that responsibly takes into account what is there. An introduction to several other models of reader-response theory will allow you to understand better the reader-oriented essay that follows as well as to see a variety of ways in which, as a reader-response critic, you might respond to literary works.

Reader-response criticism, which emerged during the 1970s, focuses on what texts do to, or in, the mind of the reader, rather than regarding a text as something with properties exclusively its own. A poem, Louise M. Rosenblatt wrote as early as 1969, "is what the reader lives through under the guidance of the text and experiences as relevant to the text." Rosenblatt knew her definition would be difficult for many to accept: "The idea that a *poem* presupposes a *reader* actively involved with a *text*," she wrote, "is particularly shocking to those seeking to emphasize the objectivity of their interpretations" (127).

Rosenblatt is implicitly referring to the formalists, the old "New Critics," when she speaks of supposedly objective interpreters shocked by the notion that readers help make poems. Formalists preferred to discuss "the poem itself," the "concrete work of art," the "real poem." And they refused to describe what a work of literature makes a reader "live through." In fact, in *The Verbal Icon* (1954), William K. Wimsatt and Monroe C. Beardsley defined as fallacious the very notion that a reader's response is part of the meaning of a literary work:

> The Affective Fallacy is a confusion between the poem and its *results* (what it *is* and what it *does*). . . . It begins by trying to derive the standards of criticism from the psychological effects of a poem and ends in impressionism and relativism. The outcome . . . is that the poem itself, as an object of specifically critical judgment, tends to disappear. (21)

Reader-response critics take issue with their formalist predecessors. Stanley Fish, author of a highly influential article entitled "Literature in the Reader: Affective Stylistics" (1970), argues that any school of criticism that would see a work of literature as an object, that would claim to describe what it *is* and never what it *does,* is guilty of misconstruing what literature and reading really are. Literature exists when it is read, Fish suggests, and its force is an affective force. Furthermore, reading is a temporal process. Formalists assume it is a spatial one as they step back and survey the literary work as if it were an object spread out before them. They may find elegant patterns in the texts they examine and reexamine, but they fail to take into account that the work is quite different to a reader who is turning the pages and being moved, or affected, by lines that appear and disappear as the reader reads.

In a discussion of the effect that a sentence penned by the seventeenth-century physician Thomas Browne has on a reader reading, Fish pauses to say this about his analysis and also, by extension, about the overall critical strategy he has largely developed: "Whatever is persuasive and illuminating about [it] . . . is the result of my substituting for one question — what does this sentence mean? — another, more operational question — what does this sentence do?" He then quotes a line from John Milton's *Paradise Lost,* a line that refers to Satan and the other fallen angels: "Nor did they not perceive their evil plight." Whereas more traditional critics might say that the "meaning" of the line is "They did perceive their evil plight," Fish relates the uncertain movement of the reader's mind *to* that half-satisfying interpretation. Furthermore, he declares that "the reader's inability to tell whether or not 'they' do perceive and his involuntary question . . . are part of the line's *meaning,* even though they take place in the mind, not on the page" (*Text* 26).

This stress on what pages *do* to minds pervades the writings of most, if not all, reader-response critics. Wolfgang Iser, author of *The Implied Reader* (1974) and *The Act of Reading: A Theory of Aesthetic Response* (1976), finds texts to be full of "gaps," and these gaps, or "blanks," as he sometimes calls them, powerfully affect the reader. The reader is forced to explain them, to connect what the gaps separate, literally to create in his or her mind a poem or novel or play that isn't *in* the text but that the text incites. Stephen Booth, who greatly influenced Fish, equally emphasizes what words, sentences, and passages "do." He stresses in his analyses the "reading experience that results" from a "multiplicity of organizations" in, say, a Shakespeare sonnet (*Essay* ix). Somctimes these organizations don't make complete sense, and sometimes they even seem curiously contradictory. But that is precisely what interests reader-response critics, who, unlike formalists, are at least as interested in fragmentary, inconclusive, and even unfinished texts as in polished, unified works. For it is the reader's struggle to *make sense* of a challenging work that reader-response critics seek to describe.

In *Self-Consuming Artifacts: The Experience of Seventeenth-Century Literature* (1972), Fish reveals his preference for literature that makes readers work at making meaning. He contrasts two kinds of literary presentation. By the phrase "rhetorical presentation," he describes literature that reflects and reinforces opinions that readers already hold; by "dialectical presentation," he refers to works that prod and provoke. A dialectical text, rather than presenting an opinion as if it were truth, challenges readers to discover truths on their own. Such a text may not even have the kind of symmetry that formalist critics seek. Instead of offering a "single, sustained argument," a dialectical text, or self-consuming artifact, may be "so arranged that to enter into the spirit and assumptions of any one of [its] . . . units is implicitly to reject the spirit and assumptions of the unit immediately preceding" (*Artifacts* 9). Such a text needs a reader-response critic to elucidate its workings. Another kind of critic is likely to try to explain why the units are unified and coherent, not why such units are contradicting and "consuming" their predecessors. The reader-response critic proceeds by describing the reader's way of dealing with the sudden twists and turns that characterize the dialectical text, making the reader return to earlier passages and see them in an entirely new light.

"The value of such a procedure," Fish has written, "is predicated on the idea of meaning as *an event*," not as something "located (presumed to be embedded) *in* the utterance" or "verbal object as a thing in itself " (*Text* 28). By redefining meaning as an event, the reader-response critic once again locates meaning in time: the reader's time. A text exists and signifies while it is being read, and what it signifies or means will depend, to no small extent, on *when* it is read. (*Paradise Lost* had some meanings for a seventeenth-century Puritan that it would not have for a twentieth-century atheist.)

With the redefinition of literature as something that only exists meaningfully in the mind of the reader, with the redefinition of the literary work as a catalyst of mental events, comes a concurrent redefinition of the reader. No longer is the reader the passive recipient of those ideas that an author has planted in a text. "The reader is *active*," Rosenblatt insists (123). Fish begins "Literature in the Reader" with a similar observation: "If at this moment someone were to ask, 'what are you doing,' you might reply, 'I am reading,' and thereby acknowledge that reading is . . . something *you do*" (*Text* 22). In "How to Recognize a Poem When You See One," he is even more provocative: "Interpreters do not decode poems: they make them" (*Text* 327). Iser, in focusing critical interest on the gaps in texts, on what is not expressed, similarly redefines the reader as an active maker. In an essay entitled "Interaction between Text and Reader," he argues that what is missing from a narrative causes the reader to fill in the blanks creatively.

Iser's title implies a cooperation between reader and text that is also implied by Rosenblatt's definition of a poem as "what the reader lives through under the guidance of the text." Indeed, Rosenblatt borrowed the term "transactional" to describe the dynamics of the reading process, which in her view involves interdependent texts and readers interacting. The view that texts and readers make poems together, though, is not shared by *all* interpreters generally thought of as reader-response critics. Steven Mailloux has divided reader-response critics into several categories, one of which he labels "subjective." Subjective critics, like David Bleich (or Norman Holland after his conversion by Bleich), assume what Mailloux calls the "absolute priority of individual selves as creators of texts" (*Conventions* 31). In other words, these critics do not see the reader's response as one "guided" by the text but rather as one motivated by deep-seated, personal, psychological needs. What they find in texts is, in Holland's phrase, their own "identity theme." Holland has argued that as readers we use "the literary work to symbolize and finally to replicate ourselves. We work out through the text our own characteristic patterns of desire" ("UNITY" 816).

Subjective critics, as you may already have guessed, often find themselves confronted with the following question: If all interpretation is a function of private, psychological identity, then why have so many readers interpreted, say, Shakespeare's *Hamlet* in the same way? Different subjective critics have answered the question differently. Holland simply has said that common identity themes exist, such as that involving an oedipal fantasy. Fish, who went through a subjectivist stage, has provided a different answer. In "Interpreting the *Variorum*," he argues that the "stability of interpretation among readers" is a function of shared "interpretive strategies." These strategies, which "exist prior to the act of reading and therefore determine the shape of what is read," are held in common by "interpretive communities" such as the one comprised by American college students reading a novel as a class assignment (*Text* 167, 171).

As I have suggested in the paragraph above, reader-response criticism is not a monolithic school of thought, as is assumed by some detractors who like to talk about the "School of Fish." Several of the critics mentioned thus far have, over time, adopted different versions of reader-response criticism. I have hinted at Holland's growing subjectivism as well as the evolution of Fish's own thought. Fish, having at first viewed meaning as the cooperative production of readers and texts, went on to become a subjectivist, and very nearly a "deconstructor" ready to suggest that all criticism is imaginative creation, fiction about literature, or *metafiction*. In developing the notion of interpretive communities, however, Fish has become more of a social, structuralist, reader-response critic; currently, he is engaged in studying reading communities and their interpretive conventions in order to understand the conditions that give rise to a work's intelligibility.

In spite of the gaps between reader-response critics and even between the assumptions that they have held at various stages of their re-
spective careers, all try to answer similar questions and to use similar
strategies to describe the reader's response to a given text. One question
these critics are commonly asked has already been discussed: Why do
individual readers come up with such similar interpretations if meaning
is not embedded *in* the work itself? Other recurring, troubling questions include the following interrelated ones: Just who *is* the reader?
(Or, to place the emphasis differently, Just who is *the* reader?) Aren't
you reader-response critics just talking about your own idiosyncratic responses when you describe what a line from *Paradise Lost* "does" in and
to "the reader's" mind? What about my responses? What if they're different? Will you be willing to say that all responses are equally valid?

Fish defines "the reader" in this way: "*the* reader is the *informed*
reader." The informed reader is someone who is "sufficiently experienced as a reader to have internalized the properties of literary discourses, including everything from the most local of devices (figures of
speech, etc.) to whole genres." And, of course, the informed reader is in
full possession of the "semantic knowledge" (knowledge of idioms, for
instance) assumed by the text (*Artifacts* 406).

Other reader-response critics use terms besides "the *informed*
reader" to define "*the* reader," and these other terms mean slightly different things. Wayne Booth uses the phrase "the implied reader" to
mean the reader "created by the work." (Only "by agreeing to play the
role of this created audience," Susan Suleiman explains, "can an actual
reader correctly understand and appreciate the work" [8].) Gerard Gen-
ette and Gerald Prince prefer to speak of "the narratee, . . . the necessary
counterpart of a given narrator, that is, the person or figure who receives a narrative" (Suleiman 13). Like Booth, Iser employs the term
"the implied reader," but he also uses "the educated reader" when he
refers to what Fish calls the "informed" or "intended" reader. Thus,
with different terms, each critic denies the claim that reader-response
criticism might lead people to think that there are as many correct interpretations of a work as there are readers to read it.

As Mailloux has shown, reader-response critics share not only questions, answers, concepts, and terms for those concepts but also strategies of reading. Two of the basic "moves," as he calls them, are to show
that a work gives readers something to do, and to describe what the
reader does by way of response. And there are more complex moves as
well. For instance, a reader-response critic might typically (1) cite direct
references to reading in the text, in order to justify the focus on reading

and show that the inside of the text is continuous with what the reader is doing; (2) show how other nonreading situations in the text nonetheless mirror the situation the reader is in ("Fish shows how in *Paradise Lost* Michael's teaching of Adam in Book XI resembles Milton's teaching of the reader throughout the poem"); and (3) show, therefore, that the reader's response is, or is perfectly analogous to, the topic of the story. For Stephen Booth, *Hamlet* is the tragic story of "an audience that cannot make up its mind." In the view of Roger Easson, Blake's *Jerusalem* "may be read as a poem about the experience of reading *Jerusalem*" (Mailloux, "Learning" 103).

Peter Rabinowitz begins the essay that follows by recalling a moment of "interpretive vertigo" in "The Dead" — the staircase scene in which Gabriel Conroy wonders what his wife is "a symbol of." He goes on to compare Gabriel's interpretive disorientation with our analogous uncertainty about "The Dead." Arguing that neither old-fashioned formalism (the old "New Criticism") nor Freudian psychoanalytic criticism can unpack the problems that the text presents, Rabinowitz proceeds not by banishing, but rather by explaining, our interpretive vertigo via a sophisticated new version of reader-response criticism that he prefers to call "reader criticism."

Rabinowitz begins with the assumptions that reading is a "rule-governed transformative activity" in which readers actively transform the text by paraphrasing and interpreting it. Among the rules we implicitly follow as we try to make sense of a text are the rules of "notice," "signification," "configuration," and "coherence" — rules telling us what parts of a narrative are important, what details have a reliable secondary or special meaning, which details fit into which familiar patterns, and how stories fit together as a whole. We may apply different rules to different kinds of texts, but, Rabinowitz insists, we will inevitably follow *some* interpretive rules. Why? To limit interpretive vertigo — because such rules can help us "to smooth away discordant details" in what we experience.

Some of the rules we follow are, Rabinowitz argues, implicit in "patterns of expectations and fulfillment" we learn as young children. Others are taught by literary criticism, including criticism of the kind attached to "The Dead" in this edition. When rules of this latter kind conflict, however, they *promote* what Rabinowitz has called "interpretive vertigo" instead of reducing it. Rather than being inherent in the text, our uncertainty about what "The Dead" means is created by just such colliding rules of reading that we, as modern readers, have been — and are being — taught to apply to such a text. Rabinowitz claims that the "Rule of Hyperdense Intertextuality" tells us that "any intertextual connection whatsoever is significant" in a work that flaunts intertextual connections. (Because Joyce went on, after writing "The Dead" and *Dubliners,* to write *Ulysses* and *Finnegans Wake,* we have been taught that Joyce wrote texts flaunting intertextual connections.) The second rule we have been taught to apply to "The Dead" is what Rabinowitz calls the "Rule of Infinite Etymology." This rule "entitles us to assume that every word brings along with it not only its meaning, but also all the associations of its etymological origins."

These two rules of signification, when applied simultaneously, create various uncertainties, ambiguities, and confusions. To complicate matters further, however, these conflicting "rules of signification" clash with a "rule of coherence," which postulates that "everything must and in fact does fit together." This "intersection of rules" creates the vertigo effect, the "unresolved dissonance in the reading process," of which Rabinowitz is speaking "by pulling readers in two mutually incompatible directions." In addition, Rabinowitz argues, there are no "rules of blockage" that help us eliminate possible readings of the text; there seems to be no "hierarchical principle" to help us choose between "rules of reading."

Rabinowitz's essay exemplifies reader-oriented criticism in that it stresses reading as a verb — an activity that takes place as readers read and reread, as texts are read and reread. Like certain subjectivist reader-response critics, Rabinowitz sees the process of reading and the interpretive product as being governed not by what is *in* the text but, rather, by what readers bring *to* the text from outside. Like reader-response critics of a more recent vintage, however, Rabinowitz also stresses reading as a (plural) noun. That is to say, he stresses the way in which accepted critical "readings" of a given text gain widespread currency within a given reading community, establish certain interpretive conventions, and thereby come to shape the way in which the text is read — which is to say, what it means. Like other reader-response critics, he draws fruitful connections between acts of "reading" or interpretation that are performed by characters within the text and the problems that we, as readers, face in interpreting the interpreters.

Finally, Rabinowitz's essay remains in the tradition of reader-oriented criticism insofar as it does not seek to stabilize the text and thereby banish our interpretive vertigo by claiming to offer an objective view of what is inside — or even outside — it. Rather, it shows us that reading and readings evolve, and that by understanding that fact we take an important step toward constructing a new, imaginative, rule-governed (though possibly still vertiginous) reading of our own.

Ross C Murfin

READER-RESPONSE CRITICISM: A SELECTED BIBLIOGRAPHY

Some Introductions to Reader-Response Criticism

Fish, Stanley E. "Literature in the Reader: Affective Stylistics." *New Literary History* 2 (1970): 123–61. Rpt. in Fish 21–67 and in Primeau 154–79.

Freund, Elizabeth. *The Return of the Reader: Reader-Response Criticism.* London: Methuen, 1987.

Holland, Norman N. "UNITY IDENTITY TEXT SELF." *PMLA* 90 (1975): 813–22.

Holub, Robert C. *Reception Theory: A Critical Introduction.* New York: Methuen, 1984.

Mailloux, Steven. "Learning to Read: Interpretation and Reader-Response Criticism." *Studies in the Literary Imagination* 12 (1979): 93–108.

———. "Reader-Response Criticism?" *Genre* 10 (1977): 413–31.

Rosenblatt, Louise M. "Towards a Transactional Theory of Reading." *Journal of Reading Behavior* 1 (1969): 31–47. Rpt. in Primeau 121–46.

Suleiman, Susan R. "Introduction: Varieties of Audience-Oriented Criticism." Suleiman and Crosman 3–45.

Tompkins, Jane P. "An Introduction to Reader-Response Criticism." Tompkins ix–xxiv.

Reader-Response Criticism in Anthologies and Collections

Garvin, Harry R., ed. *Theories of Reading, Looking, and Listening.* Lewisburg: Bucknell UP, 1981. See the essays by Cain and Rosenblatt.

Leitch, Vincent B. *American Literary Criticism from the Thirties to the Eighties.* New York: Columbia UP, 1988.

Primeau, Ronald, ed. *Influx: Essays on Literary Influence.* Port Washington: Kennikat, 1977. See the essays by Fish, Holland, and Rosenblatt.

Suleiman, Susan R., and Inge Crosman, eds. *The Reader in the Text: Essays on Audience and Interpretation.* Princeton: Princeton UP, 1980. See especially the essays by Culler, Iser, and Todorov.

Tompkins, Jane P., ed. *Reader-Response Criticism: From Formalism to Post-Structuralism.* Baltimore: Johns Hopkins UP, 1980. See especially the essays by Bleich, Fish, Holland, Prince, and Tompkins.

Reader-Response Criticism: Some Major Works

Bleich, David. *Subjective Criticism.* Baltimore: Johns Hopkins UP, 1978.

Booth, Stephen. *An Essay on Shakespeare's Sonnets.* New Haven: Yale UP, 1969.

Eco, Umberto. *The Role of the Reader.* Bloomington: Indiana UP, 1979.

Fish, Stanley Eugene. *Doing What Comes Naturally: Change, Rhetoric, and the Practice of Theory in Literary and Legal Studies.* Durham: Duke UP, 1989.

———. *Is There a Text in This Class? The Authority of Interpretive Communities.* Cambridge: Harvard UP, 1980. In this volume are collected most of Fish's most influential essays, including "Literature in the Reader: Affective Stylistics," "What It's Like to Read *L'Allegro* and *Il Penseroso*," "Interpreting the *Variorum*," "Is There a Text in This Class?" "How to Recognize a Poem When You See One," and "What Makes an Interpretation Acceptable?"

———. *Self-Consuming Artifacts: The Experience of Seventeenth-Century Literature.* Berkeley: U of California P, 1972.

———. *Surprised by Sin: The Reader in Paradise Lost.* 2nd ed. Berkeley: U of California P, 1971.

Holland, Norman N. *5 Readers Reading.* New Haven: Yale UP, 1975.

Iser, Wolfgang. *The Art of Reading: A Theory of Aesthetic Response.* Baltimore: Johns Hopkins UP, 1978.

———. *The Implied Reader: Patterns of Communication in Prose Fiction from Bunyan to Beckett.* Baltimore: Johns Hopkins UP, 1974.

Jauss, Hans Robert. *Toward an Aesthetic of Reception.* Trans. Timothy Bahti. Intro. Paul de Man. Brighton, Eng.: Harvester, 1982.

Mailloux, Steven. *Interpretive Conventions: The Reader in the Study of American Fiction*. Ithaca: Cornell UP, 1982.

———. *Rhetorical Power*. Ithaca: Cornell UP, 1989.

Messent, Peter. *New Readings of the American Novel: Narrative Theory and Its Application*. New York: Macmillan, 1991.

Prince, Gerald. *Narratology*. New York: Mouton, 1982.

Rabinowitz, Peter. *Before Reading: Narrative Conventions and the Politics of Interpretation*. Ithaca: Cornell UP, 1987.

Radway, Janice A. *Reading the Romance: Women, Patriarchy, and Popular Literature*. Chapel Hill: U of North Carolina P, 1984.

Rosenblatt, Louise M. *The Reader, the Text, the Poem: The Transactional Theory of the Literary Work*. Carbondale, IL: Southern Illinois UP, 1978.

Steig, Michael. *Stories of Reading: Subjectivity and Literary Understanding*. Baltimore: Johns Hopkins UP, 1989.

Exemplary Short Readings of Major Texts

Anderson, Howard. "*Tristram Shandy* and the Reader's Imagination." *PMLA* 86 (1971): 966–73.

Berger, Carole. "The Rake and the Reader in Jane Austen's Novels." *Studies in English Literature, 1500–1900* 15 (1975): 531–44.

Booth, Stephen. "On the Value of *Hamlet*." *Reinterpretations of English Drama: Selected Papers from the English Institute*. Ed. Norman Rabkin. New York: Columbia UP, 1969. 137–76.

Easson, Robert R. "William Blake and His Reader in *Jerusalem*." *Blake's Sublime Allegory*. Ed. Stuart Curran and Joseph A. Wittreich. Madison: U of Wisconsin P, 1973. 309–28.

Kirk, Carey H. "*Moby-Dick:* The Challenge of Response." *Papers on Language and Literature* 13 (1977): 383–90.

Leverenz, David. "Mrs. Hawthorne's Headache: Reading *The Scarlet Letter*." *The Scarlet Letter: A Case Study in Contemporary Criticism*. Ed. Ross C Murfin. Boston: Bedford–St. Martin's, 1991. 263–74.

Lowe-Evans, Mary. "Reading with a 'Nicer Eye': Responding to *Frankenstein*." *Mary Shelley, Frankenstein*. Ed. Johanna M. Smith. Case Studies in Contemporary Criticism Series. Ed. Ross C Murfin. Boston: Bedford–St. Martin's, 1992. 215–29.

Rosmarin, Adena. "Darkening the Reader: Reader-Response Criticism and *Heart of Darkness*." *Heart of Darkness: A Case Study in Contemporary Criticism*. Ed. Ross C Murfin. Boston: Bedford–St. Martin's, 1989. 148–69.

Reader-Response Approaches to Joyce

Bleich, David. "The Conception and Documentation of the Author." *Subjective Criticism*. Baltimore: Johns Hopkins UP, 1978. On *A Portrait of the Artist as a Young Man*.

Iser, Wolfgang. *The Art of Reading: A Theory of Aesthetic Response*. Baltimore: Johns Hopkins UP, 1978; London: Routledge, 1979.

——. *The Implied Reader*. Ch. 7, "Doing Things in Style: An Interpretation of 'The Oxen of the Sun' in James Joyce's *Ulysses*." Baltimore: Johns Hopkins UP, 1974. 179–95.

——. "Patterns of Communication in Joyce's *Ulysses*." *New Perspectives in German Literary Criticism*. Ed. Richard E. Armacher & Victor Lange. Princeton: Princeton UP, 1979. 320–56.

James Joyce Quarterly 16 (Fall 1978/Winter 1979), "Structuralist/Reader-Response" issue.

Ruthrof, Horst. *The Reader's Construction of Narrative*. London and Boston: Routledge, 1981.

Thomas, Brook. *James Joyce's "Ulysses": A Book of Many Happy Returns*. Baton Rouge: Louisiana State UP, 1982.

Other Work Referred to in "What Is Reader-Response Criticism?"

Wimsatt, William K., and Monroe C. Beardsley. *The Verbal Icon*. Lexington: U of Kentucky P, 1954. See especially the discussion of "The Affective Fallacy," with which reader-response critics have so sharply disagreed.

A READER-RESPONSE PERSPECTIVE

PETER J. RABINOWITZ

"A Symbol of Something": Interpretive Vertigo in "The Dead"

In a much-discussed passage in "The Dead," Gabriel Conroy gazes up a staircase at his wife Gretta: "There was grace and mystery in her attitude as if she were a symbol of something. He asked himself what is a woman standing on the stairs in the shadow, listening to distant music, a symbol of " (48). Gabriel's moment of interpretive vertigo is probably shared by many readers, especially readers who have dipped into the criticism generated by the story. Doesn't Gabriel's musing distill the text as a whole? Isn't "The Dead" similar to Gretta at this crucial moment of wonderment: simultaneously familiar (not all that different in scope or style from a story by Chekhov, for instance) and yet disturbingly unstable and distant?

Where does this ambiguity come from? Critics with different theoretical orientations, of course, would locate its source in different places. A formalist, for instance, would turn to the structure of the written text, looking for ways in which it contradicts or at least destabilizes itself by occupying contradictory positions — looking, for instance, at what Thomas Loe has called "its deliberate thematic ambiguity" (485) or untangling the multiplicity of ghostly voices that Janet Egleson Dunleavy hears in the narration. A psychoanalytic critic, in contrast, might search out the ways in which the text works on our underlying anxieties — for instance, by exploring the uncanny effects of those ghosts that Dunleavy finds or by tying the effects of the story to the male anxieties about women summarized by Freud's notorious question, "What does Woman want?"

I do not believe, however, that these approaches can really get to the heart of the matter. The narrative's formal design, after all, is fairly straightforward, especially when compared to that found in such contemporaries as Kafka, whose writings seem consciously shaped to dizzy the reader. Similarly, the story is psychologically less dense than many other texts (Balzac's "Sarrasine" or Ford Madox Ford's *The Good Soldier*) that create a similar effect. I would, therefore, like to approach the question from a different direction by examining, instead, the interpretive procedures that readers are likely to bring to bear on the text.[1]

I am starting from the premise that reading is a rule-governed transformative activity. There are, actually, three distinct assumptions involved here. First, reading is an activity. There might be no need to emphasize this, except that the word "reading" has taken on a double meaning: it refers to both an event ("I'm reading 'The Dead' ") and to the consequence of that event ("In John B. Humma's reading of 'The Dead,' Gabriel's act of reclining between the sheets is tied, symbolically, to the snow covering Ireland"). To the extent that we are trying to uncover the sources of the reader's experience of vertigo, it is this first meaning of reading — reading as a process — with which we need to concern ourselves.

Second, the activity of reading always alters the text at hand. Unless we are limiting ourselves to reading in the sense of uninflected recitation, reading is never a passive activity to which the reader contributes nothing. Rather, it is inevitably (although not exclusively) a constructive act that takes the raw material of the words on the page and builds something else from them. This is true on even the most elementary level: reading the phrase "Hamilton routs Pioneers" (which just happened to be the random headline visible after my teenage son got done with the newspaper on the day I drafted this paragraph) requires the capacity to transform it into an equivalent sentence such as "Hamilton College's basketball team beat the Utica College basketball team last night." In general, I refer to this transformative act as "interpretation." But it is important to realize that it goes well beyond what is often meant by the term. For whether we engage in activities that are traditionally considered "interpretive" (as when Ruth Bauerle tells us that "a central theme" of "The Dead" is "the 'death' of marital affection between May and John Stanislaus Joyce" [113]), or whether we attempt to describe a text in more "objective" and "neutral" terms (as when

[1]Given the broad diversity of reader critics — broader than that within many other theoretical camps — it is perhaps worthwhile placing myself explicitly with respect to some of my colleagues. In my stress on interpretive procedures — in particular those in place before the actual act of reading — I depart significantly from those, like the early Stanley Fish of "Affective Stylistics," who are concerned with the temporal process of reading as it is taking place, as well as from those (like David Bleich at the end of *Readings and Feelings*) who are interested in how *completed* interpretations are negotiated within a community. It is also worth pointing out that unlike Janice Radway in *Reading the Romance* or Norman Holland in *5 Readers Reading*, I am concerned in this essay with hypothetical, rather than concrete, flesh-and-blood readers; and unlike many subjectivist critics, my focus here is more on readers' common experiences than on their differences.

Thomas Dilworth tells us that Joyce's story falls into two parts), we are inevitably constructing something new out of it — prodding it, reconfiguring it, translating it, simplifying it, highlighting it, whatever.

I do not want to suggest that such transformative construction is the only thing that readers can or should do with a text. But it is logically prior to many of the other things we do with texts (for instance, engaging in acts of judgment); and anyone incapable of making such transformations is, in a real sense, incapable of reading. The New Critics, whose formalism dominated the teaching of literature in America for decades, denounced what they called "the heresy of paraphrase." But reading, as the New Critics were paradoxically well aware, cannot take place without paraphrase. Paraphrase, though — and herein lies the third prong of my initial premise — need not be some random, intuitive or private action. Reading is not only an activity, nor only a transformative activity. To the extent that we are talking about reading as something — like that interpretive vertigo — that can be presented, shared, and discussed meaningfully with others, it is a rule-governed activity as well: it has a foundation in more or less communally agreed-upon procedures of transformation. To put it otherwise, interpretive procedures are conventional. This does not mean, of course, that these procedures are necessarily formulated explicitly by the readers involved. Nor does it mean that they are uniform, either for all readers or for all texts. Nonetheless, reading is always grounded on selections from a repertoire of preexisting interpretive procedures that are, even if implicit, susceptible to analytic scrutiny.

There are a vast number of such interpretive procedures, and as a means of keeping them under control, I have found it useful to sort them out, roughly, into four groups.[2] First there are what I call rules of notice, rules that direct our attention to particular high points in a text. In most narratives in our culture, for instance, endings are privileged — so it is no surprise that so much critical attention has been paid to the final paragraph, even the final sentence, of "The Dead." Similarly, there is a widely applicable rule that changes in a text's direction demand special attention. Tilly Eggers, for instance, implicitly calls upon this convention of reading when she stresses the stairway scene on the grounds that, at this point, "the story shifts from a social situation to a personal experience" (379). Second, there are what I call rules of signification, procedures that allow us to draw particular meanings out of the details the rules of notice have already selected. These rules tell us, for instance,

[2]For a fuller discussion, see my *Before Reading*.

when it is appropriate to assume a religious connotation to "three" (perhaps in the tripartite descriptions of Gerard Manley Hopkins' "The Windhover," but probably not when interpreting the third strike in "Casey at the Bat"), or when it is appropriate to find a sexual meaning in dying. Third, there are rules of configuration that allow us to take the details we have noticed and fit them into a familiar pattern, thus allowing us to predict the course of the story to come. It is through application of rules of configuration that we develop expectations, and experience the satisfaction that results when they are fulfilled — as well as the surprise or frustration that results when they are not. One rule in contemporary film and television, for instance, urges us to expect an eruption of danger whenever we are shown a closeup of a character putting a key in the lock of a car door. In "The Dead," Gabriel himself engages in a fairly explicit act of configuration, although it is musical and not literary: "He knew that Mary Jane must be near the end of her piece for she was playing again the opening melody with runs of scales after every bar" (30). Finally, there are rules of coherence that allow us to fit the text together as a whole. Examples include rules that allow us to tie a work to some larger thematic abstractions, as when Adrienne Munich concludes that "in 'The Dead' Joyce said good-bye to his former way of writing" (173) or when Richard Ellmann calls it "his first song of exile" (253). Similarly, rules of coherence provide interpretive techniques to smooth away discordant details, as when David Shields accounts for the "disturbing" repetition of "falling faintly" and "faintly falling" in the last line by ironizing the conclusion (428).

Any given reader is liable to apply different sets of rules to different kinds of texts — indeed, it is possible to define genre not only in the traditional way, as a group of texts that share textual features, but also as a group of texts that appear to invite similar interpretive strategies. Thus, even a reader who has been trained in the classroom to hunt down the metaphorical play of light and dark imagery in Joseph Conrad's *Heart of Darkness* is unlikely to apply the same reading strategies when he or she processes the first sentence of Pat Booth's steamy best-seller *Malibu:* "The headlights of the Porsche probed the winding road, and the hot sun moaned through Malibu" (1) (although given the genre, he or she might well want to give the "probing" and "moaning" a sexual spin).

But as we think of literary works in this way, we have to remember that these differences are not created by the text. Although authors normally have both desires and expectations about what interpretive conventions their readers will apply, and although they often provide us with guidance as to what rules we should play by, even that advice is incomprehensible unless some framework is already in place. The reference in "The Dead" to the picture of the balcony scene in *Romeo and Juliet* (30), for instance, may well be an invitation to apply rules of configuration and to prepare ourselves for the intervention of a tragic love plot in the story of Gabriel and Gretta. But unless the reader is prepared to recognize intertextual references as predictors in this way (and unless the reader knows *Romeo and Juliet* to begin with), the invitation will be misunderstood, if it is noticed at all.

Thus, even among readers who are interested in authorial intention (and not all readers always are), different readers call on different sets of rules even when reading the same text, which is what makes interpretive disagreement. Indeed, the *same* reader may call on different rules at different times even with regard to the same text, which is one reason why a text may seem different each time we return to it.

If the rules are not produced by the literary text, where do they come from? They are implicitly (and usually inductively) taught to readers, in increasing complexity, from a very early age. Through repetition of simple narratives, we teach preschoolers certain patterns of expectations and fulfillment, which they can then use as a template when they read future texts; we teach high schoolers how to recognize and interpret metaphors. These interpretive practices are then reinforced and refined by the "criticism" that is attached to works or groups of works, whether that criticism be in the form of journal articles or newspaper reviews or coming attractions (which play an important part in our configurational activities when we watch movies) or conversations around the office coffee pot or collections such as the one you are reading now.

As a consequence, reading is never an unmediated encounter between reader and text. Rather, reading is always reading in a particular cultural context, which to a greater or lesser (but always significant) extent predetermines the nature of that reading experience. And what I would like to propose here is that "The Dead" creates vertigo in a way that Chekhov's "Lady with a Dog," for instance, does not — not because of anything in what formalists would call "the texts themselves," but rather because, in the cultural climate in which we are apt to read them, we are encouraged to apply different sets of rules to the two texts. That is, the vertigo is produced by procedures that are likely to be *already in place* before we even read the opening sentence of "The Dead." More specifically, in part because of Joyce's later writings, an academically sanctioned "way of reading" *Dubliners* has grown up among Joycean critics, especially among Joycean close readers; and it is the peculiarities of this way of reading, rather than anything in the raw material of the text itself, that generates our vertiginous response to "The Dead."

Especially in a short essay, of course, any investigation of Joyce criticism will be wildly — even criminally — sketchy. As a model for thinking about the vertigo in "The Dead" from this perspective, I think it is fair to make the preliminary generalization that our response arises from an intersection of three rules. These rules, while rarely expounded explicitly, can nonetheless be caught on the wing, inferred from the practices of academic critics (at least those who make up what Daniel Schwarz calls "the cottage industry known as Joyce scholarship" [242]), as they approach the story. They include two specially Joycean rules of signification, along with an extreme application of a more general rule of coherence.

Let me begin with the signification. First, as readers of Joyce, we are encouraged to apply what I call the Rule of Hyperdense Intertextuality: any intertextual connection whatsoever is significant. All literature operates, of course, in part through the way that it filters and reflects off other works, particularly (but not exclusively) other literary works. These connections take a variety of forms. Sometimes, for instance, we have direct explicit reference, as when Tom Stoppard's *Rosencrantz and Guildenstern are Dead* takes up Shakespeare's *Hamlet*. Sometimes, an intertextual connection can be more covert — as when Henry James apparently borrows from Ivan Turgenev's *Assya* when constructing *Daisy Miller*.[3] Sometimes, too, intertextual connections are found in a general sharing of generic procedures (for instance, the common interpretive repertoire called upon by most classical British detective stories or most utopian novels). But for the most part, readers operate on the assumption that a given text works within a specific and limited intertextual domain. Thus, readers of *The Seagull* may well decide to treat Chekhov's farcical treatment of the dead (and later stuffed) bird — an object that is used and discarded by the characters as it suits their rhetorical purposes — as an ironic commentary on Ibsen's more conventionally symbolic use of a waterbird in *The Wild Duck*. But if they do, they are apt to justify their interpretive move on the grounds that Ibsen and Chekhov share a particular domain as late nineteenth-century realistic dramatists. Even readers who interpret this way, however, may choose not to make a similar connection to the albatross in Coleridge's

---

[3]Margot Norris makes a similar distinction between what she calls "citational intertexts" and what she calls "operational intertexts" (484).

Rime of the Ancient Mariner — unless they are able to come up with an interpretively relevant domain that they believe Chekhov and Coleridge share.

Joyce, however, has the reputation of being the ultimate literary magpie. This is partly, of course, due to the complexity of *Ulysses* and especially *Finnegans Wake,* but it is also partly due to the privileging of that complexity by an influential wing of modernist criticism that esteems complexity as a literary virtue in itself. As a result, we tend to read Joyce, even early Joyce, through such critical commonplaces as Ellmann's claim that "his work ended in the vastest encyclopedia" (4) or Wilhelm Füger's claim that he exhibits an "unusually high degree of intertextuality" (87). It is no surprise, then, that many critics have come to act as if he were participating in any and all possible intertextual domains. Thus, we are encouraged not only to interpret the scene where Gabriel looks up the stairs in terms of Torvald's fantasies about Nora as a mysterious stranger in Ibsen's *A Doll's House* (Norris 486), but Darrel Mansell also urges us to see William Holman Hunt's *The Awakening Conscience* as a painting that "lie[s] behind, and figure[s] in" Gabriel's vision (487), while R. B. Kershner advises us to see it in terms of the theatrical "tableau, that staple of nineteenth-century popular entertainment" (144).

The Rule of Hyperdense Intertextuality not only encourages us to assume that any intertextual connection is interpretively relevant; it also encourages us to assume that any perceived overlap, no matter how small, is sufficient justification for claiming an intertextual connection in the first place. We can infer this rule, for instance, in Mansell's analysis of Hunt's painting, an analysis that assures us of the validity of the connection even though the key elements in Joyce's scene, the staircase and the angle of vision, are not even present in *The Awakening Conscience.* A similar interpretive process lies behind Lucy B. Maddox's argument that "Joyce has set Gabriel in relation to Othello [specifically, Verdi's rather than Shakespeare's] in much the same way he was to set Leopold Bloom in relation to the figure of Ulysses." She bases her argument not on any explicit references, but on small points of contact between the two works: for instance, "The opera begins with Otello's [Verdi's spelling] entrance during the storm at Cyprus. . . . Gabriel also enters during a storm" (271, 274).

Intensifying the complexity introduced by the Rule of Hyperdense Intertextuality, a second rule of signification is apt to be in force as we read Joyce: the Rule of Infinite Etymology, which entitles us to assume that every word brings along with it not only its meaning, but also all the associations of its etymological origins. Thus, for instance, we are urged to assume that all the proper names in the story "designate" something. Lily's name "designates her as a unified entity" (Leonard 455); Freddy Malins' name refers both to *malum* (apple) and to *malus* (bad), both of which consequently lead to a religious thematics (Lytle 195) as well as to *malean* (Celtic for monk or disciple) and to the family that kept St. Patrick's bell in the North (Torchiana 126); Bartell d'Arcy can be interpreted as a cupid figure, since his name comes from *bois d'arc* ("that tree the French thought best for arrows. Its familiar name in this country is bodark, the mock orange, whose blossom can only mock that marriage which is no longer sacramental but carnal" [Lytle 208]). It is because of this rule, for instance, that Robert Bierman is able to interpret the cooked goose at the part as "a burlesque description of Gabriel — and Ireland": for "the name Gabriel refers to a pack of spectral hounds to which are popularly attributed the Gabrielratchet: a yelping sound, possibly made by wild *geese*" (Bierman 42–43).[4]

Even by themselves, these two rules of signification are apt to contribute to our vertigo, for the particular intertextual and etymological connections themselves sometimes bring ambiguity in their wake. Thus, for instance, qualities of ambiguity in the intertexts are sometimes carried over into "The Dead" as if by infection. This contagious ambiguity is seen, for instance, when Thomas Loe not only sees "The Dead" as a novella, but also treats this generic placement as grounds for comparing it to all other novellas (including future novellas such as Franz Kafka's *Metamorphosis,* Katherine Ann Porter's *Pale Horse, Pale Rider,* and even Saul Bellow's *Seize the Day* [Loe 485]), and for assuming, in part, that the ambiguities he finds in those texts must also be characteristic of Joyce's story as well.

But it is, ultimately, a combination of interpretive procedures — the union of these rules of signification with a rule of coherence — that produces the vertigo effect of which I'm speaking, by pulling readers in two mutually incompatible directions, simultaneously multiplying meanings and demanding that the text's meaning be unified and coherent. Let me take each of these in turn.

First, the rules of signification drown readers in meaning by multiplying possible significations. Of course, different critics (indeed, different readers more generally) inevitably multiply meanings of a text. But most interpretive strategies are internally hierarchical in that they close

---

[4]Gabriel's last name reinforces the hounds and hence the goose connection: Dilworth points out that "Any Irish school boy would know that *Cu* means 'hound'" (170). See also his claim that the goose "is, symbolically, [Gabriel] and his nation" (168).

off some meanings as they open some up. Sometimes that is because of the position of the author in our culture: a Christian critic might have much to say about Dashiell Hammett's *The Maltese Falcon,* but it would in all probability not come in the form of exposing supposedly authorially sanctioned Christian imagery in the text. More usually it is because of the limits imposed by a particular theoretical perspective. If you choose to read Kafka's *The Trial* as a traditional Freudian, for instance, you give priority to certain significations — but at the same time, the very procedures that open up psychoanalytic meanings block off other possible significations (for instance, the political implications) as secondary. Similarly, a reader who reads in terms of national literary traditions would be apt to see recollections of Pushkin's *Eugene Onegin* (the normally accepted starting point of the Russian realistic novel) in Turgenev's *Assya;* such a reading strategy not only opens up that possibility, but also gives *Eugene Onegin* priority over other potential intertexts that are not part of that particular lineage.

In the generally agreed upon procedures for reading Joyce, however, there are no equivalent rules of blockage that allow us to rule some of these significances out of bounds: they open up the gates without offering any hierarchical principle to choose among those who rush to enter. That is, the very procedures that allow Maddox to find the references to Verdi's *Otello* simultaneously open the text up to Mansell's pictorial reading. The procedures that encourage us to see Gabriel's name as a reference to Bret Harte's short story *Gabriel Conroy* (Kershner 148; Gifford 113–14) and to the archangel simultaneously require us to accept its relation to the stuffed goose — and, by extension, to Chekhov's and Ibsen's dead birds as well, especially since Ibsen is implicitly called to mind by the way the story's title echoes "When We Dead Awaken."

At the same time that Joycean scholarship opens up these multiple meanings, it observes an overarching rule of coherence: everything must and in fact does fit together. Andrew Lytle phrases it succinctly: " 'The Dead' has obviously been put together by a master craftsman. The form and the subject make a perfect joinery. Nothing is left dangling; no part of it is inert" (193). Stated so abstractly, of course, this rule is fairly familiar from the kinds of close-reading practices handed down to us (in increasingly tattered form) by the New Critics; but it is applied with special rigor to Joyce, where the "nothing" and "no part" are often treated with unaccustomed strictness. "No word or sound," Paul Barolsky tells us, "is without significance" (113). Thus, for instance, Füger implicitly relies on a rule of notice that stresses climactic maxims in order to give special prominence to Gabriel's "Better pass boldly into that other world, in the fully glory of some passion, than fade and wither dismally with age" (223). But he works out its ramifications by relying on the more general rule of coherence that absolutely everything fits, which leads him to the assumption that *any* verbal repetition must be accounted for in an interpretation, and that therefore any appearance of any of these words anywhere in *Dubliners* — pass, bold, passion — must be assumed to be meaning-bearing. It is not only imagery and verbal echoing that Joyce scholarship insists we must account for: Dunleavy argues, implicitly, that even the details of rhythm in the text, too, must be explained in any full reading of the story.

The result of this intersection of rules is an unresolved dissonance in the reading process. To give but one example: John Gordon can stake out a connection between "The Dead" and Remy de Gourmont's short story "Danaette" because both have final paragraphs referring to snow and swooning; Joanna Higgins sees the final sentence as "an allusion to Roman Catholic belief expressed in the Nicene Creed" (203). R. B. Kershner, using the operas mentioned briefly in the story as intertexts, sees the ending as a sexual reversal in which "Gabriel learns to speak as Woman" (150); other critics call on operas that are not explicitly mentioned: David Cowart sees Gabriel at the end as a Tannhäuser "transcend[ing] a venereal volition" (504), while Gregory Lucente insists that Gabriel corresponds to King Mark in *Tristan und Isolde* (283–84). Dilworth, calling up yet another intertext, insists that the final scene "recalls the impotence of Malory's Fisher King" (165), while Adrienne Munich, inspired by Ellmann, sees the falling snow as a buried allusion to Homer (183–84). There is no way to eliminate any of these webs of signification (each of which, of course, extends quite far); there is surely no way to fit them all together. How can we feel anything but vertigo?

There are, I think, two things to be gained from this analysis. First, if one shares my belief that self-consciousness, in the sense of self-knowledge, is an inherently valuable thing, then coming to understand what we are doing when we are reading "The Dead" — in particular, how as readers we are constructing, rather than receiving, the experience of interpretive vertigo — is intellectually valuable in and of itself, even if it does not alter the way in which we interpret the story. This is particularly true because, as I have said, the transformative process of reading is only the first step in our experience with the story; all the subsequent steps — which might include judging the story or using its insights to alter our own lives — run the risk of being deficient if they are based on an automatic, unconsidered reading in the first place.

But this approach to thinking about the story liberates our reading as well. For as soon as we recognize that the vertigo found in the story is the product of readers rather than inherent in the text, then we open ourselves up to alternative ways of experiencing "The Dead." This is the case — and I'd like to stress this point — *even if* we wish to commit ourselves, as readers, to the attempt at uncovering of authorial intention. For this analysis raises the possibility that we are not reading the story that Joyce was trying to write at all — the possibility that we do not know, for instance, whether the text is open or closed, whether it is really a complex web of arcane references or rather a more straightforward story in a naturalist vein. In this regard, it is worth remembering that Gabriel's vertigo is an example of what Amy Mandelker has called "hermeneutic failure" (84–85), the consequence of a whole lifetime of misreading women, as other feminist readers, such as Norris, have eloquently argued as well. In particular, he abstracts Gretta as an image entirely of his own creation, as if she had no existence beyond his imagination. Our vertigo as readers may have a parallel source.

WORKS CITED

Barolsky, Paul. "Joyce's Distant Music." *Virginia Quarterly Review* 65.1 (1989): 111–18.

Bauerle, Ruth. "Date Rape, Mate Rape: A Liturgical Interpretation of 'The Dead.' " *New Alliances in Joyce Studies.* Ed. Bonnie Kime Scott. Newark: U of Delaware P, 1988.

Bierman, Robert. "Structural Elements in 'The Dead.' " *James Joyce Quarterly* 4.1 (1966): 42–45.

Bleich, David. *Readings and Feelings: An Introduction to Subjective Criticism.* Urbana: National Council of Teachers of English, 1975.

Booth, Pat. *Malibu.* New York: Ballantine, 1991.

Cowart, David. "From Nuns' Island to Monkstown: Celibacy, Concupiscence, and Sterility in 'The Dead.' " *James Joyce Quarterly* 26.4 (1989): 499–504.

Dilworth, Thomas. "Sex and Politics in 'The Dead.' " *James Joyce Quarterly* 23.2 (1986): 157–71.

Dunleavy, Janet Egleson. "The Ectoplasmic Truthtellers of 'The Dead.' " *James Joyce Quarterly* 21.4 (1984): 307–19.

Eggers, Tilly. "What Is a Woman . . . a Symbol of?" *James Joyce Quarterly* 18.4 (1981): 379–95.

Ellmann, Richard. *James Joyce*. New and rev. ed. New York: Oxford UP, 1982.

Fish, Stanley. "Affective Stylistics." *Is There a Text in This Class?: The Authority of Interpretive Communities*. Cambridge: Harvard UP, 1980.

Füger, Wilhelm. "Crosslocutions in *Dubliners*." *James Joyce Quarterly* 27.1 (1989): 87–99.

Gifford, Don. *Joyce Annotated: Notes for Dubliners and A Portrait of the Artist as a Young Man*. 2nd ed. Berkeley: U of California P, 1982.

Gordon, John. "Another Possible Joycean Source." *James Joyce Quarterly* 28.1 (1990): 292–93.

Higgens, Joanna. "A Reading of the Last Sentence of 'The Dead,' " *English Language Notes* 17 (1980): 203–207.

Holland, Norman. *5 Readers Reading*. New Haven: Yale UP, 1975.

Humma, John. "Gabriel and the Bedsheets: Still Another Reading of the Ending of 'The Dead.' " *Studies in Short Fiction* 10 (1973): 207–09.

Kershner, R. B. *Joyce, Bakhtin, and Popular Literature: Chronicles of Disorder*. Chapel Hill: U of North Carolina P, 1989.

Loe, Thomas. " 'The Dead' as Novella." *James Joyce Quarterly* 28.2 (1991): 485–97.

Lucente, Gregory L. "Encounters and Subtexts in 'The Dead': A Note on Joyce's Narrative Technique." *Studies in Short Fiction* 20.4 (1983): 281–87.

Lytle, Andrew. "A Reading of Joyce's 'The Dead.' " *Sewanee Review* 77 (1969): 193–216.

Maddox, Lucy B. "Gabriel and Otello: Opera in 'The Dead.' " *Studies in Short Fiction* 24.3 (1987): 271–77.

Mandelker, Amy. *Framing "Anna Karenina": Tolstoy, the Woman Question, and the Victorian Novel*. Columbus: Ohio State UP, 1994.

Mansell, Darrel. "William Holman Hunt's *The Awakening Conscience* and James Joyce's *The Dead*." *James Joyce Quarterly* 23.4 (1984): 487–91.

Munich, Adrienne Auslander. "Form and Subtext in Joyce's 'The Dead.' " *Modern Philology* 82.2 (1984): 173–84.

Norris, Margot. "Stifled Back Answers: The Gender Politics of Art in Joyce's 'The Dead.' " *Modern Fiction Studies* 35.3 (1989): 479–503.

Rabinowitz, Peter J. *Before Reading: Narrative Conventions and the Politics of Interpretation*. Ithaca: Cornell UP, 1987.

Radway, Janice. *Reading the Romance: Women, Patriarchy, and Popular Literature*. Chapel Hill: U of North Carolina P, 1984.

Schwarz, Daniel R. *The Transformation of the English Novel, 1890–1930*. New York: St. Martin's, 1989.

Shields, David. "A Note on the Conclusion of Joyce's 'The Dead.' " *James Joyce Quarterly* 22.4 (1985): 427–28.

Torchiana, Donald T. *Backgrounds for Joyce's Dubliners*. Boston: Allen, 1986.

The New Historicism
and
"The Dead"

WHAT IS THE NEW HISTORICISM?

The new historicism is, first of all, *new:* one of the most recent developments in contemporary theory, it is still evolving. Enough of its contours have come into focus for us to realize that it exists and deserves a name, but any definition of the new historicism is bound to be somewhat fuzzy, like a partially developed photographic image. Some individual critics that we may label new historicist may also be deconstructors, or feminists, or Marxists. Some would deny that the others are even writing the new kind of historical criticism.

All of them, though, share the conviction that, somewhere along the way, something important was lost from literary studies: historical consciousness. Poems and novels came to be seen in isolation, as urnlike objects of precious beauty. The new historicists, whatever their differences and however defined, want us to see that even the most urnlike poems are caught in a web of historical conditions, relationships, and influences. In an essay on "The Historical Necessity for — and Difficulties with — New Historical Analysis in Introductory Literature Courses" (1987), Brook Thomas suggests that discussions of Keats's "Ode on a Grecian Urn" might begin with questions such as the following: Where would Keats have seen such an urn? How did a Grecian urn end up in a museum in England? Some very important historical and political realities, Thomas suggests, lie behind and inform Keats's definitions of art, truth, beauty, the past, and timelessness. They are realities that psychoanalytic and reader-response critics, formalists and feminists and deconstructors, might conceivably overlook.

Although a number of influential critics working between 1920 and 1950 wrote about literature from a psychoanalytic perspective, the majority of critics took what might generally be referred to as the historical approach. With the advent of the New Criticism, or formalism, however, historically oriented critics almost seemed to disappear from the face of the earth. Jerome McGann writes: "a text-only approach has been so vigorously promoted during the last thirty-five years that most historical critics have been driven from the field, and have raised the flag of their surrender by yielding the title 'critic' to the victor, and accepting the title 'scholar' for themselves" (*Inflections* 17). Of course, the title "victor" has been vied for by a new kind of psychoanalytic critic, by reader-response critics, by so-called deconstructors, and by feminists since the New Critics of the 1950s lost it during the following decade. But historical scholars have not been in the field, seriously competing to become a dominant critical influence.

At least they haven't until quite recently. In the late 1970s and early 1980s new historicism first began to be practiced and articulated in the ground-breaking work of Louis Montrose and Stephen Greenblatt. Through their work and that of others, new historicism transformed the field of Renaissance Studies, and later began to influence other fields as well. By 1984, Herbert Lindenberger could write: "It comes as something of a surprise to find that history is making a powerful comeback" (16). E. D. Hirsch, Jr., has also suggested that it is time to turn back to history and to historical criticism: "Far from being naive, historically based criticism is the newest and most valuable kind . . . for our students (and our culture) at the present time" (197). McGann obviously agrees. In *Historical Studies and Literary Criticism* (1985), he speaks approvingly of recent attempts to make sociohistorical subjects and methods central to literary studies once again.

As the word *sociohistorical* suggests, the new historicism is not the same as the historical criticism practiced forty years ago. For one thing, it is informed by recent critical theory: by psychoanalytic criticism, reader-response criticism, feminist criticism, and perhaps especially by deconstruction. The new historicist critics are less fact- and event-oriented than historical critics used to be, perhaps because they have come to wonder whether the truth about what really happened can ever be purely and objectively known. They are less likely to see history as linear and progressive, as something developing toward the present.

As the word "sociohistorical" also suggests, the new historicists view history as a social science and the social sciences as being properly historical. McGann most often alludes to sociology when discussing the future of literary studies. "A sociological poetics must be recognized not only as relevant to the analysis of poetry, but in fact as central to the analysis" (*Inflections* 62). Lindenberger cites anthropology as particularly useful in the new historical analysis of literature, especially anthropology as practiced by Victor Turner and Clifford Geertz. Geertz, who has related theatrical traditions in nineteenth-century Bali to forms of political organization that developed during the same period, has influenced some of the most important critics writing the new kind of historical criticism. Due in large part to Geertz's influence, new historicists such as Stephen Greenblatt have asserted that literature is not a sphere apart or distinct from the history that is relevant to it. That is what old historical criticism tended to do, to present history as information you needed to know before you could fully appreciate the separate world of art. Thus the new historicists have discarded old distinctions between literature, history, and the social sciences, while blurring other boundaries. They have erased the line dividing historical and literary materials, showing that the production of one of Shakespeare's plays was a political act and that the coronation of Elizabeth I was carried out with the same care for staging and symbol lavished on a work of dramatic art.

In addition to breaking down barriers that separate literature and history, history and the social sciences, new historicists have reminded us that it is treacherously difficult to reconstruct the past as it really was — rather than as we have been conditioned by our own place and time to believe that it was. And they know that the job is utterly impossible for anyone who is unaware of the difficulty and of the nature of his or her own historical vantage point. "Historical criticism can no longer make any part of [its] sweeping picture unselfconsciously, or treat any of its details in an untheorized way," McGann wrote in 1985 (*Historical Studies* 11). *Unselfconsciously* and *untheorized* are key words here; when the new historicist critics of literature describe a historical change, they are highly conscious of, and even likely to discuss, the *theory* of historical change that informs their account. They know that the changes they happen to see and describe are the ones that their theory of change allows or helps them to see and describe. And they know, too, that their theory of change is historically determined. They seek to minimize the distortion inherent in their perceptions and representations by admitting that they see through preconceived notions; in other words, they learn and reveal the color of the lenses in the glasses that they wear.

All three of the critics whose recent writings on the so-called back-to-history movement have been quoted thus far — Hirsch, Lindenberger, and McGann — mention the name of the late Michel Foucault. As much an archaeologist as a historian and as much a philosopher as either, Foucault in his writings brought together incidents and phenomena from areas of inquiry and orders of life that we normally regard as unconnected. As much as anyone, he encouraged the new historicist critic of literature to redefine the boundaries of historical inquiry.

Foucault's views of history were influenced by Friedrich Nietzsche's concept of a *wirkliche* ("real" or "true") history that is neither melioristic nor metaphysical. Foucault, like Nietzsche, didn't understand history as development, as a forward movement toward the present. Neither did he view history as an abstraction, idea, or ideal, as something that began "In the beginning" and that will come to THE END, a moment of definite closure, a Day of Judgment. In his own words, Foucault "abandoned [the old history's] attempts to understand events in terms of . . . some great evolutionary process" (*Discipline and Punish* 129). He warned new historians to be aware of the fact that investigators are themselves "situated." It is difficult, he reminded them, to see present cultural practices critically from within them, and on account of the same cultural practices, it is almost impossible to enter bygone ages. In *Discipline and Punish: The Birth of the Prison* (1975), Foucault admitted that his own interest in the past was fueled by a passion to write the history of the present.

Like Marx, Foucault saw history in terms of power, but his view of power owed more perhaps to Nietzsche than to Marx. Foucault seldom viewed power as a repressive force. Certainly, he did not view it as a tool of conspiracy used by one specific individual or institution against another. Rather, power represents a whole complex of forces; it is that which produces what happens. Thus, even a tyrannical aristocrat does not simply wield power, because he is formed and empowered by discourses and practices that constitute power. Viewed by Foucault, power is "positive and productive," not "repressive" and "prohibitive" (Smart 63). Furthermore, no historical event, according to Foucault, has a single cause; rather, it is intricately connected with a vast web of economic, social, and political factors.

A brief sketch of one of Foucault's major works may help clarify some of his ideas. *Discipline and Punish* begins with a shocking but accurate description of the public drawing and quartering of a Frenchman who had botched his attempt to assassinate King Louis XV. Foucault proceeds, then, by describing rules governing the daily life of modern Parisian felons. What happened to torture, to punishment as public spectacle? he asks. What complex network of forces made it disappear? In working toward a picture of this "power," Foucault turns up many interesting puzzle pieces, such as that in the early revolutionary years of the nineteenth century, crowds would sometimes identify with the prisoner and treat the executioner as if *he* were the guilty party. But Foucault sets forth a related reason for keeping prisoners alive, moving punishment indoors, and changing discipline from physical torture into mental rehabilitation: colonization. In this historical period, people were needed to establish colonies and trade, and prisoners could be used for that purpose. Also, because these were politically unsettled times, governments needed infiltrators and informers. Who better to fill those roles than prisoners pardoned or released early for showing a willingness to be rehabilitated? As for rehabilitation itself, Foucault compares it to the old form of punishment, which began with a torturer extracting a confession. In more modern, "reasonable" times, psychologists probe the minds of prisoners with a scientific rigor that Foucault sees as a different kind of torture, a kind that our modern perspective does not allow us to see as such.

Thus, a change took place, but perhaps not so great a change as we generally assume. It may have been for the better or for the worse; the point is that agents of power didn't make the change because mankind is evolving and, therefore, more prone to perform good-hearted deeds. Rather, different objectives arose, including those of a new class of doctors and scientists bent on studying aberrant examples of the human mind.

Foucault's type of analysis has recently been practiced by a number of literary critics at the vanguard of the back-to-history movement. One of these critics, Stephen Greenblatt, has written on Renaissance changes in the development of both literary characters and real people. Like Foucault, he is careful to point out that any one change is connected with a host of others, no one of which may simply be identified as the cause or the effect. Greenblatt, like Foucault, insists on interpreting literary devices as if they were continuous with other representational devices in a culture; he turns, therefore, to scholars in other fields in order to better understand the workings of literature. "We wall off literary symbolism from the symbolic structures operative elsewhere," he writes, "as if art alone were a human creation, as if humans themselves were not, in Clifford Geertz's phrase, cultural artifacts." Following Geertz, Greenblatt sets out to practice what he calls "anthropological or cultural criticism." Anthropological literary criticism, he continues, addresses itself "to the interpretive constructions the members of a society apply to their experience," since a work of literature is itself an interpretive construction, "part of the system of signs that constitutes a given culture." He suggests that criticism must never interpret the past without at least being "conscious of its own status as interpretation" (4).

Not all of the critics trying to lead students of literature back to history are as "Foucauldian" as Greenblatt. Some of these new historicists owe more to Marx than to Foucault. Others, like Jerome McGann, have followed the lead of Soviet critic M. M. Bakhtin, who was less likely than Marx to emphasize social class as a determining factor. (Bakhtin was more interested in the way that one language or style is the parody of an older one.) Still other new historicists, like Brook Thomas, have clearly been more influenced by Walter Benjamin, best known for essays such as "Theses on the Philosophy of History" and "The Work of Art in the Age of Mechanical Reproduction."

Moreover, there are other reasons not to declare that Foucault has been the central influence on the new historicism. Some new historicist critics would argue that Foucault critiqued old-style historicism to such an extent that he ended up being antihistorical or, at least, nonhistorical. As for his commitment to a radical remapping of relations of power and influence, cause and effect, in the view of some critics, Foucault consequently adopted too cavalier an attitude toward chronology and facts. In the minds of other critics, identifying and labeling a single master or central influence goes against the very grain of the new historicism. Practitioners of the new historicism have sought to decenter the study of literature and move toward the point where literary studies overlap with anthropological and sociological studies. They have also struggled to see history from a decentered perspective, both by recognizing that their own cultural and historical position may not afford the best understanding of other cultures and times and by realizing that events seldom have any single or central cause. At this point, then, it is appropriate to pause and suggest that Foucault shouldn't be seen as *the* cause of the new historicism, but as one of several powerful, interactive influences.

It is equally useful to suggest that the debate over the sources of the movement, the differences of opinion about Foucault, and even my own need to assert his importance may be historically contingent; that is to say, they may all result from the very *newness* of the new historicism itself. New intellectual movements often cannot be summed up or represented by a key figure, any more than they can easily be summed up or represented by an introduction or a single essay. They respond to disparate influences and almost inevitably include thinkers who represent a wide range of backgrounds. Like movements that are disintegrating, new movements embrace a broad spectrum of opinions and positions.

But just as differences within a new school of criticism cannot be overlooked, neither should they be exaggerated, since it is the similarity among a number of different approaches that makes us aware of a new movement under way. Greenblatt, Hirsch, McGann, and Thomas all started with the assumption that works of literature are simultaneously influenced by and influencing reality, broadly defined. Thus, whatever their disagreements, they share a belief in referentiality — a belief that literature refers to and is referred to by things outside itself — that is fainter in the works of formalist, poststructuralist, and even reader-response critics. They believe with Greenblatt that the "central concerns" of criticism "should prevent it from permanently sealing off one type of discourse from another or decisively separating works of art from the minds and lives of their creators and their audiences" (5).

McGann, in his introduction to *Historical Studies and Literary Criticism,* turns referentiality into a rallying cry:

> What will not be found in these essays . . . is the assumption, so common in text-centered studies of every type, that literary works are self-enclosed verbal constructs, or looped intertextual fields of autonomous signifiers and signifieds. In these essays, the question of referentiality is once again brought to the fore. (3)

In "Keats and the Historical Method in Literary Criticism," he outlines a program for those who have rallied to the cry. These procedures, which he claims are "practical derivatives of the Bakhtin school," assume that historicist critics, who must be interested in a work's point of origin and in its point of reception, will understand the former by studying biography and bibliography. After mastering these details, the critic must then consider the expressed intentions of the author, because, if printed, these intentions have also modified the developing history of the work. Next, the new historicist must learn the history of the work's reception, as that body of opinion has become part of the platform on which we are situated when we study the book. Finally, McGann urges the new historicist critic to point toward the future, toward his or her *own* audience, defining for its members the aims and limits of the critical project and injecting the analysis with a degree of self-consciousness that alone can give it credibility (*Inflections* 62).

In the essay that follows, Michael Levenson begins by reminding us that in Joyce's Ireland it was unusually apparent that literature is not independent of history and politics. In 1907, John Synge's play *The Playboy of the Western World* provoked riots in Ireland, with Irish nationalists raising "angry objections to Synge's 'slander' of Irish . . . dignity." Joyce, Levenson tells us, "eagerly followed the controversy. . . . The *Playboy* affair made clear that in the midst of an ongoing colonial struggle the boundaries between art and politics were highly permeable, where they existed at all."

Levenson argues that, as a consequence of Joyce's political awareness, "the relation of history to the literary life" stands "at the center of Joyce's fiction." Indeed, within most of his works may be found "a body of concerns which have marked the most influential readings of new historicist critics — the interpenetration of literary and nonliterary discourse; the circulation of words, beliefs, and emotions between personal and public life; the serpentine paths of power and its concealed effects."

This is not to say that Joyce was entirely pleased by the politicized nature of his aesthetic situation, or that he relished the role of being what, in retrospect, we might call a proto-new historicist. In fact, Levenson argues that, through "The Dead," Joyce sought to negotiate an internal, personal conflict between "a purified aestheticism which coolly disregarded the claims of politics" and "a cultural nationalism which demanded that art participate in the struggle against imperial domination." (Gabriel Conroy and Miss Ivors exemplify these conflicting attitudes, the former character being as *a*political as the latter is political.) Through the story, Joyce also examines the "entanglement of personal identity within the matrix of social discourses" (another subject of new historicist inquiry), using Gabriel to show the psychic toll exacted by all the "stresses and conflicts" inherent in "an unresolved Irish nationality."

Joyce's mixed feelings about the complex political situation emerging in the Ireland of his day may be seen in the range of his opinions about specific separatist initiatives. He defended the national autonomy movement led by the Sinn Fein ("Ourselves") party. Yet he opposed the campaign to bring back the Irish language and viewed the movement to "purify" the Irish "race" as being both foolish and wrong. "What race, or what language . . . can boast of being pure today?" Joyce asked. "And no race has no less right to utter such a boast than the race now living in Ireland." Joyce thus attempted to refute both extremes and develop a third way; in condemning both the English colonialists and the Irish revivalists, he located his quest for personal integrity in exile.

Joyce's understanding of the contemporary political situation was characterized by a sophistication appreciated by new historicist critics, for he did not view Ireland and England in terms of an "us versus them" dichotomy. Nor did he view English power as simply oppressive, or revolution as a simple political act. He understood the consciousness of the Irish to be, in Levenson's words, a "colonized consciousness"; thus, he found it difficult to see "how an uncompromised resistance was possible." He realized that power is not only exercised in physical shows of authority, but that it also resides in the dominant representational discourse. As a result, he did not see how Ireland, so much a product of long-standing English influence, could readily become an independent Catholic culture.

Levenson's analysis of "The Dead" in many ways parallels Joyce's analysis of the Irish predicament. For he unravels the complexity of Joyce's response to Irish separatist efforts using the same kind of thick description Joyce uses to describe the complexity of Ireland's situation. "It is tempting to see Joyce's refusal of this militant triad of race, language, and nation as a sign of his enlightened cosmopolitanism," Levenson admits. But he eschews this easy historical explanation for a more complex account, which he offers with the typical, self-historicizing tentativeness of the new historicist critic. "In larger part, though, it surely reflects the delicate politics of culture which [Joyce] was trying to negotiate. His position as an aspiring professional writer, who lived by plying his verbal trade, meant that the very instruments of his livelihood were placed in jeopardy by the revivalist program of the Gaelic League." Engaged in a "political struggle to preserve the conditions of a professional writing identity," Joyce offered a critique of the emerging Irish culture that is itself open to critique. Like Levenson's analysis — and this introduction — it is a product of its times.

Ross C Murfin

THE NEW HISTORICISM:
A SELECTED BIBLIOGRAPHY

The New Historicism: Further Reading

Graff, Gerald, and Gerald Gibbons, eds. *Criticism in the University*. Evanston: Northwestern UP, 1985. This volume, which contains Hirsch's essay, "Back to History," in the section entitled "Pedagogy and Polemics," also includes sections devoted to the historical backgrounds of academic criticism; the influence of Marxism, feminism, and critical theory in general on the new historicism; and varieties of "cultural criticism."

Hirsch, E. D., Jr. "Back to History." Graff and Gibbons 189–97.

History and . . . Special issue, *New Literary History* 21 (1990). See especially the essays by Carolyn Porter, Rena Fraden, Clifford Geertz, and Renato Rosaldo.

Howard, Jean. "The New Historicism in Renaissance Studies." *English Literary Renaissance* 16 (1986): 13–43.

Lindenberger, Herbert. *The History in Literature: On Value, Genre, Institutions*. New York: Columbia UP, 1990.

———. "Toward a New History in Literary Study." *Profession: Selected Articles from the Bulletins of the Association of Departments of English and the Association of the Departments of Foreign Languages*. New York: MLA, 1984. 16–23.

Liu, Alan. "The Power of Formalism: The New Historicism." *English Literary History* 56 (1989): 721–71.

McGann, Jerome. *The Beauty of Inflections: Literary Investigations in Historical Method and Theory*. Oxford: Clarendon-Oxford UP, 1985.

———. *Historical Studies and Literary Criticism*. Madison: U of Wisconsin P, 1985. See especially the introduction and the essays in the following sections: "Historical Methods and Literary Interpretations" and "Biographical Contexts and the Critical Object."

Montrose, Louis Adrian. "Renaissance Literary Studies and the Subject of History." *English Literary Renaissance* 16 (1986): 5–12.

Morris, Wesley. *Toward a New Historicism*. Princeton: Princeton UP, 1972.

Thomas, Brook. "The Historical Necessity for — and Difficulties with — New Historical Analysis in Introductory Courses." *College English* 49 (1987): 509–22.

———. *The New Historicism and Other Old-Fashioned Topics*. Princeton: Princeton UP, 1991.

————. "Walter Benn Michaels and the New Historicism: Where's the Difference?" *Boundary 2* 18 (1991): 118–59.

Veeser, Harold, ed. *The New Historicism*. New York: Routledge, 1989.

Wayne, Don E. "Power, Politics and the Shakespearean Text: Recent Criticism in England and the United States." *Shakespeare Reproduced: The Text in History and Ideology*. Ed. Jean Howard and Marion O'Conner. New York: Methuen, 1987. 47–67.

The New Historicism: Influential Examples

New Historicism has taken its present form less through the elaboration of basic theoretical postulates and more through certain influential examples. The works listed represent some of the most important contributions guiding research in this area.

American Literary History. A journal devoted to new historicist and cultural criticism; the first issue was Spring 1989. New York: Oxford UP.

Brown, Gillian. *Domestic Individualism: Imagining Self in Nineteenth-Century America*. Berkeley: U of California P, 1990.

Dollimore, Jonathan. *Radical Tragedy: Religion, Ideology and Power in the Drama of Shakespeare and His Contemporaries*. Brighton, Eng.: Harvester, 1984.

Dollimore, Jonathan, and Alan Sinfield, eds. *Political Shakespeare: New Essays in Cultural Materialism*. Manchester, Eng.: Manchester UP, 1985. See especially the essays by Dollimore, Greenblatt, and Tennenhouse.

Goldberg, Jonathan. *James I and the Politics of Literature*. Baltimore: Johns Hopkins UP, 1983.

Greenblatt, Stephen. *Renaissance Self-Fashioning from More to Shakespeare*. Chicago: U of Chicago P, 1980. See ch. 1 and the chapter on *Othello* entitled "The Improvisation of Power."

————. *Shakespearean Negotiations: The Circulation of Social Energy in Renaissance England*. Berkeley: U of California P, 1985. See especially "The Circulation of Social Energy" and "Invisible Bullets: Renaissance Authority and Its Subversion, *Henry IV* and *Henry V*."

Marcus, Leah. *Puzzling Shakespeare: Local Reading and Its Discontents*. Berkeley: U of California P, 1988.

Michaels, Walter Benn. *The Gold Standard and the Logic of Natural-

ism: American Literature at the Turn of the Century. Berkeley: U of California P, 1987.

Montrose, Louis Adrian. " 'Shaping Fantasies': Figurations of Gender and Power in Elizabethan Culture." *Representations* 2 (1983): 61–94. One of the most influential early new historicist essays.

Mullaney, Steven. *The Place of the Stage: License, Play, and Power in Renaissance England*. Chicago: U of Chicago P, 1987.

Representations. This quarterly journal, printed by the University of California Press, regularly publishes new historicist studies and cultural criticism.

Sinfield, Alan. *Literature, Politics, and Culture in Postwar Britain*. Berkeley: U of California P, 1989.

Tennenhouse, Leonard. *Power on Display: The Politics of Shakespeare's Genres*. New York and London: Methuen, 1986.

Foucault and His Influence

As I point out in the introduction to the new historicism, some new historicists would question the "privileging" of Foucault implicit in this section heading ("Foucault and His Influence") and the following one ("Other Writers and Works"). They might cite the greater importance of one of these other writers or point out that to cite a central influence or a definitive cause runs against the very spirit of the movement.

Foucault, Michel. *The Archaeology of Knowledge*. Trans. A. M. Sheridan Smith. New York: Harper, 1972.

———. *Discipline and Punish*. Trans. Alan Sheridan. New York: Pantheon, 1978.

———. *The History of Sexuality*, vol. 1. Trans. Robert Hurley. New York: Pantheon, 1978.

———. *Language, Counter-Memory, Practice*. Ed. Donald F. Bouchard. Trans. Bouchard and Sherry Simon. Ithaca: Cornell UP, 1977.

———. *The Order of Things: An Archaeology of the Human Sciences*. New York: Vintage, 1973.

———. *Politics, Philosophy, Culture*. Ed. Lawrence D. Kritzman. Trans. Alan Sheridan *et al*. New York: Routledge, 1988.

———. *Power/Knowledge*. Ed. Colin Gordon. Trans. Colin Gordon *et al*. New York: Pantheon, 1980.

———. *Technologies of the Self*. Ed. Luther H. Martin, Huck Gutman, and Patrick H. Hutton. Amherst: U of Massachusetts P, 1988.

Dreyfus, Hubert L. and Paul Rabinow. *Michel Foucault: Beyond Structuralism and Hermeneutics.* Chicago: U of Chicago P, 1983.

Sheridan, Alan. *Michel Foucault: The Will to Truth.* New York: Tavistock, 1980.

Smart, Barry. *Michel Foucault.* New York: Ellis Horwood and Tavistock, 1985.

Other Writers and Works of Interest to New Historicist Critics

Bakhtin, M. M. *The Dialogic Imagination: Four Essays.* Ed. Michael Holquist. Trans. Caryl Emerson. Austin: U of Texas P, 1981. Bakhtin wrote many influential studies on subjects as varied as Dostoyevsky, Rabelais, and formalist criticism. But this book, in part due to Holquist's helpful introduction, is probably the best place to begin reading Bakhtin.

Benjamin, Walter. "The Work of Art in the Age of Mechanical Reproduction." [1936] *Illuminations.* Trans. Harry Zohn. New York: Schocken, 1969.

Fried, Michael. *Absorption and Theatricality: Painting and Beholder in the Works of Diderot.* Berkeley: U of California P, 1980.

Geertz, Clifford. *The Interpretation of Cultures.* New York: Basic Books, 1973.

———. *Negara: The Theatre State in Nineteenth-Century Bali.* Princeton: Princeton UP, 1980.

Goffman, Erving. *Frame Analysis.* New York: Harper, 1974.

Jameson, Fredric. *The Political Unconscious.* Ithaca: Cornell UP, 1981.

Koselleck, Reinhart. *Futures Past.* Trans. Keith Tribe. Cambridge: MIT P, 1985.

Said, Edward. *Orientalism.* New York: Columbia UP, 1978.

Recent Historical and New Historicist Studies of Joyce and Irish Literature

Eagleton, Terry, Fredric Jameson, and Edward W. Said. *Nationalism, Colonialism, and Literature.* Minneapolis: U of Minnesota P, 1990.

Foster, John Wilson. *Fictions of the Irish Literary Revival.* Syracuse: Syracuse UP, 1987.

Frazier, Adrian. *Behind the Scenes: Yeats, Horniman, and the Struggle for the Abbey Theatre.* Berkeley: U of California P, 1990.

Hawkins, Hunt. "Joyce as a Colonial Writer." *CLA Journal* 35 (1992): 400–10.

Hutchinson, John. *The Dynamics of Cultural Nationalism: The Gaelic Revival and the Creation of the Irish Nation State.* London: Allen, 1987.

Lloyd, David. *Nationalism and Minor Literature: James Clarence Mangan and the Emergence of Irish Cultural Nationalism.* Berkeley: U of California P, 1987.

Luftig, Victor and Mark Wollaeger. "Why 'Joyce and History'? Why Now?" *James Joyce Quarterly* 28 (1991): 745–48.

Macdonagh, Oliver, W. F. Mandle, and Pauric Travers, eds. *Irish Culture and Nationalism, 1750–1950.* Dublin: Macmillan, 1983.

Manganiello, Dominic. *Joyce's Politics.* London: Routledge, 1980.

———. "The Politics of the Unpolitical in Joyce's Fictions." *James Joyce Quarterly* 29 (1992): 41–58.

Platt, L. H. "Joyce and the Anglo-Irish Revival: The Triestine Lectures." *James Joyce Quarterly* 29 (1992): 259–66.

Spoo, Robert. "Joyce's Attitudes Toward History: Rome, 1906–07." *Journal of Modern Literature* 14 (1988): 481–97.

A NEW HISTORICIST PERSPECTIVE

MICHAEL LEVENSON

Living History in "The Dead"

Given the odd shape of our century, in which the last years so eerily mimic the first, it should not appear paradoxical to say that three quarters of a century before we knew the phrase, James Joyce was a New Historicist: under the political pressures of his moment, he was made to encounter a set of problems which contemporary literary criticism has also been made to confront. At the center of Joyce's fiction is the relation of history to the literary life, a question that led him to a body of concerns which have marked the most influential readings of New Historicist critics — the interpenetration of literary and nonliterary discourse; the circulation of words, beliefs, and emotions between personal and public life; and the serpentine paths of power and its concealed effects. "The Dead" is a story written at a moment of colonial resistance when fiction-making came under special pressure to define its relation to politics; it is also a story that forcibly brings the question of history inside the terms of its personal narrative.[1]

During one of the first crises in a fiction that follows a quick rhythm of crisis, Gabriel Conroy has an uncomfortable exchange with the nationalist Miss Ivors who has deduced his identity as G. C., book reviewer for *The Daily Express*.[2] Because she thinks of the journal as an instrument of British domination, she playfully accuses him of being a "West Briton," namely one who fails to acknowledge an independent Irish identity and who regards Ireland as merely a western province of Britain. Surprisingly agitated by Miss Ivors's provoking tease, Gabriel struggles to find a response.

> He did not know how to meet her charge. He wanted to say that literature was above politics. But they were friends of many years' standing and their careers had been parallel, first at the University and then as teachers: he could not risk a grandiose phrase with her. He continued blinking his eyes and trying to smile and murmured lamely that he saw nothing political in writing reviews of books. (31)

Several features of this passage will eventually come into play, but at the moment the telling aspect is Gabriel's meditation on the relationship between politics and literature. For Gabriel to insist that literature was "above politics" is too "grandiose" a claim, suggesting as it does a hierarchy that assigns a superior value to the literary life. Timidly, he contents himself with saying that there is "nothing political" in book-reviewing, a view that ignores the question of hierarchy and insists merely on the irreducible *differences* of literature and politics, in effect placing the two practices in separate zones of human experience.

What is a context for literature? In the cultural and political turmoil of turn-of-the-century Ireland, this question became sharply pointed. When national struggle is cast in terms of a restored cultural identity, then literary practice can no longer be seen as a domain apart. During the first decade of the century, Irish literary activity often served as the arena of politics, and during the months of Joyce's work on "The Dead" in late 1906 and early 1907, the collision of realms suddenly became conspicuous. The decisive event was the rioting over the perfor-

---

[1] John V. Kelleher's 1965 essay on "The Dead" in *The Review of Politics* set the initial terms for discussion of the story's social contexts, and it convincingly established that no reading of the story can afford to ignore its high historical specificity.

[2] Joyce himself had reviewed books for the *Daily Express*, this being only one of many (ambiguous) links between author and character in "The Dead."

mance of John Synge's *The Playboy of the Western World* in February 1907. The play's comic debunking of certain cherished ideals led to a fierce reaction, with many active nationalists raising angry objections to Synge's 'slander' of Irish beauty, Irish dignity, Irish womanhood. Joyce, who was living out a few months of his exile in Rome, eagerly followed the controversy, clearly sensing that here was a foretaste of a feast being laid for him. The *Playboy* affair made clear that in the midst of an ongoing colonial struggle the boundaries between art and politics were highly permeable, where they existed at all.

A few months later, Thomas Kettle published a review of *Chamber Music*, Joyce's book of poems, which had recently appeared in Dublin. In the context of a sympathetic reading, Kettle notes that "The inspiration of the book is almost entirely literary. There is no trace of the folklore, folk dialect, or even the national feeling that have coloured the work of practically every writer in contemporary Ireland" (Ellmann 261). It cannot have surprised Joyce to be described in these terms; he had himself cherished many misgivings about the lyric idealism of his early poems. But the publication of *Chamber Music,* hard upon the riots over Synge's play, displayed the terms of conflict Joyce was seeking to negotiate in "The Dead": on the one side, a purified aestheticism that coolly disregarded the claims of politics, and on the other side a cultural nationalism that demanded that art participate in the struggle against imperial domination.

In the competing attitudes of Gabriel and Miss Ivors, "The Dead" registers these two strong and contesting forces. Gabriel's (unspoken) position represents a militant aestheticism, which placed the claims of politics on a lower rank of importance; Miss Ivors's view, on the other hand, represents an engaged cultural politics, which derided the elitist pretensions of dreamy artists. Joyce's early writing career developed in dialogue with these two rival positions, both of which struck him as badly disabling in themselves. Much of his struggle in the early years of the century was to formulate a position strong enough to answer these two challenges, and "The Dead" itself incorporates the languages of both aestheticism and Revivalist politics in order to contest each of them, not by escaping their reach, but by engaging them with one another in ways that will allow a third term, a third posture to precipitate out of the reaction.

Certainly the dominant milieu of "The Dead" is the milieu of a genteel aestheticism, marked not only by Gabriel's own role as professor and book reviewer but more immediately by the musical interests of the Morkan family, which provide the occasion for the annual party. The world of amateur musical performance, of piano and voice instruction, of fine food and literate discussion, constitutes a closed domestic sphere in which the arts serve as both an intrinsic source of pleasure and a solace for life's hardships. Within this demure realm of self-willed propriety, where the greatest (conscious) worry is whether Freddy Malins will turn up drunk, the amiably combative Miss Ivors stands out as an isolated provocation, reassuringly outnumbered by the art-loving traditionalists. And yet, the sharp contrast between her easy confidence and Gabriel's fragility helps to remind us that behind Miss Ivors stands a multitude. Although at the party she is alone of her political kind, she metonymically summons the growing forces of Irish nationalism, which stood as a serious challenge to the social posture of both Gabriel and his creator.

In the interval between Joyce's completing the other stories in *Dubliners* and his beginning to compose "The Dead," the agitation against British rule in Ireland had conspicuously intensified. But at least as striking as the anticolonial passion was the diversity of its forms. While the Irish members of parliament continued to work for a Home Rule solution achieved through legal negotiation with the British, the newly formed party Sinn Fein ("Ourselves") was casting aside the parliamentary enterprise as both futile and degrading. The flourishing Gaelic League aimed to keep clear of political entanglements in order to sustain the interest (of all parties and both religions) in the revival of the Irish language. At the Irish National Theatre W. B. Yeats, a Protestant, sought to reanimate the island's legendary past, while D. P. Moran, editor of the influential journal *The Leader,* scorned the efforts of 'sourface' Protestants, campaigning instead for an "Irish Ireland" anchored in a separate Catholic consciousness and distinct Catholic traditions.[3] Any adequate representation of Irish political life in this period must respect the sheer profusion of views diffused within the national consciousness and also must acknowledge the (mistaken) sense of climax that had begun to prevail.

Living in Trieste and Rome, Joyce followed this political fury as closely as he could: hungry for information, he complained that no one in Ireland would take the trouble to send him newspapers. Situated at a

[3] In a recent essay, "The Catholic Revival and 'The Dead,' " Willard Potts has made a strenuous argument for the influence of Moran on the political workings of the story. Although the claim for the story's specific debt to Moran's work is excessive, the historical recovery of the divided character of the Irish nationalist movement is important. Particularly useful is Potts's demonstration of the conflict between Protestant and Catholic wings of the struggle.

great physical remove from the milieu that gave him the materials of his fiction, Joyce had only limited access to the rapid eddies of political and cultural debate; general critical appeals to "the mood of the time" fail to capture the particular determinacy of his social engagement. Some aspects of the social tumult were obscure to him; to some others he remained indifferent. A close scrutiny of his reactions makes clear that he was chiefly preoccupied by two strains of political discourse that would leave visible marks on "The Dead": the national autonomy movement of Sinn Fein, and the Irish language campaign.

In 1904 the journalist Arthur Griffith had collected a number of his essays into a pamphlet called *The Resurrection of Hungary,* which caused a sensation and which laid the groundwork for the emergence of Sinn Fein the following year. Griffith took the precedent of Hungary's struggle for national self-determination as the working model for the Irish struggle against British colonial rule. What this meant in practice was a refusal to participate in parliamentary procedures, a boycott of British goods, and a coordinated program to develop Irish education and Irish industry. That Ireland should seek to secure its own growth as a nation, independent of any relations with either the British economy or the British political system, was Griffith's proposal, which quickly became a leading element of the anti-imperial cause.

Against the wariness of his brother Stanislaus, Joyce defended the broad outlines of the Sinn Fein strategy: "I believe that its policy would benefit Ireland very much" (*Letters* 102).[4] His interest in the resurgent nationalism of Sinn Fein was no doubt a significant cause of Joyce's changing attitudes toward his homeland. The well-known letter of 1906, in which he regrets the severity of the earlier *Dubliners* stories and their failure to render the beauty and hospitality of Ireland, must be seen not only as a literary recognition but also as a new political acknowledgment, an appreciation of the claims of Irish nationalism (*Letters* 110).

During the months leading up to the writing of "The Dead" Joyce was struggling with the implications of Sinn Fein politics — the implications for Ireland, and the implications for his fiction. Without doubt the keenest difficulty for him came in the proposals for restoring ancient

---

[4]His one hesitation came from his confessedly uncertain socialist convictions, which led to the view that "if the Irish question exists, it exists for the Irish proletariat chiefly" (*Letters* 111). But as Joyce pondered the issues over the next several months, he found a way to accommodate Sinn Fein to his socialism: "Of course I see that its success would be to substitute Irish for English capital but no-one, I suppose, denies that capitalism is a stage of progress. The Irish proletariat has yet to be created" (*Letters* 125).

Irish culture as the living sign of independent nationhood. Joyce had long-standing distaste for the turn to Irish legend in the poetry and drama of Yeats, but far more consequential was his resistance to the call for a literature written in the Irish language. At an important moment of self-recognition, Joyce wrote to his brother, "If the Irish programme did not insist on the Irish language I suppose I could call myself a nationalist" (*Letters* 125).

That the vexing language issue had laid a strong grip on Joyce's attention is shown by his lecture "Ireland, Island of Saints and Sages," read in Italian and delivered in Trieste on April 27, 1907. At the opening of that talk, Joyce nods respectfully at the striking success of the Gaelic League in promoting the use of Irish in contemporary civic life:

> In Dublin, the names of the streets are printed in both languages. The League organises concerts, debates, and socials at which the speaker of *beurla* (that is, English) feels like a fish out of water, confused in the midst of a crowd that chatters in a harsh and guttural tongue. In the streets, you often see groups of young people pass by speaking Irish perhaps a little more emphatically than is necessary. The members of the League write to each other in Irish, and often the poor postman, unable to read the address, must turn to his superior to untie the knot. (*Critical Writings* 156)

The leading figure behind the Gaelic League's accomplishment was its founder and president, Douglas Hyde. In a celebrated essay on "The Necessity for De-Anglicising Ireland" Hyde had narrated a story of decline according to which contemporary Ireland has fallen from the organic early history, which is the only basis for its nationhood:

> If we take a bird's eye view of our island to-day, and compare it with what it used to be, we must be struck by the extraordinary fact that the nation which was once, as every one admits, one of the most classically learned and cultured nations in Europe, is now one of the least so; how one of the most reading and literary peoples has become one of the *least* studious and most *un*-literary, and how the present art products of one of the quickest, most sensitive, and most artistic races on earth are now only distinguished for their hideousness. (*Language* 153)

For Hyde, the great crime of colonization rests on the basis of language. The near obliteration of Irish has been the surest means of English domination, and adapting a passage from Joubainville, Hyde writes that England "has definitely conquered us, she has even imposed upon us her language, that is to say, the form of our thoughts during every instant of our existence" (*Language* 159–60). No one, of course, was better suited than Joyce to understand the intimacy between a language and an identity. The radical entanglement of selfhood within linguistic structures, within the rhythms, the music, the conventions, and the cliches of language is a root perception in his literary project. There should be no difficulty, then, in grasping the anxiety that is so palpable in his reflections on the anticolonial struggle.

Joyce saw clearly the coherence in the tie that connected Griffith and Hyde, the tie between the struggle for economic autonomy and the revival of an Irish language. He saw the coherence, and he contested it, by formulating a rival view of nationhood and a rival view of language. From Joyce's perspective, both Sinn Fein and the Gaelic League tended toward a theory of racial identity, which he described as "the old pap of racial hatred" (*Letters* 111). Indeed Hyde had been brutally explicit in arguing that the only effective response to "the devouring demon of Anglicization" (*Language* 178) was "to cultivate everything that is most racial, most smacking of the soil, most Gaelic, most Irish" (*Language* 169).

In his Trieste lecture Joyce bitterly agreed that the crimes of imperial Britain were brutal and disabling, but he placed no hope in the purification of an Irish race. There was no longer any such purity to retrieve. A diversity of racial and linguistic strains had for so long intermingled that "it is useless to look for a thread that may have remained pure and virgin without having undergone the influence of a neighbouring thread. What race, or what language . . . can boast of being pure today? And no race has less right to utter such a boast than the race now living in Ireland" (*Critical Writings* 165–66). With cold equanimity Joyce condemns both the conquering English and the naive Irish revivalists, concluding that the only hope for personal integrity lies in exile: "No one who has any self-respect stays in Ireland, but flees afar as though from a country that has undergone the visitation of an angered Jove" (*Critical Writings* 171).

It is tempting to see Joyce's refusal of this militant triad of race, language, and nation as a sign of his enlightened cosmopolitanism. In larger part, though, it surely reflects the delicate politics of culture, which he was attempting to negotiate. His position as an aspiring professional writer who lived by plying his verbal trade meant that the very instruments of his livelihood were placed in jeopardy by the revivalist program of the Gaelic League. His words were his laboring implements; the prospect of learning Irish in order to become a Gaelic writer must have been scarcely imaginable. It is not too much to say that in the years 1906–07, Joyce was engaged in a political struggle to preserve the conditions of a professional writing identity — political because it required him on the one hand to contest the British legal power, which blocked the publication of his earlier stories (on grounds of indecency), and on the other hand to fend off the Irish national demands for an art that kept faith with an "Irish Ireland." To his brother he conveyed the belief that "either *Sinn Fein* or Imperialism will conquer the present Ireland. As it is, I am content to recognise myself an exile: and, prophetically, a repudiated one" (*Letters* 125). Here as elsewhere Joyce identifies a political basis for his literary exile.

Gabriel Conroy, of course, has not fled Ireland, and self-respect is indeed hard for him to attain. Like so many of Joyce's fictional incarnations, Conroy shares just enough with his creator to make the contrasts stand out. He has a literary sensibility and shares Joyce's suspicion of the revivalist project without sharing his resolve to forge an alternative. Just such an unsettled personal bearing is what Douglas Hyde had derided as the bane of the Irish: "we have ceased to be Irish without becoming English." This puts well Gabriel Conroy's impossible fate. Living on in Ireland without putting his colonial identity in any question, he occupies a murky zone in which character can achieve no hard outlines.

In this connection, a telling ambiguity appears in Gabriel's nervous response to Miss Ivors's challenge. When she asks why he travels in France and Belgium "instead of visiting your own land," he answers that "it's partly to keep in touch with the languages and partly for a change." Her rejoinder is sharp: "haven't you your own language to keep in touch with — Irish?" "Well," says Gabriel, "if it comes to that, you know, Irish is not my language." And then when Miss Ivors presses further, insisting that he acknowledge his "own people, and [his] own country," he erupts: "O, to tell you the truth . . . I'm sick of my own country, sick of it!" (32).

These two impulsive reactions seem to chime harmoniously as tones of revulsion from the revivalist program, but a notable difference separates them. For while Gabriel denies that Irish is his language, he implicitly accepts Ireland as his nation — "my own country" — sick of it though he may be. Deep paradoxes in the theory of modern nationhood collect around this highly unsteady posture. Implicated as a citizen of his country and yet estranged from such a fundamental source of national identity as a separate language, Gabriel bears internally the stresses and conflicts of an unresolved Irish nationality. He is no more autonomous or coherent than the country that contains him.

Such entanglement of personal identity within the matrix of social discourses is an abiding concern of "The Dead," much as it is a working assumption of current New Historicist inquiry. The task of securing an integral selfhood merges with the task of formulating a context — a set of customs and rituals, a matrix of values, a distribution of status — in which a self might live. The Morkan party in "The Dead" represents just such a matrix of rituals and discourses: it has its own cherished values (music, gentility, family dignity); its own well-entrenched customs (performance, after-dinner oratory); its own mythology (Aunt Julia might have been a grand success as a singer); its own reassuringly familiar scapegrace (Freddy Malins); and its own ratifying narrative histories. The fictive construction of the party milieu is, among other things, a distinctly sociological act: Joyce's presentation of an enclosed social formation — traditional, Catholic, apolitical — with its elaborate mechanisms for self-confirmation and self-preservation.

Nevertheless, from its opening lines "The Dead" renders its characters not as figures within a static social form but as participants in an inescapably historical process, suffused with a consciousness of time. That the celebration is an "annual dance" (21) which was "always a great affair" (21); that it has gone on for "years and years," (21) for "as long as anyone could remember" (21); that it began indeed "a good thirty years ago if it was a day" (22) enforces the historical character of this private life. The appeal to the past becomes a major source of validation; so Gabriel caressingly recalls "the tradition of genuine warm-hearted courteous Irish hospitality, which our forefathers have handed down to us and which we in turn must hand down to our descendants" (43).

Under the pressure of Miss Ivors's nationalist critique, Gabriel moves into place the heavy armaments of tradition; and yet the story records this characteristic movement of reaction only to emphasize its own fragility. The pomposity of his rhetoric is one sign of strain, as is his private view of his aunts as "only two ignorant old women" (35). But beyond the failure of conviction in Gabriel's own traditionalism stands the pervasive evocation of an aging that is a decline. Gabriel's fading aunts give one visible sign, and his first encounter with the servant Lily gives another. To his jaunty tease — "I suppose we'll be going to your wedding one of these fine days" — she bitterly responds, "The men that is now is only all palaver and what they can get out of you" (23). Soon after, Lily herself becomes the subject of "historical" inquiry, when Aunt Kate observes that "She's not the girl she was at all" (26). The diverse instances of this motif — Ireland's loss of the canons of hospitality, the withering of Kate and Julia, the decline of romantic and marriageable men into mere "palaver," Lily's fall from innocence — accumulate to suggest that the stability implied by the ritual of the annual dance is a false stability that cannot disguise the marked logic of historical decay.

At an awkward moment, when the conversation turns to the weather, Mary Jane remarks, "They say . . . we haven't had snow like it for thirty years" (50), thus dating the last great storm at the time she came to live with Aunts Kate and Julia and the party began its annual ritual. The force of the detail is to create the image of a bounded historical phase, a thirty-year epoch, the length of generation, whose end is all too easy to envisage. Here is a social formation that has devised its own collective myths and personal narratives but that can scarcely conceal the tensions that accompany its aging. The end points to this phase are marked by two great blizzards, and beyond those snowy boundaries there is only a remote elusive past or an inconceivable future.

For those Irish nationalists with whom the story is in continual, restless dialogue, the past is not shadowy, nor is the future inconceivable. For both Hyde and Griffith, though with quite different emphases, a repressed Irish history points unmistakably to the postcolonial epoch. For Hyde, the "deanglicized" national future is written in Gaelic, and when an Irish tongue can again speak its language, it will speak the suppressed truth of its national identity. For Griffith, the vital relic is the suspended Irish constitution of 1782, which stands as the basis for the struggle against British rule. In both cases, the path from past to future was clearly marked: it was only a matter of rousing the will to resist the tyranny of the present.

Although Joyce shared the loathing of British domination, he skeptically distrusted any course promising a quick escape from the morass into the clearing of nationhood. If imperial domination has been so massive — if, as Hyde put it, the conquering English have imposed "the form of our thoughts during every instant of our existence" (160) — then for Joyce it was difficult to see how an uncompromised resistance was possible. Where will they come from, those resisting thoughts that will somehow subvert a total domination? Hyde does not pause over this conundrum, but the self-defeating character of the colonized consciousness is one of Joyce's great subjects.

The attempt to construct a stable self-identity from within a radically unstable community is the acutely painful spectacle that Joyce plays out through Gabriel Conroy. Crucially, the investment in Gabriel's personal solidity is not his concern alone but is rendered as a broader social desire. "It's such a relief," Aunt Kate tells Gretta "that Gabriel is here. I always feel easier in my mind when he's here" (26). He is, in effect, the party's officialdom, its symbol of firm authority, its constabulary, its instrument of power. The task of policing Freddy Malins, who, after all, shows himself to be the most harmless of threats, displays Gabriel's role as the figure of domestic control, a role consolidated during his speech and, just as reassuringly, at his carving of the meats. A rich description of the well-laid table culminates with military resonance: decanters of cut glass standing "as sentries to a fruit-stand," (38) and "three squads of bottles of stout and ale and minerals, drawn up according to the colours of their uniforms" (38) — at which point Gabriel appears.

> Gabriel took his seat boldly at the head of the table and, having looked to the edge of the carver, plunged his fork firmly into the goose. He felt quite at ease now for he was an expert carver and liked nothing better than to find himself at the head of a well-laden table. (38)

Wielding his expert knife, presiding over "the noise of orders and counter-orders" (39), Gabriel consolidates the desire for a regulating authority which promises to control disturbance, to promote civility, and to perform all the little ceremonies sanctioning the communal life.

No reader should doubt that in representing the wavering rhythms of an evening party, "The Dead" is representing the political fragility of Ireland. The triumph of festivity — the generous circulation of food and feeling — is indeed conspicuous, making good on Joyce's resolve to overcome the "scrupulous meanness" (*Selected Letters* 134) of his earlier stories in favor of fair acknowledgment of Irish hospitality. But even during the moments of fond mutual regard and common exultation, the stresses are ineradicable.[5] Here is colonial Ireland at its best — so "The Dead" implies — and yet even at its best, it is decaying and fragile: the moments of collective self-affirmation, painfully achieved, bear signs of insupportable tension. Refusing to acknowledge the political provocations that circulate in their festive midst, content to surround themselves with the allure of art and literature, these colonial

---

[5]Vincent Pecora has written persuasively of the complex career of "generosity" and "hospitality" in "The Dead." He rightly emphasizes the apparently harmless comic aside, in which Gabriel describes the party's guests as "victims" of Aunt Kate's and Aunt Julia's hospitality, and shows the radical ambiguity in Joyce's gesture of artistic reparation (Pecora 233–45).

subjects manufacture a simulacrum of autonomy. Its hollowness is not only enforced by its reliance on *English* cultural tradition, neatly captured by the scene from *Romeo and Juliet* hanging on the wall, but emphatically by the inability to suppress a distinctly *Irish* provocation, first articulated by Miss Ivors and then embodied, in the story's climax, by Gretta Conroy.

For Joyce, colonial subjection is by no means the only obstacle to Irish recovery; but it is a blocking force so thick and heavy and ancient that it disables all who live within its encircling shadow. The colonized consciousness has all its other vulnerabilities heightened, and the sharp pathos in the life of Gabriel Conroy is that he aims to construct an emancipated personal identity, cultured and cosmopolitan, within an unemancipated milieu. Naively believing that he can liberate himself from inside the colonial constraint, he repeatedly aspires to a condition of self-ratifying autonomy, only to meet a failure that appears structurally inevitable. As Joyce tersely puts it in his lecture, "The economic and intellectual conditions that prevail in [Ireland] do not permit the development of individuality" (*Critical Writings* 171). "The Dead" reinforces this historical claim that the conflicts of colonialism have grown too sharp and too obtrusive in Ireland; at every step there looms the reminder that perfection of the self has grown impossible.

The historical record indeed makes clear that in those years at the beginning of the century, the general political uncertainty put the meaning of individual Irish lives into active question. Even as a decisive outcome to the anti-imperial struggle eluded reach, the vast number of competing postures ensured a ceaseless conflict of interpretations over the value of particular life-choices. If literary activity became charged — the riots over *The Playboy of the Western World* being only one exemplary instance — it was at least in part because so much of the struggle was necessarily a struggle over *representation:* over how to represent history, language, and the obligations of art. In the absence of a determining conflict with imperial British power, such representational issues became invested with even more resonance than usual.

The exercise of power appears in "The Dead" precisely as the power of representation, as the ability to control the texture of subjective response through authoritative verbal acts. Whether the occasion is Gabriel's dispute with Miss Ivors, or his after-dinner speech, or the supper discussion of Irish tenors, or, climactically, Gabriel's last conversation with Gretta — the resonant question is, Whose speech will triumph? Whose verbal construction of the collective experience will dominate, and in dominating, will dictate the terms by which individuals understand their own lives?

To speak of power as the power of representational discourse is not to deny that Joyce saw the physical basis of authority that undergirds colonial rule. When Gabriel "pilots" a tipsy Freddy Malins into the party (28), the small physical gesture might stand as a metonymy for an entire apparatus of imperial control. Far more dramatically, when an erotically charged Gabriel longs "to crush [Gretta's] body against his, to overmaster her" (54), the fantasy suggests the physical power that lies beneath the gauze of romance. And yet, while Joyce gives such quiet reminders of physical power and bodily violence, he locates drama in the acts of representation through which colonized subjects comprehend their fate. For those Irish who live within the circle of English domination, either in resistance or in capitulation, the immediate struggle is over the elaboration of a discourse, a broad narrative, within which lives might receive meaning. As Joyce's writing shows in many diverse ways, the significance of a life depends on the frame that surrounds it.

If Miss Ivors and the nationalists control the terms of political understanding, then not only will Gabriel's life be seen as a fraud, he will see himself as a fraud. Alternatively, if Gabriel can prevail, as he attempts to do with his after-dinner speech, then Miss Ivors and her like will be marked as the "sceptical" and "thought-tormented" representatives of a "less spacious age" (43). Gabriel's choice of this last metaphor ("less spacious") is revealing. The contest in "The Dead" is repeatedly cast as a battle to control the widest frame, the broadest space of social meaning.

In the story's last scene, when Gabriel is swept with high waves of love and lust, he not only anticipates a passionate night, he anticipates a new personal history within which to locate the events of his marriage. He wants to recover his wife's love by changing the design in which she locates it. As he himself remembers scenes of their early intimacy, he longs "to recall to her those moments, to make her forget the years of their dull existence together and remember only their moments of ecstasy" (52). He wants, in short, to rewrite the banal history of their marriage by placing it within the more "spacious" narrative of passion achieved, forgotten, recovered.

In the event, and fatefully, Gabriel is unable to control the movement of contexts, unable to achieve an historical revaluation that will preserve value, assign identities, and save a marriage through its times of stress. Gretta, it turns out, has a story of her own, a context of her own, which is wider than her life with Gabriel and which encloses his story within its awful reach. That Gretta loved Michael Furey before he met her, that she has felt a passion keener than any he has known — these are not only brutally painful facts in themselves, but they also place Gabriel within a rival setting. Having listened to her helplessly, he dreads that "Perhaps she had not told him all the story"; perhaps not, but she has told him enough to make clear "how poor a part he, her husband, had played in her life" (58). What links love and citizenship for Joyce, marriage, and Ireland, is that they both entangle a self within surroundings that threaten to crush its struggle for integrity.[6] In the final paragraphs of Gabriel's surrender, he swooningly yields to powers wider than his own.

Joyce himself, choosing exile, sought to escape exactly those forces, emanating from deep within the colonial state, that combine to break Gabriel Conroy. And yet, Joyce was not content merely to live outside the grip of his home colony, merely to escape the fatal tangle of political tension.[7] Against the threat of being absorbed within a larger frame, he set out to contain the container, to swallow those who would swallow him in their contexts. The characteristic strategy of his work is to bring *inside the fiction* exactly those pressures that surround it in the living world. This is how "The Dead" articulates a third place beyond the alternatives of nationalist politics and apolitical aesthetics: to represent them is to occupy a site distinct from them.

The virtuosity of the final image in the story — the snow that is "general all over Ireland" (59) — may lie not in any symbolic register, but in its sheer blank literalism. The odd piece of phrasing, "general all over," enforces the brutally direct condition: no Irish place is free from snow. Through these final paragraphs, the word "all" — "all the story," "all becoming shades," "all the living and the dead," "all over Ireland"

---

[6] A letter of November 1906 suggests that modern marriage was no more satisfactory a form of community than modern nationhood: "Perhaps my view of life is too cynical but it seems to me that a lot of this talk about love is nonsense. A woman's love is always maternal and egoistic. A man, on the contrary, side by side with his extraordinary cerebral sexualism and bodily fervour (from which women are normally free) possesses a fund of genuine affection for the 'beloved' or 'once beloved' object. I am no friend of tyranny, as you know, but if many husbands are brutal the atmosphere in which they live . . . is brutal and few wives and homes can satisfy the desire for happiness" (*Letters* 130).

[7] In the spring of 1907, Joyce wrote of "certain ideas I would like to give form to," and suggested they may be "purely personal." "I have no wish," he immediately goes on, "to codify myself as anarchist or socialist or reactionary" (*Letters* 151–52). After his long thought on the national question, he reaches the political impasse that leads into the complex social thought of "The Dead."

(59) — stretches the panorama into a nearly inconceivable universality. Here at the last is a frame wider than any other, a frame that surrounds even vast and bitter divisions of religion, politics, class, gender. Snow is the final, brutally simple context that now lies over all the lines of stress, which have thrust cracks through the narrative surface of the story.

And yet, if the snow that ends "The Dead" is in one respect a revenge upon the workings of history, an act of defiant literary will that assimilates political struggle within the universalizing image of "all the living and the dead," it is not that alone. The snow, after all, is general all over *Ireland*. And in the sudden release of the narrative eye to scan the entire snowy Irish island, the story's last sentence evokes the geography of a separate national identity. An Ireland covered in snow, however one understands the symbolic valence, has achieved a unity that its colonial status has long blocked. In such a way does the exile in Trieste send home his equivocal historical gift: a storm-driven Ireland flattened into the shape of a nation.

WORKS CITED

Ellmann, Richard. *James Joyce*. New York: Oxford UP, 1982.

Hyde, Douglas. *Language, Lore and Lyrics*. Ed. Brendan O Conaire. Blackrock: Irish Academic, 1986.

Joyce, James. "Ireland, Island of Saints and Sages." *The Critical Writings of James Joyce*. Ed. Ellsworth Mason and Richard Ellmann. New York: Viking, 1959.

———. *Letters of James Joyce*. vol. 2. Ed. Richard Ellmann. New York: Viking, 1966.

———. *Selected Letters of James Joyce*. Ed. Richard Ellmann. New York: Viking, 1957.

Kelleher, John V. "Irish Mythology in James Joyce's 'The Dead.' " *Review of Politics* 27 (1965): 414–33.

Pecora, Vincent. " 'The Dead' and the Generosity of the Word." *PMLA* 101 (1986): 233–45.

Potts, Willard. "The Catholic Revival and 'The Dead.' " *Joyce Studies Annual* 2 (1991): 3–26.

Feminist Criticism
and
"The Dead"

WHAT IS FEMINIST CRITICISM?

Feminist criticism comes in many forms, and feminist critics have a variety of goals. Some are interested in rediscovering the works of women writers overlooked by a masculine-dominated culture. Others have revisited books by male authors and reviewed them from a woman's point of view to understand how they both reflect and shape the attitudes that have held women back.

Since the early 1970s three strains of feminist criticism have emerged, strains that can be categorized as French, American, and British. These categories should not be allowed to obscure either the global implications of the women's movement or the fact that interests and ideas have been shared by feminists from France, Great Britain, and the United States. British and American feminists have examined similar problems while writing about many of the same writers and works, and American feminists have recently become more receptive to French theories about femininity and writing. Historically speaking, however, French, American, and British feminists have examined similar problems from somewhat different perspectives.

French feminists have tended to focus their attention on language, analyzing the ways in which meaning is produced. They have concluded that language as we commonly think of it is a decidedly male realm. Drawing on the ideas of the psychoanalytic philosopher Jacques Lacan, French feminists remind us that language is a realm of public discourse. A child enters the linguistic realm just as it comes to grasp its separateness from its mother, just about the time that boys identify with their father, the family representative of culture. The language learned reflects a binary logic that opposes such terms as active/passive, masculine/feminine, sun/moon, father/mother, head/heart, son/daughter, intelligent/sensitive, brother/sister, form/matter, phallus/vagina, reason/emotion. Because this logic tends to group with masculinity such qualities as light, thought, and activity, French feminists have said that the structure of language is phallocentric: it privileges the phallus and, more generally, masculinity by associating them with things and values more appreciated by the (masculine-dominated) culture. Moreover, French feminists believe, "masculine desire dominates speech and posits woman as an idealized fantasy-fulfillment for the incurable emotional lack caused by separation from the mother" (Jones 83).

In the view of French feminists, language is associated with separation from the mother. Its distinctions represent the world from the male point of view, and it systematically forces women to choose: either they can imagine and represent themselves as men imagine and represent them (in which case they may speak, but will speak as men) or they can choose "silence," becoming in the process "the invisible and unheard sex" (Jones 83).

But some influential French feminists have argued that language only *seems* to give women such a narrow range of choices. There is another possibility, namely that women can develop a *feminine* language. In various ways, early French feminists such as Annie Leclerc, Xavière Gauthier, and Marguerite Duras have suggested that there is something that may be called *l'écriture féminine:* women's writing. Recently, Julia Kristeva has said that feminine language is "semiotic," not "symbolic." Rather than rigidly opposing and ranking elements of reality, rather than symbolizing one thing but not another in terms of a third, feminine language is rhythmic and unifying. If from the male perspective it seems fluid to the point of being chaotic, that is a fault of the male perspective.

According to Kristeva, feminine language is derived from the preoedipal period of fusion between mother and child. Associated with the maternal, feminine language is not only threatening to culture, which is patriarchal, but also a medium through which women may be creative in new ways. But Kristeva has paired her central, liberating claim — that truly feminist innovation in all fields requires an understanding of the relation between maternity and feminine creation — with a warning. A feminist language that refuses to participate in "masculine" discourse, that places its future entirely in a feminine, semiotic discourse, risks being politically marginalized by men. That is to say, it risks being relegated to the outskirts (pun intended) of what is considered socially and politically significant.

Kristeva, who associates feminine writing with the female body, is joined in her views by other leading French feminists. Hélène Cixous, for instance, also posits an essential connection between the woman's body, whose sexual pleasure has been repressed and denied expression, and women's writing. "Write your self. Your body must be heard," Cixous urges; once they learn to write their bodies, women will not only realize their sexuality but enter history and move toward a future based on a "feminine" economy of giving rather than the "masculine" economy of hoarding (Cixous 250). For Luce Irigaray, women's sexual pleasure (*jouissance*) cannot be expressed by the dominant, ordered, "logical," masculine language. She explores the connection between women's sexuality and women's language through the following analogy: as women's *jouissance* is more multiple than men's unitary, phallic pleasure ("woman has sex organs just about everywhere"), so "feminine" language is more diffusive than its "masculine" counterpart. ("That is undoubtedly the reason . . . her language . . . goes off in all directions and . . . he is unable to discern the coherence," Irigaray writes [101–03].)

Cixous's and Irigaray's emphasis on feminine writing as an expression of the female body has drawn criticism from other French feminists. Many argue that an emphasis on the body either reduces "the feminine" to a biological essence or elevates it in a way that shifts the valuation of masculine and feminine but retains the binary categories. For Christine Fauré, Irigaray's celebration of women's difference fails to address the issue of masculine dominance, and a Marxist-feminist, Catherine Clément, has warned that "poetic" descriptions of what constitutes the feminine will not challenge that dominance in the realm of production. The boys will still make the toys, and decide who gets to use them. In her effort to redefine women as political rather than as sexual beings, Monique Wittig has called for the abolition of sexual categories that Cixous and Irigaray retain and revalue as they celebrate women's writing.

American feminist critics have shared with French critics both an interest in and a cautious distrust of the concept of feminine writing.

Annette Kolodny, for instance, has worried that the "richness and variety of women's writing" will be missed if we see in it only its "feminine mode" or "style" ("Some Notes" 78). And yet Kolodny herself proceeds, in the same essay, to point out that women *have* had their own style, which includes reflexive constructions ("she found herself crying") and particular, recurring themes (clothing and self-fashioning are two that Kolodny mentions; other American feminists have focused on madness, disease, and the demonic).

Interested as they have become in the "French" subject of feminine style, American feminist critics began by analyzing literary texts rather than philosophizing abstractly about language. Many reviewed the great works by male writers, embarking on a revisionist rereading of literary tradition. These critics examined the portrayals of women characters, exposing the patriarchal ideology implicit in such works and showing how clearly this tradition of systematic masculine dominance is inscribed in our literary tradition. Kate Millett, Carolyn Heilbrun, and Judith Fetterley, among many others, created this model for American feminist criticism, a model that Elaine Showalter came to call "the feminist critique" of "male-constructed literary history" ("Poetics" 25).

Meanwhile another group of critics including Sandra Gilbert, Susan Gubar, Patricia Meyer Spacks, and Showalter herself created a somewhat different model. Whereas feminists writing "feminist critique" have analyzed works by men, practitioners of what Showalter used to refer to as "gynocriticism" have studied the writings of those women who, against all odds, produced what she calls "a literature of their own." In *The Female Imagination* (1975), Spacks examines the female literary tradition to find out how great women writers across the ages have felt, perceived themselves, and imagined reality. Gilbert and Gubar, in *The Madwoman in the Attic* (1979), concern themselves with well-known women writers of the nineteenth century, but they too find that general concerns, images, and themes recur, because the authors that they treat wrote "in a culture whose fundamental definitions of literary authority are both overtly and covertly patriarchal" (45).

If one of the purposes of gynocriticism is to (re)study well-known women authors, another is to rediscover women's history and culture, particularly women's communities that have nurtured female creativity. Still another related purpose is to discover neglected or forgotten women writers and thus to forge an alternative literary tradition, a canon that better represents the female perspective by better representing the literary works that have been written by women. Showalter, in *A Literature of Their Own* (1977), admirably began to fulfill this purpose, providing a remarkably comprehensive overview of women's writing through three of its phases. She defines these as the "Feminine, Feminist, and Female" phases, phases during which women first imitated a masculine tradition (1840–80), then protested against its standards and values (1880–1920), and finally advocated their own autonomous, female perspective (1920 to the present).

With the recovery of a body of women's texts, attention has returned to a question raised in 1978 by Lillian Robinson: Doesn't American feminist criticism need to formulate a theory of its own practice? Won't reliance on theoretical assumptions, categories, and strategies developed by men and associated with nonfeminist schools of thought prevent feminism from being accepted as equivalent to these other critical discourses? Not all American feminists believe that a special or unifying theory of feminist practice is urgently needed; Showalter's historical approach to women's culture allows a feminist critic to use theories based on nonfeminist disciplines. Kolodny has advocated a "playful pluralism" that encompasses a variety of critical schools and methods. But Jane Marcus and others have responded that if feminists adopt too wide a range of approaches, they may relax the tensions between feminists and the educational establishment necessary for political activism.

The question of whether feminism weakens or fortifies itself by emphasizing its separateness — and by developing unity through separateness — is one of several areas of debate within American feminism. Another area of disagreement touched on earlier, between feminists who stress universal feminine attributes (the feminine imagination, feminine writing) and those who focus on the political conditions experienced by certain groups of women at certain times in history, parallels a larger distinction between American feminist critics and their British counterparts.

While it has been customary to refer to an Anglo-American tradition of feminist criticism, British feminists tend to distinguish themselves from what they see as an American overemphasis on texts linking women across boundaries and decades and an underemphasis on popular art and culture. They regard their own critical practice as more political than that of American feminists, whom they have often faulted for being uninterested in historical detail. They would join such American critics as Myra Jehlen to suggest that a continuing preoccupation with women writers might create the danger of placing women's texts outside the history that conditions them.

In the view of British feminists, the American opposition to male stereotypes that denigrate women has often led to counterstereotypes of feminine virtue that ignore real differences of race, class, and culture among women. In addition, they argue that American celebrations of individual heroines falsely suggest that powerful individuals may be immune to repressive conditions and may even imply that *any* individual can go through life unconditioned by the culture and ideology in which she or he lives.

Similarly, the American endeavor to recover women's history — for example, by emphasizing that women developed their own strategies to gain power within their sphere — is seen by British feminists like Judith Newton and Deborah Rosenfelt as an endeavor that "mystifies" male oppression, disguising it as something that has created for women a special world of opportunities. More important from the British standpoint, the universalizing and "essentializing" tendencies in both American practice and French theory disguise women's oppression by highlighting sexual difference, suggesting that a dominant system is impervious to political change. By contrast, British feminist theory emphasizes an engagement with historical process in order to promote social change.

In the essay that follows, Margot Norris begins by setting Joyce's work in the contexts of late nineteenth- and early twentieth-century feminism. She remarks, for instance, on the fact that as early as 1900 the young Joyce "wrote in the *Fortnightly Review* praising Ibsen's insightful representation of women." She also reveals, however, that "a long critical tradition has assumed Joyce's hostility" toward feminism.

Before turning to "The Dead," which she considers "an excellent opportunity for exploring the question of Joyce's feminism or misogyny," Norris expands on the distinction between French feminist criticism and the "Anglo-American" alternative. (In this introduction, the latter approach has been simply called "American" in order to distinguish it from a different, particularly British feminism grounded in Marxist and cultural criticism.) Norris sees American feminist criticism as being rooted in the historical tradition of "liberal feminism" that stretches from William Godwin and Mary Wollstonecraft through John Stuart Mill and Virginia Woolf. "The progressive ideology of this feminist tradition," she explains, "produced a rhetorical investment in moral improvement and social hope. . . . Joyce's representations of women fail badly in the light of this rhetorical demand."

By contrast, Norris then suggests, "French feminism . . . comes . . . in part through experimental modernism (in the case of Hélène Cixous, *through* Joyce)." It is thus extremely sympathetic to "an antirepresentational, antirealist strategy" of writing. Indeed, Norris suggests, Joyce's late, "highly experimental writing, . . . which proclaims itself as having nothing significant to tell the reader, acts out, in the view of French feminism, a set of values (antidogmatism, undecidability, playfulness) that can be designated as feminine writing (*écriture féminine*) in distinction to a patriarchal writing that arrogates truth, knowledge, and authority to itself."

In the end, Norris does not side with those American feminists who, because of their "representational and polemical approach," position Joyce in a long line of patriarchal writers who have misrepresented women through weak, flawed female characters and biased, chauvinistic narrators. Nor does she exclusively take a French, "performative and rhetorical approach (that pays attention to *how* saying works)," one that would lead her to conclude that the text of "The Dead" amounts to "a feminist critique of a patriarchal society that is hidebound and hardbound." Instead, she leans toward the French interpretation by bringing up several points which, no matter what Joyce's intent, have the effect of undermining the audible male bourgeois (patriarchal) narrative voice centered in Gabriel's point of view.

Because "The Dead" contains, in her view, feminist *and* antifeminist aspects and strategies, Norris approaches it from both vantage points, finding in the charming and civilized narrator (who Norris says "takes Gabriel's position") and "the graceless, vulgar, blurting voices of the women" characters "the narration's collusion with patriarchy." On the other hand, Norris also finds Joyce's narrative to be antipatriarchal in nature insofar as its gaps and discrepancies allow us to see that "the institution and practice of art is as exclusionary as all other institutional practices."

Late in the essay, Norris juxtaposes two sentences that sum up the American and French perspectives, in that order. In so doing she resolves the question about whether Joyce was feminist or misogynist by sidestepping it, that is, by showing us that, viewed from different feminist perspectives, the text of "The Dead" can be misogynist *and* feminist. "The narration," she writes, "intent on making Gabriel remarkable and the women unremarkable, has brushed away . . . challenges by Lily and Molly Ivors as female misunderstandings, and has foregrounded an aestheticized representation of Gretta whose function is to certify Gabriel's poesy, passion, and benign compassion." Then she continues in a French feminist view:

> The text's feminism, its possibilities for political critique, are lodged in the detachability of the narrator and his project from a larger textual project that supplements and challenges the narrator's

version of events and people — not with commentary or another voice, but by posing problems within the narration that encourage, and reward, readerly skepticism, query, and challenge.

Norris thus suggests that although the narrative voice is patriarchal and misogynist, it contains gaps and contradictions that encourage the reader to ask questions and raise objections, thereby enabling the text ultimately to perform a feminist function.

Ross C Murfin

FEMINIST CRITICISM: A SELECTED BIBLIOGRAPHY

French Feminist Theories

Beauvoir, Simone de. *The Second Sex.* 1953. Trans. and ed. H. M. Parshley. New York: Bantam, 1961.

Cixous, Hélène. "The Laugh of the Medusa." Trans. Keith Cohen and Paula Cohen. *Signs* 1 (1976): 875–94.

Cixous, Hélène, and Catherine Clément. *The Newly Born Woman.* Trans. Betsy Wing. Minneapolis: U of Minnesota P, 1986.

French Feminist Theory. Special issue, *Signs* 7.1 (1981).

Irigaray, Luce. *This Sex Which Is Not One.* Trans. Catherine Porter. Ithaca: Cornell UP, 1985.

Jones, Ann Rosalind. "Writing the Body: Toward an Understanding of *L'Écriture féminine.*" Showalter, *New Feminist Criticism* 361–77.

Kristeva, Julia. *Desire in Language: A Semiotic Approach to Literature and Art.* Ed. Leon S. Roudiez. Trans. Thomas Gora, Alice Jardine, and Roudiez. New York: Columbia UP, 1980.

Marks, Elaine, and Isabelle de Courtivron, eds. *New French Feminisms: An Anthology.* Amherst: U of Massachusetts P, 1980.

Moi, Toril, ed. *French Feminist Thought: A Reader.* Oxford: Basil Blackwell, 1987.

British and American Feminist Theories

Belsey, Catherine, and Jane Moore, eds. *The Feminist Reader: Essays in Gender and the Politics of Literary Criticism.* New York: Basil Blackwell, 1989.

Benhabib, Seyla, and Drucilla Cornell, eds. *Feminism as Critique: On the Politics of Gender*. Minneapolis: U of Minnesota P, 1987.

Collins, Patricia Hill. *Black Feminist Thought: Knowledge, Consciousness, and the Politics of Empowerment*. Boston: Unwin Hyman, 1990.

de Lauretis, Teresa, ed. *Feminist Studies/Critical Studies*. Bloomington: Indiana UP, 1986.

Feminist Readings: French Texts/American Contexts. Special issue, *Yale French Studies* 62 (1982). Essays by Jardine and Spivak.

Fuss, Diana. *Essentially Speaking: Feminism, Nature and Difference*. New York: Routledge, 1989.

Herndl, Diana Price, and Robyn Warhol, eds. *Feminisms: An Anthology of Literary Theory and Criticism*. New Brunswick, NJ: Rutgers UP, 1991.

hooks, bell. *Ain't I a Woman?: Black Women and Feminism*. Boston: South End, 1981.

Keohane, Nannerl O., Michelle Z. Rosaldo, and Barbara C. Gelpi, eds. *Feminist Theory: A Critique of Ideology*. Chicago: U of Chicago P, 1982.

Kolodny, Annette. "Dancing Through the Minefield: Some Observations on the Theory, Practice, and Politics of a Feminist Literary Criticism." Showalter, *New Feminist Criticism* 144–67.

The Lesbian Issue. Special issue, *Signs* 9 (Summer 1984).

Malson, Micheline, et al., eds. *Feminist Theory in Practice and Process*. Chicago: U of Chicago P, 1986.

Rich, Adrienne. *On Lies, Secrets, and Silence: Selected Prose, 1966–1979*. New York: Norton, 1979.

Showalter, Elaine. "Toward a Feminist Poetics." Showalter, *New Feminist Criticism* 125–43.

———, ed. *The New Feminist Criticism: Essays on Women, Literature, and Theory*. New York: Pantheon, 1985.

The Feminist Critique

Fetterley, Judith. *The Resisting Reader: A Feminist Approach to American Fiction*. Bloomington: Indiana UP, 1978.

Greer, Germaine. *The Female Eunuch*. New York: McGraw, 1971.

Millett, Kate. *Sexual Politics*. Garden City: Doubleday, 1970.

Robinson, Lillian S. *Sex, Class, and Culture*. 1978. New York: Methuen, 1986.

Wittig, Monique. *Les Guérillères*. Trans. David Le Vay. 1969. New York: Avon, 1973.

Woolf, Virginia. *A Room of One's Own*. New York: Harcourt, 1929.

Women's Writing and Creativity

Abel, Elizabeth, ed. *Writing and Sexual Difference*. Chicago: U of Chicago P, 1982.

Abel, Elizabeth, Marianne Hirsch, and Elizabeth Langland, eds. *The Voyage In: Fictions of Female Development*. Hanover: UP of New England, 1983.

Auerbach, Nina. *Communities of Women: An Idea in Fiction*. Cambridge: Harvard UP, 1978.

Christian, Barbara. *Black Feminist Criticism: Perspectives on Black Women Writers*. New York: Pergamon, 1985.

Gilbert, Sandra M., and Susan Gubar. *The Madwoman in the Attic: The Woman Writer and the Nineteenth-Century Literary Imagination*. New Haven: Yale UP, 1979.

Jacobus, Mary, ed. *Women Writing and Writing about Women*. New York: Barnes, 1979.

Miller, Nancy K., ed. *The Poetics of Gender*. New York: Columbia UP, 1986.

Newton, Judith Lowder. *Women, Power and Subversion: Social Strategies in British Fiction, 1778–1860*. Athens: U of Georgia P, 1981.

Poovey, Mary. *The Proper Lady and the Woman Writer: Ideology as Style in the Works of Mary Wollstonecraft, Mary Shelley, and Jane Austen*. Chicago: U of Chicago P, 1984.

Showalter, Elaine. *A Literature of Their Own: British Women Novelists from Brontë to Lessing*. Princeton: Princeton UP, 1977.

Marxist and Class Analysis

Barrett, Michèle. *Women's Oppression Today: Problems in Marxist Feminist Analysis*. London: Verso, 1980.

Delphy, Christine. *Close to Home: A Materialist Analysis of Women's Oppression*. Trans. and ed. Diana Leonard. Amherst: U of Massachusetts P, 1984.

Hartsock, Nancy C. M. *Money, Sex, and Power: Toward a Feminist Historical Materialism*. Boston: Northeastern UP, 1985.

Kaplan, Cora. *Sea Changes: Culture and Feminism*. London: Verso, 1986.

Mitchell, Juliet. *Woman's Estate*. New York: Pantheon, 1971.

Newton, Judith, and Deborah Rosenfelt, eds. *Feminist Criticism and Social Change: Sex, Class and Race in Literature and Culture.* New York: Methuen, 1985.

Sargent, Lydia, ed. *Women and Revolution: A Discussion of the Unhappy Marriage of Marxism and Feminism.* Montreal: Black Rose, 1981.

Women's History/Women's Studies

Bridenthal, Renate, and Claudia Koonz, eds. *Becoming Visible: Women in European History.* Boston: Houghton, 1977.

Farnham, Christie, ed. *The Impact of Feminist Research in the Academy.* Bloomington: Indiana UP, 1987.

Kelly, Joan. *Women, History and Theory.* Chicago: U of Chicago P, 1984.

McConnell-Ginet, Sally, et al., eds. *Woman and Language in Literature and Society.* New York: Praeger, 1980.

Mitchell, Juliet, and Ann Oakley, eds. *The Rights and Wrongs of Women.* London: Penguin, 1976.

Newton, Judith L., et al., eds. *Sex and Class in Women's History.* London: Routledge, 1983.

Riley, Denise. *"Am I That Name?": Feminism and the Category of "Women" in History.* Minneapolis: U of Minnesota P, 1988.

Rowbotham, Sheila. *Woman's Consciousness, Man's World.* Harmondsworth: Penguin, 1973.

Schipper, Mineke, ed. *Unheard Words: Women and Literature in Africa, the Arab World, Asia, the Caribbean, and Latin America.* London: Allison, 1985.

Scott, Joan Wallach. *Gender and the Politics of History.* New York: Columbia UP, 1988.

Smith-Rosenberg, Carroll. *Disorderly Conduct: Visions of Gender in Victorian America.* New York: Knopf, 1985.

Feminism and Other Critical Approaches

Armstrong, Nancy, ed. *Literature as Women's History I.* A special issue of *Genre* 19–20 (1986–87).

Benstock, Shari. *Textualizing the Feminine: On the Limits of Genre.* Norman: U of Oklahoma P, 1991.

Diamond, Irene, and Lee Quinby, eds. *Feminism and Foucault: Reflections on Resistance.* Boston: Northeastern UP, 1988.

Elliot, Patricia. *From Mastery to Analysis: Theories of Gender in Psychoanalytic Criticism.* Ithaca: Cornell UP, 1990.

Feminist Studies 14 (1988). Special issue on feminism and deconstruction.

Gallop, Jane. *The Daughter's Seduction: Feminism and Psychoanalysis.* Ithaca: Cornell UP, 1982.

Keller, Evelyn Fox. *Reflections on Gender and Science.* New Haven: Yale UP, 1985.

Meese, Elizabeth, and Alice Parker, eds. *The Difference Within: Feminism and Critical Theory.* Amsterdam/Philadelphia: John Benjamins, 1989.

Penley, Constance, ed. *Feminism and Film Theory.* New York: Routledge, 1988.

Feminist Approaches to Joyce

Benstock, Shari. "City Spaces and Women's Places in Joyce's Dublin." *James Joyce: The Augmented Ninth.* Ed. Bernard Benstock. Syracuse: Syracuse UP, 1988. 293–307.

———. *Women of the Left Bank.* Austin: U of Texas P, 1986.

Church, Margaret. "The Adolescent Point of View Toward Women in Joyce's *Portrait.*" *Irish Renaissance Annual* 2 (1981): 158–65.

Cixous, Hélène. "Joyce: The (r)use of writing." *Post-Structuralist Joyce.* Ed. Derek Attridge and Daniel Ferrer. Cambridge: Cambridge UP, 1984. 15–30.

Devlin, Kimberly J. "The Female Eye: Joyce's Voyeuristic Narcissists." *New Alliances in Joyce Studies.* Ed. Bonnie Kime Scott. Newark: U of Delaware P, 1988. 135–43.

French, Marilyn. *The Book as World.* Cambridge: Harvard UP, 1975.

———. "Women in Joyce's Dublin." *James Joyce: The Augmented Ninth.* Ed. Bernard Benstock. Syracuse: Syracuse UP, 1988. 267–72.

Henke, Suzette. *James Joyce and the Politics of Desire.* New York: Routledge, 1990.

Henke, Suzette, and Elaine Unkeless, eds. *Women in Joyce.* Urbana: U of Illinois P, 1982.

Modern Fiction Studies 35 (Autumn 1989). "Feminist Readings of Joyce" issue.

Norris, Margot. *The Decentered Universe of "Finnegans Wake."* Baltimore: Johns Hopkins UP, 1974.

———. "Portraits of the Artist as a Young Lover." *New Alliances in*

Joyce Studies. Ed. Bonnie Kime Scott. Newark: U of Delaware P, 1988. 144–52.

Scott, Bonnie Kime. *James Joyce*. Feminist Readings Series. Brighton, Eng.: Harvester P; Atlantic Highlands: Humanities P Intl., 1987.

———. *Joyce and Feminism*. Bloomington: Indiana UP, 1984.

A FEMINIST PERSPECTIVE

MARGOT NORRIS

Not the Girl She Was at All: Women in "The Dead"

I. Historical and Theoretical Context

Joyce wrote in the context of an awareness of late nineteenth- and early twentieth-century feminism, whose polemics jostled his own early publications and permeated the literary paternity of a hero of his adolescence, Henrik Ibsen. His essay ("The Day of the Rabblement") protesting the expulsion of Ibsen and other Continental dramatists from the stage of the Irish Literary Theatre was published privately, in the face of college censorship, along with Francis Skeffington's advocacy of equal status for women at the university ("A Forgotten Aspect of the University Question"). The first installment of *Portrait* appeared in the issue of *The Egoist* in which Dora Marsden protested Christabel Pankhurst's advocacy of chastity for the control of venereal disease (Scott 51). In 1900 the eighteen-year-old Joyce wrote in *The Fortnightly Review*, praising Henrik Ibsen's insightful representation of women in *When We Dead Awaken* with the feminist figure of implicit androgyny, "Ibsen's knowledge of humanity is nowhere more obvious than in his portrayal of women. He amazes one by his painful introspection. He seems to know them better than they know themselves. Indeed, if one may say so of an extremely virile man, there is a curious admixture of the woman in his nature" ("Ibsen's New Drama" 64). Yet in assessing whether Joyce was submerged in or repelled by this intellectual feminist climate, a long critical tradition has assumed Joyce's hostility. Richard Ellmann's interpretation of the ideological separation of Joyce and Skeffington's essays — construing their preface, "each writer is responsible only for what appears under his own name," to mean that "neither agreed with the other's position" (88) — put in place the notion that the young Joyce did not wish his own freethinking to be tarred with Skeffington's feminist brush. The possibility that Joyce and Skeffington might have regarded their texts to function as complementary pleas for a progressive Irish literacy, with stage and university as merely alternative venues, is thereby suppressed. Likewise, Carolyn Heilbrun insisted in 1982 that "Joyce admired Ibsen and ignored his most profound contribution," and described him as "a man who hates women. Ought one rather to call him a misogynist, a man who hates women for becoming what he has determined they should be?" (215). Yet Joyce could not have been clearer that this was not so, than in his defense of Ibsen to Arthur Power:

> You ignore the spirit which animated him. The purpose of *The Doll's House,* for instance, was the emancipation of women, which has caused the greatest revolution in our time in the most important relationship there is — that between men and women; the revolt of women against the idea that they are the mere instruments of men. (35)

Joyce's story "The Dead" provides an excellent opportunity for exploring the question of Joyce's feminism or misogyny in terms of the feminist textual strategies that were, and are, available — technically and politically — to the male author. This issue, in turn, is worth exploring theoretically within a historical context before turning to "The Dead" itself, in order to elucidate the intellectual complexions of the feminist critical traditions within which modern readers interpret texts. Anglo-American feminism, whose hostility to Joyce is best typified in the work of Sandra Gilbert and Susan Gubar, grows out of the philosophical traditions of the British Enlightenment (the thought of William Godwin and Mary Wollstonecraft, for example) whose inspiration by the French Revolution gave way, in the nineteenth century, to the liberal feminism produced by the utilitarianism of John Stuart Mill. The progressive ideology of this feminist tradition produced a rhetorical investment in moral improvement and social hope that culminates, in twentieth-century writing, in powerful feminist polemics (like Virginia Woolf's *A Room of One's Own*) and utopian female representations and self-representations (like the artist Lily Briscoe in Woolf's *To the Lighthouse*). Joyce's representations of women fail badly in the light of this rhetorical demand. Gilbert and Gubar, for example, complain that in making Molly Bloom so ignorant, depriving her of the Greek that would let her understand not only "metempsychosis" but, implicitly, the classical Odyssean intertext in which she herself is embedded, he foreclosed the historical possibilities of a more progressive type of female representation, "Molly's bewilderment at the classic concepts of 'metempsychosis' and her implicit metamorphosis of it into the babble of 'Met him pike hoses' exemplify the parrot-like blankness with which Joyce's women respond to abstract concepts" (232).

In contrast, French feminism, the other dominant feminist tradition to have shaped textual criticism in the last twenty years, comes to feminism in part through experimental modernism (in the case of Hélène Cixous, *through Joyce*) and therefore finds itself far more comfortable with an antirepresentational, antirealist strategy of writing woman. Itself ahistorical (French feminism appears to "forget" its own intellectual antecedents in a Nietzschean gesture), poststructuralist feminism pays relatively little attention to what writers say about women, or how women are represented, in favor of exploring how the activity of saying may itself act as a gendering of a text. Joyce's later highly experimental writing, the inauthoritative textuality of *Finnegans Wake*, which proclaims itself as having nothing significant to tell the reader, acts out, in the view of French feminism, a set of values (antidogmatism, undecidability, playfulness) that can be designated as feminine writing (*écriture féminine*) in distinction to a patriarchal writing that arrogates truth, knowledge, and authority to itself (Kristeva 92). If these two feminist approaches to texts are held distinct, as a representational and polemical approach (that pays attention to *what* is said) contrasted with a performative and rhetorical approach (that pays attention to *how* saying works), then the possibility opens for reading a text, like "The Dead" — with its disappointing representations of women — as nonetheless *performing* feminist gestures and a feminist critique of art and society.

II. The Male Narrator and the Female Back Answer

Joyce performs in "The Dead" not only a critique of patriarchy, but a critique of his own art as contributing to the oppression and the silencing of women. These critiques are not overt, however, because they are lodged not in the narration, in what is said by the text, but rather in gaps, contradictions, silences, in what is *not* said by the narration. "The Dead" must therefore be read not as one text but as two texts: a "loud" or audible male narration challenged and disrupted by a "silent" or discounted female countertext that does not, in the end, succeed in making itself heard. "The Dead" itself thematizes this complicated textual operation in the homely gesture of what I call "the stifled back answer," which derives from the opening description of Lily, the servant girl, but which also describes the text that represses its own oppressive practices with respect to women, inscribes a protest against them, and then silences or stifles that protest. The Morkans, we learn, get on well with Lily — "But the only thing they would not stand was back answers" (22). We are prompted here, I would argue, to think of the text of "The Dead" as a narration itself unwilling to allow a series of back answers that nonetheless disrupt it: "The men that is now is only all palaver and what they can get out of you" (23), "West Briton!" (33), "There's a nice husband for you, Mrs Malins" (34), "And if I were in Julia's place I'd tell that Father Healy straight up to his face . . . " (37), "And why couldn't he have a voice too? . . . Is it because he's only a black?" (40). If we can think of these as back answers that are repeatedly stifled by the text, then the status of female protest in the text — voiced, then silenced; sounded but rejected; there, but negated — becomes visible to us as something whose fate is *staged*, rather than articulated, by the story.

If the two texts of the story can be understood as a male voice repeatedly disrupted by female back answers, then the rather handsome narration, with its conspicuously attractive prose, can begin to be suspected by a skeptical or resisting reader as fitting Lily's description of male discourse, when she says, "The men that is now is only all palaver and what they can get out of you" (23). The suspicion that the narration may be seductive male palaver can then alert us to the possibility that the voice that narrates "The Dead" promotes the interests and values of the story's male protagonist, and must therefore not be trusted to be "innocent," disinterested, or fair. The narrative voice has a bourgeois agenda: to produce a flattering picture of Irish middle-class life whose center of security and reliability is Gabriel Conroy, paterfamilias to a family of women. But the narrator does not merely promote patriarchy; his donnée (and one is justified in gendering this voice male on the basis of its aims and functions) is to make a subtle and philosophical argument about perfectability, to present the story of a cultured, progressive, cosmopolitan man — the very opposite of the drunkards and failures who populate the other stories of *Dubliners* — who nonetheless has blind spots and egotisms that he is shown capable of transcending. Ideologically, the plot of the story promotes the liberal and humane values of a civilized life that puts particularly great store in art, artistic sensibility, and idealism. Not only is Gabriel Conroy not a philistine, for all of his prosperity and respectability, but he is shown to possess the language of a poet and the passions of a lover. The shock of confronting his wife's secret love, and the recognition that she does not perceive him as he perceives himself, forces him to refine his self-image into a transcendent epiphany of his own fallibility and mortality. The narrator is allowed to participate rhetorically in Gabriel's achievement of a higher philosophical vision by producing a breathtaking peroration: an immense panoramic perspective vested in the hushed diction of equanimity and peace, and cloaked in the power of a dominant metaphor, as the snow stands for the indiscriminate universality of death, and its metaphysical acceptance:

> Yes, the newspapers were right: snow was general all over Ireland. It was falling on every part of the dark central plain, on the treeless hills, falling softly upon the Bog of Allen and, farther westward, softly falling into the dark, mutinous Shannon waves. . . . His soul swooned slowly as he heard the snow falling, . . . like the descent of their last end, upon all the living and the dead. (59)

III. The Critical Molly

It is easy to be charmed by this (male) narrative voice with its considerable poetic talents, and consequently to dislike the graceless, vulgar, blurting voices of the women, produced by an urgent need to protest an offense, an injustice, an oppression. This critical or readerly position is thematized by the function of Molly Ivors in the story, whom Gabriel pictures as ungenerous, ungracious, and hypercritical for failing to be seduced by the beautiful phrases of his review of Browning ("He repeated to himself a phrase he had written in his review: *One feels that one is listening to a thought-tormented music*" [34] because her focus is fixed on its institutional context — the pro-British *Daily Express*. The reader is put in a similar quandary of assuming either the benign, bookish posture of Gabriel ("But that did not make him a West Briton surely. The books he received for review were almost more welcome than the paltry cheque" [31]) or the strident polemic of Miss Ivors ("Well, I'm ashamed of you, said Miss Ivors frankly. To say you'd write for a rag like that" [31]). The issue raised between this man and woman who are described as intellectually equal ("their careers had been parallel, first at the University and then as teachers" [31]) is the issue raised by the text itself: whether or not art is above politics, and whether or not there is something political about the reading of books.

I would argue that the narration takes Gabriel's position ("He wanted to say that literature was above politics" [31]) not only ideologically but in the polemical form Gabriel himself feels he must relinquish ("he could not risk a grandiose phrase with her" [31]). The narrations's gorgeous prose makes the implicit point, in its grandiose phrasing, that there should be nothing political in either the reading or the reviewing of books, and makes readers and viewers embarrassed for turning quizzical eyes, like Molly Ivors's prominent "rabbit's eyes" (33), upon "The Dead" to subject this highly aestheticized story to an ideological cross-examination. The reader — and especially the female reader — is thus caught in an uncomfortable and contradictory position: tempted by the story's stylistic beauty and civilized sentiments to offer a celebratory encomium that is spoiled, like the Morkans' party by the disruptive Miss Ivors, by the need to prod and query the disruptions and gaps in the story's treatment of its women. Although the altercation we hear between Gabriel and Molly Ivors concerns the politics of Irish nationalism, their discussion (which may include the subject of advanced education for Irish women — "she spoke of the University question and Gabriel felt more at ease" [31]) — may be seen as a paradigmatic articulation of the problem of a feminist reading of "The Dead" itself. "The Dead" tries to argue, I would suggest, that its treatment of women is above politics, while clearly demonstrating that it is not. Joyce thus has it both ways with this story: producing one of the finest examples of aesthetic modernism riddled with its own self-critique.

IV. The Aestheticized Gretta

Gabriel Conroy's party can be said to have been troubled by the unexpected challenges of three women, who confront his complacencies in order of increasing intimacy, as servant, colleague, and wife. This nicely ordered scheme elides the reader's most significant challenge, which is posed by Julia Morkan and her sister, and which bears on the silencing of female art. Thus the problem of female insertion into art is explored from its polar positions: woman as objet d'art (Gretta Conroy) and woman as producer of art (Julia Morkan). Gabriel's representation of his wife may therefore be seen to thematize the text's treatment of women — that is, as mirroring how Joyce, the male author, treats the female figure in his text. Joyce stages his own gender project in Gabriel's aestheticization of Gretta, when, seeing her atop the stair listening to an indistinct song, he transforms her both into a beautiful painting ("*Distant Music* he would call the picture if he were a painter" [48]) and into beautiful prose ("There was grace and mystery in her attitude as if she were a symbol of something. He asked himself what is a woman standing on the stairs in the shadow, listening to distant music, a symbol of" [48]). But by making male artistic activity in the moment of homage to the woman explicit, Joyce is able to externalize its politics by implicitly intertexting it with contemporary versions of the Pygmalion myth. This fable of the artist who sculpts a statue of a woman, and falls in love with it, figures the displacement of woman by the male's aesthetic imago of her: as in Shaw's staging of the social construction of femininity by the narcissistic male more interested in his own creative powers than in woman, and Robert Browning's sinister Duke of Ferrara, preferring a painting of his last duchess over a living bride.

Gabriel's romantic gesture in lyricizing his wife's beauty on the stair, like Romeo at Juliet's balcony, is ironized by placing it in context with his other more prosaic gestures that constitute the social oppression needed to make the wife sufficiently blank, a social and emotional stranger, whose identity and features he can then sketch or write as he will. He writes her rapturously, to be sure — "Their children, his writing, her household cares had not quenched all their souls' tender fire" (52); but that script elides or erases the rest ("He longed to recall to her those moments, to make her forget the years of their dull existence together and remember only their moments of ecstasy" [52]). We catch glimpses of that 'dull existence' at the story's beginning, in Gabriel's uxorious display before his aunts — "Gabriel's solicitude was a standing joke with them" (25) — when we learn of his various controls over what his wife and children wear, eat, and do: "He's really an awful bother, what with green shades for Tom's eyes at night and making him do the dumb-bells, and forcing Eva to eat the stirabout. The poor child! And she simply hates the sight of it! . . . O, but you'll never guess what he makes me wear now" (25). The implicit intertextuality of Ibsen's *A Doll's House,* which is also the story of a Christmas season party spoiled by a wife's revelation, foregrounds the troublesome ambiguity that draws a fine line between the solicitous husband and the domestic martinet. Torvald Helmer's infantilizing ban on his wife's macaroons betrays the suffocating paternalism that can mask domestic tyranny as loving care, but whose oppressive effect Gretta inadvertently captures in a joking submarine metaphor that pictures herself submerged in a threatening environment from which only Gabriel's appliances and prescriptions can save her — "The next thing he'll buy me will be a diving suit" (25).

Gretta Conroy's 'dull existence' clearly has its complexities and oppressions, including an interfering and coercive husband, a disapproving and ungrateful mother-in-law who required burdensome nursing care before her death, and a disesteemed provincial background ("she had once spoken of Gretta as country cute" [30]) that her husband obliges her to suppress and disown ("O do go, Gabriel, she cried, I'd love to see Galway again. — You can go if you like, said Gabriel coldly" [33]). This erasure of Gretta's Galway background plays a crucial role in the plot because it allows Gretta's revelation of Michael Furey's love to result from Gabriel's own interdictions on Gretta's subjectivity and that leaching of her identity that makes her his romantic stranger on the stair, that blank page upon which Gabriel can write his tender images of her (or their rhetorical substitute, his feigned poetic inadequacy to do so — *"Is it because there is no word tender enough to be your name?"*). It is further significant that although Gretta herself is not a feminist figure, her revelation and self-revelation, her retrieval of buried memories and longings for home, are triggered by a feminist, by Molly Ivors's prodding and Gabriel's response of a defensive foreclosure of Gretta's homesickness. Gretta's blurted back answer to his discourtesy — "There's a nice husband for you, Mrs Malins" (34) — is as disregarded by the narrator as by Mrs. Malins herself, who copes with her own exile to Scotland by excessively idealizing her new life, "Mrs Malins, without adverting to the interruption, went on to tell Gabriel what beautiful places there were in Scotland and beautiful scenery" (34). The text, likewise, refuses to advert to Gretta's interruption until she in turn interrupts Gabriel's erotic agenda in the Gresham — and possibly averts mate rape, as Ruth Bauerle has argued ("A dull anger began to gather again at the back of his mind and dull fires of lust began to glow angrily in his veins" [55]) — by retrieving her own version of Romeo and Juliet in the image of Michael Furey wooing her under a dripping tree and dying for love of her.

V. The Silenced Julia

The narration of "The Dead" is not innocent, objective, or sympathetic toward the women it represents, and must be heard with acute skepticism. This is especially true in the case of the marginal figures, the elderly Morkan spinsters and the servant Lily, whose situations can be retrieved in their oppressiveness only by reading against the ideological grain and the affirmative tone of the narrative voice. Julia Morkan's story, especially, must be revised, because her case crucially bears on women's relationship to art, and clarifies, in a sense, why men drown out women's voices and stories in art. Julia Morkan's story, as it unfolds the night of the party, and as it is staged by the narrative voice, represents the silencing of female art.

The wedge that opens our insight into the narrator's fallibility is a discrepancy or 'lie' in the account of Julia's life. The flattering introduction to the Morkans' household, with its emphasis on their bourgeois solidity and social self-sufficiency, tells us that "Julia, though she was quite grey, was still the leading soprano in Adam and Eve's" (22). Kate Morkan's outburst after the triumph of Julia's song before dinner makes it clear that this is no longer true — "it's not at all honourable for the pope to turn out the women out of the choirs that have slaved there all their lives and put little whipper-snappers of boys over their heads" (36). Something has happened to Julia Morkan's job with the choir, and if she still sings in it at all, it is certainly no longer as lead soprano. This missing event, which the narrator seems either not to know or not to register at the story's beginning, and that is treated with such scant interest and sympathy by the narration that the reader is little alerted to its enormous significance, clearly has catastrophic implications for the lives of the aging Morkan sisters, one of whom is nearly driven to heresy in her outrage at the pope's banning female singers from church ("O, I don't question the pope's being right. I'm only a stupid old woman and I wouldn't presume to do such a thing. But there's such a thing as common everyday politeness and gratitude" [37]). The event, which Kate alludes to but the story never names, concerns a papal document (a *Motu Proprio*) issued by Pope Pius X on November 22, 1903 — that is, about six weeks before the date of the Morkans' Christmas party — ousting women from church choirs: "It follows from the same principle that the singers of the church have a real liturgical office, and that woman, therefore, being incapable of such an office, cannot be admitted to the choir. If high voices, such as treble and alto, are wanted, these parts must be sung by boys, according to the ancient custom of the Church" (Hayburn 228). Joyce thus introduces into "The Dead," by way of an allusion, a stunning historical instance of female exclusion from the practice of art on pure grounds of sexual discrimination decreed by a doctrinally infallible and therefore (to Catholic women) incontrovertible authority: the pope himself. This extra-textual intrusion into the story deserves to be interrogated and evaluated, for it is hardly gratuitous. The question it raises is whether in addition to the social and economic losses of livelihood and prestige it costs Julia Morkan, the papal decree constitutes a loss to art itself. Joyce answers this question by having Julia Morkan sing before the party guests and before the reader in order to demonstrate her art. The result is a performance of a fiendishly difficult operatic aria — George Linley's arrangement of Vincenzo Bellini's *Son Vergin Vezzosa* from *I Puritani* — that, if performed as the text describes it, would constitute an operatic tour de force by a coloratura soprano. The narrator describes Julia Morkan's singing with two extraordinary compliments. The first is technical — "Her voice, strong and clear in tone, attacked with great spirit the runs which embellish the air and though she sang very rapidly she did not miss even the smallest of the grace notes" (35) — but the second is metaphorical and rapturous, "To follow the voice, without looking at the singer's face, was to feel and share the excitement of swift and secure flight" (35). Lest we doubt the narrator's judgment, Joyce supplements it with the opinion of Leopold Bloom, the hero of Joyce's *Ulysses* (1922), himself an occasional impresario who knows music, who certifies that Dubliners took Julia Morkan seriously as a singer to the end of her life: "Great song of Julia Morkan's. Kept her voice up to the very last. Pupil of Michael Balfe's, wasn't she?" (8.416).

Bloom's information is doubly relevant to assessing Julia's fate both in life and in narrative in "The Dead." Bloom confirms that Julia, who seems a bit haggard and fey at the party in spite of narrative assurances that she is younger and less feeble than her sister, succumbed to Gabriel's prophecy of his aunt's imminent death, and was buried by June 16, 1904. Thus a little more than six months after the papal destruction of her career, Julia Morkan is dead, and while there is no proof of a causal link between the two events, readers may at least wonder if Joyce did not write into "The Dead" the concealed story of a female artist murdered by gender discrimination. Her performance of *Arrayed for the Bridal* becomes, retrospectively, her swan song — perhaps her last public performance, given her expulsion from the choir, and therefore a rather poignant and momentous event in the narrative of "The Dead." Why does the narrator never draw our attention to this hidden drama of two sisters whose lives are destroyed and whose faith is tainted with bitterness and frustration? Why does the narrator tell us that Julia learned needlework at school and "worked" scenes from Shakespeare in wools (that is, became a producer of kitsch and pudding [41]), but not that she might have studied music with Michael Balfe, Ireland's most famous composer in the late Victorian age, and that she might have possessed a rare talent? Why does the narrative expend precious descriptive time upon a dinner table discussion of operatic trivia without contending with why the far more compelling and highly topical issue of the pope's recent silencing of women's sacred music is patronizingly stifled ("we really are all hungry and when we are hungry we are all very quarrelsome" [37]). The answer is no doubt analogous to why the dinner party will not discuss the "negro" singer at the *Gaiety* — "And why couldn't he have a voice too? asked Freddy Malins sharply. Is it because he's only a black?" (40). The institution and practice of art are as exclusionary as all other institutional practices, and a homely old grey spinster (whose face the narrator veils, "To follow the voice, without looking at the singer's face," before being able to hear the glory of her song) is not considered eligible to be a great artist any more than a black singer, however marvelous his voice, may be allowed on to the legitimate stage. Joyce thus politicizes not only the dinner table discussion of art, but the narrative practice that reports it in his own text.

VI. Other Dublin Women

Once the reader begins to suspect the narration's collusion with patriarchy in "The Dead," skepticism becomes uncontrollable, and the text becomes a ground of ongoing critical labor and testing for the reader. Every narrative account of a woman's experience may now be treated as potentially unreliable and reread as a politicized vignette. The 'problem' with Lily, who blatantly contravenes narrative assurances that she does not give back answers by blurting out one of the sharpest and most unprovoked, now invites scrutiny and reinterpretation. Gabriel's innocent question ("I suppose we'll be going to your wedding one of these fine days with your young man, eh?" [23]) can be transformed into a gauge of Lily's sexual maturation and availability when coupled with Gabriel's odd ocular gesture in the pantry. Alone with Lily in the small, secluded room, Gabriel "looked up at the pantry ceiling, which was shaking with the stamping and shuffling of feet on the floor above, listened for a moment to the piano and then glanced at the girl, who was folding his overcoat carefully at the end of a shelf" (23). Does Gabriel calculate their privacy before launching the prelude of a suggestive advance toward Lily, and does her instant and strong retort — "The men that is now is only all palaver and what they can get out of you" (23) — suggest that Gabriel has a predatory reputation that has put Lily on her guard and let her arm herself against him in advance? Is Gabriel's gold coin a gratuitous generosity to a rude and nervous servant or practiced hush money to stop her agitation? The issue is undecidable — and Julia's remark, "I'm sure I don't know what has come over her lately. She's not the girl she was at all" (26), suggests that Lily has recently been sexually burnt in some other way and is spilling her bitterness onto Gabriel by mere association. But the narrator would nonetheless be capable of concealing Gabriel's mental or actual philandering from the reader, and Gabriel's question at the story's end, "He wondered at his riot of emotions of an hour before. From what had it proceeded?" (58) remains unanswered except by overdetermination. We are entitled to wonder, as Gabriel wonders of Gretta — "Perhaps she had not told him all the story" (58) — if the narrator has told us all the story.

Other women in the story internalize the narrator's own compulsion to put a good face on everything and admit no unpleasantnesses, conflicts, and irregularities in the bourgeois existence whose virtues are so carefully recorded and cultivated by the story. Mrs. Malins, whose infirmity might betoken a small stroke of some sort indicated by her slight stutter (33), transforms her exile to Scotland and dependency on her daughter's family into a compulsive idyll — "Her son-in-law brought them every year to the lakes and they used to go fishing. Her son-in-law was a splendid fisher. One day he caught a fish, a beautiful big fish, and the man in the hotel boiled it for their dinner" (34). The discrepancy between Mrs. Malins's uncontrollable utopianism and her son's alcoholic disarray suggests that Freddy is left to symptomatize the social irregularities and human frailties that his mother so rigorously represses. Freddy's anomalous business (Gabriel tells Gretta about the sovereign Freddy borrowed "at Christmas, when he opened that little Christmas-card shop in Henry Street" [54]) makes him a purveyor of idyllic Christmas scenes and sentiments which, in real life, he makes it his business to disrupt and demystify. Freddy Malins functions as a "seer" in "The Dead" — as an ideological innocent who does not know that old women and blacks can't be great artists, and who thus lives to contravene social cant of the kind his mother lives by. Mrs. Malins, however, is left to embody the bloated and immobilized complacency that comes of internalizing unexamined bourgeois pieties and hypocrisies of a good life. The narrator thus can be seen to serve as Mrs. Malins's more sophisticated double.

Mary Jane Morkan too may be seen as a female who has internalized the oppressions of her situation and thus transformed herself into a model spinster-in-training, "talented, cheerful, hard-working and the best of nieces" (44), a woman as technically proficient — but lacking melody — as her music ("Mary Jane was playing her Academy piece, full of runs and difficult passages. . . . He liked music but the piece she was playing had no melody for him and he doubted whether it had any melody for the other listeners" [29]). Mary Jane appears to have be-

come an attenuated younger version of her aunts, lacking their residues
of brilliance and fire, but with their own bourgeois self-complacencies
replicated in her. Driven by economic responsibility ("the main prop of
the household" [22]), she toadies to her pupils from "the better-class
families on the Kingstown and Dalkey line" (22) who might be scandal-
ized by Freddy Malins's behavior ("They would not wish for worlds
that any of Mary Jane's pupils should see him under the influence"
[22]). Mary Jane's minute attempts to modernize herself appear to have
been stifled ("she had also suggested apple sauce for the goose but Aunt
Kate had said that plain roast goose without apple sauce had always
been good enough for her and she hoped she might never eat worse"
[38–39]) by Aunt Kate whose own political and social protest against
the pope Mary Jane in turn stifles.

   The various young women in the story are differentiated according
to their social functions in relation to others. Miss Daly is clearly a peer
of Mary Jane's and therefore mirrors her as general dogsbody, playing
waltzes, carving the ham, serving as dancing partner when needed ("O,
Miss Daly, you're really awfully good, after playing for the last two
dances, but really we're so short of ladies to-night" [28]). Miss Furlong,
on the other hand, is privileged as one of Mary Jane's pupils, presumably from a 'better-class' family, judging by her fastidious recoil from
the drunken Mr. Browne's familiarities, "Miss Furlong, who was one of
Mary Jane's pupils, asked Miss Daly what was the name of the pretty
waltz she had played" (27–28), and her equally prissy critique of the
contralto praised by Bartell D'Arcy, "but Miss Furlong thought she had
a rather vulgar style of production" (39). Miss Furlong, the only pupil
who seems to participate in the musical conversation over dinner, also
appears to be served first at table — "Miss Furlong, what shall I send
you? he asked. A wing or a slice of the breast?" (38).

   Miss O'Callaghan's function can only be inferred on slender evidence. But it seems that in spite of the fact that Bartell D'Arcy
was paired with Miss Daly for quadrilles (28), the conceited young
singer — who we know from *Ulysses* once kissed Molly Bloom on the
choir stairs — may have chosen Miss O'Callaghan for this particular
evening's flirtation and seduction. The two of them are pointedly left
alone together upstairs while Gabriel tells the Johnny story to the re-
maining company, and the question of what they were doing must be
linked to another mystery involving the haphazard and illogical performance of *The Lass of Aughrim*. This performance is so privileged by its
centrality to the plot that we scarcely notice how offhand, and tattered,
it actually is: "The song seemed to be in the old Irish tonality and the

singer seemed uncertain both of his words and of his voice" (49). Why would Bartell D'Arcy, who successfully resisted, all night, the importunities of Mary Jane and Gretta that he perform, sing a song whose words and melody seem unfamiliar to him when his voice, for which he is rightfully anxious, is still hoarse from a cold? His desire to please Miss O'Callaghan, who perhaps requested a private concert, provides a plausible answer that further serves to make the Conroys' aesthetic and romantic responses to the ballad highly ironic. In effect, the Conroys would have been seduced by a song of seduction they were never intended to hear; in the ballad the victim goes off into the night, alone, in a cab with the philandering tenor. Miss O'Callaghan can thus also be seen to serve as a figure of the unresisting reader, seduced by the narrative's intentions without regard to its verbal and logical dissonances.

"The Dead" represents a community of women whose relationships are politically heterogeneous — mutually supportive, oppressive, liberative without consistency — and the story thus seems committed to offering a liberal, pluralistic representation of Irish women. But that is not the narrator's aim, whose selective plot emphases and rhetorical colorations have put the representations of women in the service of a self-congratulatory affirmation of an oppressive patriarchal status quo. The narration, intent on making Gabriel remarkable and the women unremarkable, has brushed away his challenges by Lily and Molly Ivors as female misunderstandings and has foregrounded an aestheticized representation of Gretta, whose function is to certify Gabriel's poesy, passion, and benign compassion. The text's feminism, its possibilities for political critique, are lodged in the detachability of the narrator and his project from a larger textual project that supplements and challenges the narrator's version of events and people — not with commentary or another voice, but by posing problems within the narration that encourage and reward readerly skepticism, query, and challenge. Insofar as feminism can be construed as a critical act, the text of "The Dead" can be construed as a signifying activity that uses narration as merely one tool for the implementation of knowledge and meaning in the story, and that supplements this single, authoritative, stifling voice with the eloquent silencings and silences of women that in turn speak alternative stories and open alternative interpretations. The young Joyce learned a concept of dramaturgy from the politically progressive Ibsen that extended far beyond political theme and content to the issue of modes of representation and distributions of knowledge, and that translated itself generically, in fiction, into the activity of a performative text. Insofar as feminism can be construed as a call to political activism, "The Dead" refuses to instruct readers about female oppression and thereby refuses to assume a patriarchal role in relation to the reader; rather it presents readers with textual problems that they must labor to puzzle, understand, and solve for themselves. "The Dead" constructs its own readers, as all texts do, but constructs them along the same female models that it thematizes in the story. Readers can choose whether to behave with the pleased passivity of a Mrs. Malins, indulged in their reading like Mrs. Malins in her sea crossing ("She answered placidly that she had had a beautiful crossing and that the captain had been most attentive to her" [33]). They can abdicate as critics, like Mary Jane Morkan who "intervened pacifically" to stifle her aunt's protest against injustice in the interest of preserving personal disinterest, bland civility, and uncontroversial politeness. Or they can take the least popular stance in the story — disruptive, challenging, critical, and activist — and risk losing the patina of intellectual graciousness that Gabriel praises so warmly, but that historically colludes with retarding political criticism and reform. The story allows the feminist reader to take sides against Gabriel and resist his admonition — "But we are living in a sceptical, and if I may use the phrase, a thought-tormented age: and sometimes I fear that this new generation, educated or hypereducated as it is, will lack those qualities of humanity, of hospitality, of kindly humour which belonged to an older day" (43). Like Molly Ivors, we may run down the stairs that Gretta Conroy will soon occupy so picturesquely, and go on to our own critical projects outside the confines of the male narration, leaving the company of other readers puzzled and perturbed like the society of Dubliners.

WORKS CITED

Bauerle, Ruth. "Date Rape, Mate Rape: A Liturgical Interpretation of 'The Dead.'" *New Alliances in Joyce Studies.* Ed. Bonnie Kime Scott. Newark: U of Delaware P, 1988. 113–25.

Ellmann, Richard. *James Joyce.* Oxford: Oxford UP, 1983.

Gilbert, Sandra M., and Susan Gubar. *No Man's Land: The Place of the Woman Writer in the Twentieth Century.* Vol. 1. New Haven: Yale UP, 1988.

Hayburn, Robert F. *Papal Legislation on Sacred Music 95 A.D. to 1977 A.D.* Collegeville, MN: Liturgical, 1979.

Heilbrun, Carolyn G. "Afterword." *Women in Joyce.* Ed. Suzette

Henke and Elaine Unkeless. Urbana: U of Illinois P, 1982. 215–16.

Joyce, James. "Ibsen's New Drama." *The Critical Writings.* Ed. Ellsworth Mason and Richard Ellmann. Ithaca: Cornell UP, 1989.

———. *Ulysses: The Corrected Text.* Ed. Hans Walter Gabler with Wolfhard Steppe and Claus Melchior. New York: Vintage-Random, 1986.

Kristeva, Julia. *Desire in Language.* Ed. Leon S. Roudiez. Trans. Thomas Gora, Alice Jardine, and Leon S. Roudiez. New York: Columbia UP, 1980.

Norris, Margot. "Stifled Back Answers: The Gender Politics of Art in Joyce's 'The Dead.'" *Modern Fiction Studies* 35 (1989): 479–503.

Power, Arthur. *Conversations with James Joyce.* Ed. Clive Hart. Chicago: U of Chicago P, 1974.

Scott, Bonnie Kime. *Joyce and Feminism.* Bloomington: Indiana UP, 1984.

Deconstruction
and
"The Dead"

WHAT IS DECONSTRUCTION?

Deconstruction has a reputation for being the most complex and forbidding of contemporary critical approaches to literature, but in fact almost all of us have, at one time, either deconstructed a text or badly wanted to deconstruct one. Sometimes when we hear a lecturer effectively marshal evidence to show that a book means primarily one thing, we long to interrupt and ask what he or she would make of other, conveniently overlooked passages, passages that seem to contradict the lecturer's thesis. Sometimes, after reading a provocative critical article that *almost* convinces us that a familiar work means the opposite of what we assumed it meant, we may wish to make an equally convincing case for our former reading of the text. We may not think that the poem or novel in question better supports our interpretation, but we may recognize that the text can be used to support *both* readings. And sometimes we simply want to make that point: texts can be used to support seemingly irreconcilable positions.

To reach this conclusion is to feel the deconstructive itch. J. Hillis Miller, the preeminent American deconstructor, puts it this way: "Deconstruction is not a dismantling of the structure of a text, but a demonstration that it has already dismantled itself. Its apparently solid ground is no rock but thin air" ("Stevens' Rock" 341). To deconstruct a text isn't to show that all the high old themes aren't there to be found in it. Rather, it is to show that a text — not unlike DNA with its double helix — can have intertwined, opposite "discourses" — strands of narrative, threads of meaning.

Ultimately, of course, deconstruction refers to a larger and more complex enterprise than the practice of demonstrating that a text means contradictory things. The term refers to a way of reading texts practiced by critics who have been influenced by the writings of the French philosopher Jacques Derrida. It is important to gain some understanding of Derrida's project and of the historical backgrounds of his work before reading the deconstruction that follows, let alone attempting to deconstruct a text. But it is important, too, to approach deconstruction with anything but a scholar's sober and almost worshipful respect for knowledge and truth. Deconstruction offers a playful alternative to traditional scholarship, a confidently adversarial alternative, and deserves to be approached in the spirit that animates it.

Derrida, a philosopher of language who coined the term "deconstruction," argues that we tend to think and express our thoughts in terms of opposites. Something is black but not white, masculine and therefore not feminine, a cause rather than an effect, and so forth. These mutually exclusive pairs or dichotomies are too numerous to list but would include beginning/end, conscious/unconscious, presence/absence, speech/writing, and construction/destruction (the last being the opposition that Derrida's word deconstruction tries to contain and subvert). If we think hard about these dichotomies, Derrida suggests, we will realize that they are not simply oppositions; they are also hierarchies in miniature. In other words, they contain one term that our culture views as being superior and one term viewed as negative or inferior. Sometimes the superior term seems only subtly superior (*speech, masculine, cause*), whereas sometimes we know immediately which term is culturally preferable (*presence* and *beginning* and *consciousness* are easy choices). But the hierarchy always exists.

Of particular interest to Derrida, perhaps because it involves the language in which all the other dichotomies are expressed, is the hierarchical opposition speech/writing. Derrida argues that the "privileging" of speech, that is, the tendency to regard speech in positive terms and writing in negative terms, cannot be disentangled from the privileging of presence. (Postcards are written by absent friends; we read Plato because he cannot speak from beyond the grave.) Furthermore, according to Derrida, the tendency to privilege both speech and presence is part of the Western tradition of *logocentrism*, the belief that in some ideal beginning were creative *spoken* words, words such as "Let there be light," spoken by an ideal, *present* God. According to logocentric tradition, these words can now only be represented in unoriginal speech or writing (such as the written phrase in quotation marks above). Derrida doesn't seek to reverse the hierarchized opposition between speech and writing, or presence and absence, or early and late, for to do so would be to fall into a trap of perpetuating the same forms of thought and expression that he seeks to deconstruct. Rather, his goal is to erase the boundary between oppositions such as speech and writing, and to do so in such a way as to throw the order and values implied by the opposition into question.

Returning to the theories of Ferdinand de Saussure, who invented the modern science of linguistics, Derrida reminds us that the association of speech with present, obvious, and ideal meaning and writing with absent, merely pictured, and therefore less reliable meaning is suspect, to say the least. As Saussure demonstrated, words are *not* the things they name and, indeed, they are only arbitrarily associated with those things. Neither spoken nor written words have present, positive, identifiable attributes themselves; they have meaning only by virtue of their difference from other words (*red, read, reed*). In a sense, meanings emerge from the gaps or spaces between them. Take *read* as an example. To know whether it is the present or past tense of the verb — whether it rhymes with *red* or *reed* — we need to see it in relation to some other word (for example, *yesterday*).

Because the meanings of words lie in the differences between them and in the differences between them and the things they name, Derrida suggests that all language is constituted by *différance,* a word he has coined that puns on two French words meaning "to differ" and "to defer": words are the deferred presences of the things they "mean," and their meaning is grounded in difference. Derrida, by the way, changes the *e* in the French word *différence* to an *a* in his neologism *différance;* the change, which can be seen in writing but cannot be heard in spoken French, is itself a playful, witty challenge to the notion that writing is inferior or "fallen" speech.

In *De la grammatologie* [*Of Grammatology*] (1967) and *Dissemination* (1972), Derrida begins to redefine writing by deconstructing some old definitions. In *Dissemination,* he traces logocentrism back to Plato, who in the *Phaedrus* has Socrates condemn writing and who, in all the great dialogues, powerfully postulates that metaphysical longing for origins and ideals that permeates Western thought. "What Derrida does in his reading of Plato," Barbara Johnson points out, "is to unfold dimensions of Plato's *text* that work against the grain of (Plato's own) Plato-nism" (xxiv). Remember: that is what deconstruction does according to Miller; it shows a text dismantling itself.

In *Of Grammatology,* Derrida turns to the *Confessions* of Jean-Jacques Rousseau and exposes a grain running against the grain. Rous-seau, another great Western idealist and believer in innocent, noble origins, on one hand condemned writing as mere representation, a corruption of the more natural, childlike, direct, and therefore unde-vious speech. On the other hand, Rousseau admitted his own tendency to lose self-presence and blurt out exactly the wrong thing in public. He confesses that, by writing at a distance from his audience, he often ex-pressed himself better: "If I were present, one would never know what I was worth," Rousseau admitted (Derrida, *Of Grammatology* 142). Thus, writing is a *supplement* to speech that is at the same time *necessary.* Barbara Johnson, sounding like Derrida, puts it this way: "Recourse to writing . . . is necessary to recapture a presence whose lack has not been preceded by any fullness" (Derrida, *Dissemination xii*). Thus, Derrida shows that one strand of Rousseau's discourse made writing seem a sec-ondary, even treacherous supplement, while another made it seem nec-essary to communication.

Have Derrida's deconstructions of *Confessions* and the *Phaedrus* ex-plained these texts, interpreted them, opened them up and shown us what they mean? Not in any traditional sense. Derrida would say that anyone attempting to find a single, correct meaning in a text is simply imprisoned by that structure of thought that would oppose two read-ings and declare one to be right and not wrong, correct rather than incorrect. In fact, any work of literature that we interpret defies the laws of Western logic, the laws of opposition and noncontradiction. In the views of poststructuralist critics, texts don't say "A and not B." They say "A and not-A," as do texts written by literary critics, who are also in-volved in producing creative writing.

Miller has written that the purpose of deconstruction is to show "the existence in literature of structures of language which contradict the law of non-contradiction." Why find the grain that runs against the grain? To restore what Miller has called "the strangeness of literature," to reveal the "capacity of each work to surprise the reader," to demon-strate that "literature continually exceeds any formula or theory with which the critic is prepared to encompass it" (Miller, *Fiction* 5).

Although its ultimate aim may be to critique Western idealism and logic, deconstruction began as a response to structuralism and to formalism, another structure-oriented theory of reading. (Deconstruction, which is really only one kind of a poststructuralist criticism, is sometimes referred to as poststructuralist criticism, or even as poststructuralism.)

Structuralism, Robert Scholes tells us, may now be seen as a reaction to modernist alienation and despair (3). Using Saussure's theory as Derrida was to do later, European structuralists attempted to create a *semiology,* or science of signs, that would give humankind at once a scientific and a holistic way of studying the world and its human inhabitants. Roland Barthes, a structuralist who later shifted toward poststructuralism, hoped to recover literary language from the isolation in which it had been studied and to show that the laws that govern it govern all signs, from road signs to articles of clothing. Claude Lévi-Strauss, a structural anthropologist who studied everything from village structure to the structure of myths, found in myths what he called *mythemes,* or building blocks, such as basic plot elements. Recognizing that the same mythemes occur in similar myths from different cultures, he suggested that all myths may be elements of one great myth being written by the collective human mind.

Derrida could not accept the notion that structuralist thought might someday explain the laws governing human signification and thus provide the key to understanding the form and meaning of everything from an African village to a Greek myth to Rousseau's *Confessions.* In his view, the scientific search by structural anthropologists for what unifies humankind amounts to a new version of the old search for the lost ideal, whether that ideal be Plato's bright realm of the Idea or the Paradise of Genesis or Rousseau's unspoiled Nature. As for the structuralist belief that texts have "centers" of meaning, in Derrida's view that derives from the logocentric belief that there is a reading of the text that accords with "the book as seen by God." Jonathan Culler, who thus translates a difficult phrase from Derrida's *L'Écriture et la différence* [*Writing and Difference*] (1967) in his book *Structuralist Poetics* (1975), goes on to explain what Derrida objects to in structuralist literary criticism:

> [When] one speaks of the structure of a literary work, one does so from a certain vantage point: one starts with notions of the meaning or effects of a poem and tries to identify the structures responsible for those effects. Possible configurations or patterns that make no contribution are rejected as irrelevant. That is to say, an intuitive understanding of the poem functions as the "centre" . . . : it is both a starting point and a limiting principle. (244)

For these reasons, Derrida and his poststructuralist followers reject the very notion of "linguistic competence" introduced by Noam Chomsky, a structural linguist. The idea that there is a competent reading "gives a privileged status to a particular set of rules of reading, . . . granting preeminence to certain conventions and excluding from the realm of language all the truly creative and productive violations of those rules" (Culler, *Structuralist Poetics* 241).

Poststructuralism calls into question assumptions made about literature by formalist, as well as by structuralist, critics. Formalism, or the New Criticism as it was once commonly called, assumes a work of literature to be a freestanding, self-contained object, its meanings found in the complex network of relations that constitute its parts (images, sounds, rhythms, allusions, and so on). To be sure, deconstruction is somewhat like formalism in several ways. Both the formalist and the deconstructor focus on the literary text; neither is likely to interpret a poem or a novel by relating it to events in the author's life, letters, historical period, or even culture. And formalists, long before deconstructors, discovered counterpatterns of meaning in the same text. Formalists find ambiguity and irony, deconstructors find contradiction and undecidability.

Here, though, the two groups part ways. Formalists believe a complete understanding of a literary work is possible, an understanding in which even the ambiguities will fulfill a definite, meaningful function. Poststructuralists confront the apparently limitless possibilities for the production of meaning that develop when the language of the critic enters the language of the text. They cannot accept the formalist view that a work of literary art has organic unity (therefore, structuralists would say, a "center"), if only we could find it.

Undecidability, as Paul de Man came to define it, is a complex notion easily misunderstood. There is a tendency to assume it refers to readers who, when forced to decide between two or more equally plausible and conflicting readings motivated by the same text, throw up their hands and decide that the choice can't be made. But undecidability in fact debunks this whole notion of reading as a decision-making process carried out on texts by readers. To say we are forced to choose or decide — or that we are unable to do so — is to locate the problem of undecidability falsely outside ourselves, and to make it reside within a text to which we come as another. The poststructuralist concept of undecidability, we might say, deconstructs the either/or type distinction or opposition that structuralists and formalists have made between reader and text. It entails what de Man calls the "mutual obliteration" not only of propositions apparently opposed but also of the subject/ object relation.

Poststructuralists break with formalists, too, over an issue they have debated with structuralists. The issue involves metaphor and metonymy, two terms for different kinds of rhetorical *tropes,* or figures of speech. *Metonymy* refers to a figure that is chosen to stand for something that it is commonly associated with, or with which it happens to be contiguous or juxtaposed. When said to a waitress, "I'll have the cold plate today" is a metonymic figure of speech for "I'll eat the cold food you're serving today." We refer to the food we want as a plate simply because plates are what food happens to be served on and because everyone understands that by *plate* we mean food. A *metaphor,* on the other hand, is a figure of speech that involves a special, intrinsic, nonarbitrary relationship with what it represents. When you say you are blue, if you believe that there is an intrinsic, timeless likeness between that color and melancholy feeling — a likeness that just doesn't exist between sadness and yellow — then you are using the word *blue* metaphorically.

Although both formalists and structuralists make much of the difference between metaphor and metonymy, Derrida, Miller and de Man have contended with the distinction deconstructively. They have questioned not only the distinction but also, and perhaps especially, the privilege we grant to metaphor, which we tend to view as the positive and superior figure of speech. De Man, in *Allegories of Reading* (1979), analyzes a passage from Proust's *Swann's Way,* arguing that it is about the nondistinction between metaphor and metonymy — and that it makes its claim metonymically. In *Fiction and Repetition: Seven English Novels* (1982), Miller connects the belief in metaphorical correspondences with other metaphysical beliefs, such as those in origins, endings, transcendence, and underlying truths. Isn't it likely, deconstructors keep implicitly asking, that every metaphor was once a metonym, but that we have simply forgotten what arbitrary juxtaposition or contiguity gave rise to the association that now seems mysteriously special?

The hypothesis that what we call metaphors are really old metonyms may perhaps be made clearer by the following example. We used the word *Watergate* as a metonym to refer to a political scandal that began in the Watergate building complex. Recently, we have used part of the building's name (*gate*) to refer to more recent scandals (*Irangate*). However, already there are people who use and "understand" these terms who are unaware that Watergate is the name of a building. In the future, isn't it possible that *gate,* which began as part of a simple metonym, will seem like the perfect metaphor for scandal — a word that suggests corruption and wrongdoing with a strange and inexplicable rightness?

This is how deconstruction works: by showing that what was prior and privileged in the old hierarchy (for instance, metaphor and speech) can just as easily seem secondary, the deconstructor causes the formerly privileged term to exchange properties with the formerly devalued one. Causes become effects and (d)evolutions become origins, but the result is neither the destruction of the old order or hierarchy nor the construction of a new one. It is, rather, *deconstruction*. In Robert Scholes's words, "If either cause or effect can occupy the position of an origin, then origin is no longer originary; it loses its metaphorical privilege" (88).

Once deconstructed, literal and figurative can exchange properties, so that the prioritizing between them is erased: all words, even dog and cat, are understood to be figures. It's just that we have used some of them so long that we have forgotten how arbitrary and metonymic they are. And, just as literal and figurative can exchange properties, criticism can exchange properties with literature, in the process coming to be seen not merely as a supplement — the second, negative, and inferior term in the binary opposition creative writing/literary criticism — but rather as an equally creative form of work. Would we write if there were not critics — intelligent readers motivated and able to make sense of what is written? Who, then, depends on whom?

"It is not difficult to see the attractions" of deconstructive reading, Jonathan Culler has commented. "Given that there is no ultimate or absolute justification for any system or for the interpretations from it," the critic is free to value "the activity of interpretation itself, . . . rather than any results which might be obtained" (*Structuralist Poetics* 248). Not everyone, however, has so readily seen the attractions of deconstruction. Two eminent critics, M. H. Abrams and Wayne Booth, have observed that a deconstructive reading "is plainly and simply parasitical" on what Abrams calls "the obvious or univocal meaning" (Abrams 457–58). In other words, there would be no deconstructors if critics did not already exist who can see and show central and definite meanings in texts. Miller responded in an essay entitled "The Critic as Host," in which he not only deconstructed the oppositional hierarchy (host/parasite), but also the two terms themselves, showing that each derives from two definitions meaning nearly opposite things. *Host* means "hospitable welcomer" and "military horde." *Parasite* originally had a positive connotation; in Greek, *parasitos* meant "beside the grain" and referred to a friendly guest. Finally, Miller suggests, the words *par-*

asite and *host* are inseparable, depending on one another for their meaning in a given work, much as do hosts and parasites, authors and critics,
structuralists and poststructuralists.

In the essay that follows, John Paul Riquelme describes Gabriel
Conroy as a "self-deluded person who is startled into a process of reconsidering what he has thought about himself and about those around
him," a man who has come to see two opposing perspectives. Whether
he has decided to give up his illusions — or whether in coming to "see
double" he has merely lost his identity — is open to debate among
readers. For Riquelme, however, that point of disagreement is but one
of many that the text engenders. Indeed, as he sees it, "The Dead" fosters a *general* "skepticism concerning the adequacy" of *all* "determinate
readings." Like Gabriel, the story sees double and, hence, causes us "to
question any absolute separation of the ostensible opposites that are important in it, including the living and the dead."

Riquelme goes on to wonder how a single text can engender opposite meanings, each powerfully supported by evidence. In considering
why such conflicting responses cannot be merged into any "harmonizing interpretive synthesis," Riquelme explains that "the story's language
and structure contain inherently heterogeneous elements whose double
antithetical character resists being resolved into a single reading." The
story's meanings thus remain "perplexingly multiple and in flux."

Among the antithetical elements Riquelme identifies are its realist
and antirealist modes. For although " 'The Dead' . . . creates the impression that it is a story about actual, ordinary experience rendered in a
circumstantial, straightforward way by an anonymous narrator," its
"language is at times not determinate and not referential." The story
can thereby leave basic questions unanswered — questions such as Who
speaks? and What is happening? It is often difficult to tell whether
thoughts or images belong to the third-person narrator or whether they
amount to free indirect discourse, that is, a representation of the workings of Gabriel's mind by that omniscient narrator. And as Riquelme
points out, the text often "evokes experiences and meanings that cannot
be convincingly understood as actual, literal ones."

Surprisingly, the discontinuity created by realist and antirealist
modes is also created by doublings and repetitions, which tend to break
rather than create continuity. For example, an image (such as snow)
may be the product of Gabriel's consciousness here and an aspect of
third-person narration there; figurative the first time, literal the next; a
figure for the living and then, suddenly, a figure for the dead.

Riquelme's essay is, of course, deconstructive in its tendency to show oppositions, contradictions, and undecidabilities within a text. To show them, Riquelme, like other deconstructors, practices close reading, paying special attention to textual "echoes" and to figures of speech, or tropes. (Whereas de Man focused on the metaphor/metonymy distinction, Riquelme analyzes the contradictory effects of the rhetorical trope known as "chiasmus.") He also shares with other poststructuralist critics an interest in etymology, particularly the way in which the duplicity of words and phrases is often grounded in the fact that they have meant different and even opposite things at different moments in history.

If Riquelme stopped here, however, his approach and critical habits would not be terribly different from those of an old-fashioned formalist, or New Critic. Formalists, after all, liked to write about the ambiguity of texts, and their writings were characterized by close reading, special attention to figures of speech, and an interest in etymology. What makes Riquelme's essay distinctively deconstructive is the conviction that *all* texts — not just one particularly beautiful one — are fundamentally against themselves. What Riquelme says about "The Dead" he would say "in some measure about every literary text," namely, that it "frustrates the possibility that readers could ever agree on a single definitive interpretation, one that is decisively superior to all the other alternatives." Thus, the skepticism that the story fosters with regard to the adequacy of determinate readings it fosters toward *all* stories — even as all stories (including Riquelme's) foster skepticism concerning the adequacy of determinate reading.

Ross C Murfin

DECONSTRUCTION:
A SELECTED BIBLIOGRAPHY

Deconstruction, Poststructuralism, and Structuralism: Introduction, Guides, and Surveys

Arac, Jonathan, Wlad Godzich, and Wallace Martin, eds. *The Yale Critics: Deconstruction in America*. Minneapolis: U of Minnesota P, 1983. See especially the essays by Bové, Godzich, Pease, and Corngold.

Berman, Art. *From the New Criticism to Deconstruction: The Reception of Structuralism and Post-Structuralism*. Urbana: U of Illinois P, 1988.

Butler, Christopher. *Interpretation, Deconstruction, and Ideology: An Introduction to Some Current Issues in Literary Theory*. Oxford: Oxford UP, 1984.

Cain, William E. "Deconstruction in America: The Recent Literary Criticism of J. Hillis Miller." *College English* 41 (1979): 367–82.

Culler, Jonathan. *On Deconstruction: Theory and Criticism After Structuralism*. Ithaca: Cornell UP, 1982.

———. *Structuralist Poetics: Structuralism, Linguistics and the Study of Literature*. Ithaca: Cornell UP, 1975. See especially ch. 10.

Esch, Deborah. "Deconstruction." *Redrawing the Boundaries: The Transformation of English and American Literary Studies*. Ed. Stephen Greenblatt and Giles Gunn. New York: MLA, 1992. 374–91.

Gasché, Rodolphe. "Deconstruction as Criticism." *Glyph* 6 (1979): 177–215.

Jay, Gregory. *America the Scrivener: Deconstruction and the Subject of Literary History*. Ithaca: Cornell UP, 1990.

Jefferson, Ann. "Structuralism and Post Structuralism." *Modern Literary Theory: A Comparative Introduction*. Totowa, NJ: Barnes, 1982. 84–112.

Leitch, Vincent B. *American Literary Criticism from the Thirties to the Eighties*. New York: Columbia UP, 1988. See especially ch. 10 ("Deconstructive Criticism").

———. *Deconstructive Criticism: An Advanced Introduction and Survey*. New York: Columbia UP, 1983.

Lentricchia, Frank. *After the New Criticism*. Chicago: U of Chicago P, 1981.

Melville, Stephen W. *Philosophy Beside Itself: On Deconstruction and Modernism*. Theory and History of Literature 27. Minneapolis: U of Minnesota P, 1986.

Norris, Christopher. *Deconstruction and the Interests of Theory*. Oklahoma Project for Discourse and Theory 4. Norman: U of Oklahoma P, 1989.

———. *Deconstruction: Theory and Practice*. London: Methuen, 1982. Rev. ed. London: Routledge, 1991.

Raval, Suresh. *Metacriticism*. Athens: U of Georgia P, 1981.

Scholes, Robert. *Structuralism in Literature: An Introduction*. New Haven: Yale UP, 1974.

Sturrock, John. *Structuralism and Since*. New York: Oxford UP, 1975.

Selected Works by Jacques Derrida and Paul de Man

de Man, Paul. *Allegories of Reading*. New Haven: Yale UP, 1979. See especially ch. 1 ("Semiology and Rhetoric").

―――. *Blindness and Insight*. New York: Oxford UP, 1971. Minneapolis: U of Minnesota P, 1983. The 1983 edition contains important essays not included in the original edition.

―――. *The Resistance to Theory*. Minneapolis: U of Minnesota P, 1986.

Derrida, Jacques. *Acts of Literature*. Ed. Derek Attridge. New York: Routledge, 1992. Includes a helpful editor's introduction on Derrida and literature.

―――. *Dissemination*. 1972. Trans. Barbara Johnson. Chicago: U of Chicago P, 1981. See especially the concise, incisive "Translator's Introduction," which provides a useful point of entry into this work and others by Derrida.

―――. *Margins of Philosophy*. Trans. Alan Bass. Chicago: U of Chicago P, 1982.

―――. *Of Grammatology*. Trans. Gayatri C. Spivak. Baltimore: Johns Hopkins UP, 1976. Trans. of *De la Grammatologie*. 1967.

―――. *The Postcard: From Socrates to Freud and Beyond*. Trans. with intro. Alan Bass. Chicago: U of Chicago P, 1987.

―――. *Writing and Difference*. 1967. Trans. Alan Bass. Chicago: U of Chicago P, 1978.

Essays in Deconstruction and Poststructuralism

Barthes, Roland. *S/Z*. Trans. Richard Miller. New York: Hill, 1974. In this influential work, Barthes turns from a structuralist to a poststructuralist approach.

Bloom, Harold, et al., eds. *Deconstruction and Criticism*. New York: Seabury, 1979. Includes essays by Bloom, de Man, Derrida, Miller, and Hartman.

Chase, Cynthia. *Decomposing Figures*. Baltimore: Johns Hopkins UP, 1986.

Harari, Josué, ed. *Textual Strategies: Perspectives in Post-Structuralist Criticism*. Ithaca: Cornell UP, 1979.

Johnson, Barbara. *The Critical Difference: Essays in the Contemporary Rhetoric of Reading*. Baltimore: Johns Hopkins UP, 1980.

————. *A World of Difference.* Baltimore: Johns Hopkins UP, 1987.

Krupnick, Mark, ed. *Displacement: Derrida and After.* Bloomington: Indiana UP, 1987.

Miller, J. Hillis. *Ariadne's Thread: Story Lines.* New Haven: Yale UP, 1992. See especially the discussion of "anastomosis" in Joyce, 156–64.

————. *The Ethics of Reading: Kant, de Man, Eliot, Trollope, James, and Benjamin.* New York: Columbia UP, 1987.

————. *Fiction and Repetition: Seven English Novels.* Cambridge, MA: Harvard UP, 1982.

————. *Hawthorne and History, Defacing It.* Oxford: Basil Blackwell, 1991. Contains a bibliography of Miller's work from 1955–1990.

————. "Stevens' Rock and Criticism as Cure." *Georgia Review* 30 (1976): 5–31, 330–48.

Ulmer, Gregory L. *Applied Grammatology.* Baltimore: Johns Hopkins UP, 1985.

Other Work Referred to in "What Is Deconstruction?"

Abrams, M. H. "Rationality and the Imagination in Cultural History." *Critical Inquiry* 2 (1976): 447–64.

Poststructuralist Approaches to Joyce

Attridge, Derek. *Peculiar Language: Literature as Difference from the Renaissance to James Joyce.* Ithaca: Cornell UP, 1988.

Attridge, Derek, and Daniel Ferrer, eds. *Post-Structuralist Joyce: Essays from the French.* Cambridge: Cambridge UP, 1984.

Derrida, Jacques. "Ulysses Gramophone: Hear Say Yes in Joyce." *James Joyce: The Augmented Ninth.* Ed. Bernard Benstock. Syracuse: Syracuse UP, 1988. 27–75. Rpt. in *Acts of Literature.* "Plato's Pharmacy," an essay published in *Dissemination,* contains a footnote indicating the influence of Joyce's *Finnegans Wake* on Derrida.

McGee, Patrick. *Paperspace.* Lincoln: U of Nebraska P, 1988.

Riquelme, John Paul. "Joyce's 'The Dead': The Dissolution of the Self and the Police." *Style* 25 (1991): 488–505.

————. *Teller and Tale in Joyce's Fiction: Oscillating Perspectives.* Baltimore: Johns Hopkins UP, 1983.

Stewart, Garrett. *Reading Voices: Literature and the Phonotext.* Berkeley: U of California P, 1990. See especially ch. 6 ("'An Earsighted View': Joyce's 'Modality of the Audible'") 232–58.

A DECONSTRUCTIONIST PERSPECTIVE

JOHN PAUL RIQUELME

For Whom the Snow Taps: Style and Repetition in "The Dead"

> Who in the rainbow can draw the line where the violet tint ends and the orange tint begins? Distinctly we see the difference of the colors, but where exactly does the first blendingly enter into the other?
>
> —HERMAN MELVILLE, *Billy Budd*

In "The Crack-Up," a series of brief meditations on his breakdown, F. Scott Fitzgerald claims "the test of a first-rate intelligence is the ability to hold two opposed ideas in the mind at the same time, and still retain the ability to function" (69). His statement is relevant for understanding Gabriel Conroy's situation at the end of "The Dead" and our own situation as readers. It is because, when Gabriel encounters a series of events that undermine his sense of identity, his previously held attitudes and perspectives fade, and the new ones that begin to form are superimposed on them, as in a palimpsest. Although our perspective does not and cannot coincide completely with Gabriel's, by means of the narrator's style the reader experiences a version of Gabriel's ambiguous position between selves and voices. Gabriel begins to see double in a process that may enable him to move beyond a monocular, self-serving mode of vision. But the process may instead undermine his identity and leave him a broken man.

Fitzgerald contrasts the ability to think oppositionally with a self-destructive delusion that tries unsuccessfully to turn its back on unpleasant elements of reality. The "tendency [of the self-delusion] is to refuse to face things as long as possible by retiring into an infantile dream — but one is continually startled out of this by various contacts with the world" (75). In "The Dead" Gabriel Conroy provides an example of a self-deluded person who is startled into a process of reconsidering what

he has thought about himself and about those around him. But there
are difficulties in establishing precisely what the effect on Gabriel at the
story's end is and what it will be in the future. These and related difficulties contribute to the lack of consensus among readers concerning
Gabriel's actions and thoughts in the concluding pages.

The differences of interpretive opinion can take various forms, including ones reflecting the two possibilities already mentioned: that Gabriel learns something that helps him to develop or that he is destroyed.
In the wake of Gabriel's encounters with Lily, Miss Ivors, and his wife,
he has in the view of some readers begun to disburden himself in a painful but salutary way of illusions that had kept him from accepting those
around him, including his wife, on terms of equality. Consequently, in
the future he is likely to be a different person: more honest, humble,
and accepting of others. His apparent decision to travel west, expressed
in the final paragraph, would in this reading mean his acceptance of his
wife's Irish background as an important and valuable part of his own
identity. In the view of others, the effect on Gabriel is largely destruc-
tive. That is, he does not begin giving up his illusions in a way that
suggests he will behave more admirably and compassionately in the future. Instead he just gives up; he undergoes something like a death,
represented by his decision to travel westward, from which there can be
no adequate recovery. The one reading sees Gabriel in a positive light
becoming more alive to the realities of life; the other, more negative
interpretation places him among the dead. "The Dead," however, can
lead us to question any absolute separation of the ostensible opposites
that are important in it, including the living and the dead. The story can
also foster skepticism concerning the adequacy of determinate readings,
whether they applaud or decry what happens to Gabriel Conroy, that
treat "The Dead" as at base realistic.

How can the same story encourage two such different readings?
And why is it not possible to merge these and other conflicting responses, each supported by aspects of the text, into an interpretive synthesis that will satisfy every reader? No such harmonizing interpretive
synthesis is possible because the story's language and its structure contain inherently heterogeneous elements whose double antithetical character resists being resolved into a single reading. This fact about "The
Dead," and in some measure about every literary text, frustrates the
possibility that readers could ever agree on a single definitive interpretation, one that is decisively superior to all the other alternatives. The
story is not meaningless and it will not support indiscriminately any
meaning that a reader might want to ascribe to it. Instead, its meanings

are perplexingly multiple and in flux in ways that can startle us out of resting content with single-minded readings that slight one or another aspect of the story's language, structure, actions, and implications.

In the case of "The Dead," the interpretive multiplicity arises in part because of the story's ambiguous status as a piece of realistic writing. "The Dead" is and is not realistic. On the one hand, it creates the impression that it is a story about actual, ordinary experience rendered in a circumstantial, straightforward way by an anonymous narrator whose language presents a determinate slice of reality. On the other hand, the language is at times not determinate and not referential, or not that only or even primarily. It points to or evokes experiences and meanings that cannot be convincingly understood as actual, literal ones. At those times, its style can encourage the reader to wonder Who speaks? and What is happening? while it also places obstacles in the path of our answering those questions. Like Gabriel, the reader is addressed in unexpected ways that can trigger a kind of thinking that involves holding conflicting perspectives in mind simultaneously without losing what Fitzgerald calls "the ability to function."

We can see the story's heterogeneous, dissonant character in the repetitions that many readers notice and try to account for in their responses. These include the repeated references to the snow and Gabriel's repeated encounters with women, which he finds disquieting. The natural world and social encounters, verbal and imagistic repetition on the one hand and repeated actions informed by desire and habit on the other, that appear initially to be unrelated become linked through their recurring juxtaposition in the story's network of seemingly realistic details. These different but connected elements in the story embody two kinds of repetition that may occur in conjunction to some degree in all fictional prose narratives. The conjunction is particularly emphatic in "The Dead" because of the story's comparative brevity. Rather than occurring at greater distance from each other amidst a denser presentation of realistic details and actions, as they likely would in a novel, these forms of repetition occur in such small compass in "The Dead" that it is difficult to overlook them. Frequent repetitions of images and scenes can have an effect like that of the unlikely coincidences that sometimes occur in narratives; their insistent, even mechanical, quality can disturb the realistic illusion. "The Dead"'s curious character arises as well from salient aspects of its style, especially the narrator's use of free indirect discourse, the report of the character's thoughts in the third person and the past tense, using words and phrases that seem at times to originate with the character in the present time of the action. Aspects of scene,

imagery, action, thought, and style work together to reveal the story's
implications and simultaneously to impede any easy formulation of
them.

The style reaches a resonant moment of concluding intensity in the
well-known final sentence. Here the verbal and imagistic repetition of
the snow presents, as is the case of many earlier passages, something
from the natural world that is part of the scene. But the repetition occurs in language that evokes the character's thoughts as part of a verbal
trajectory that brings the narrative to a close with the phrase that also
serves as the story's beginning and title, "the dead":

> His soul swooned slowly as he heard the snow falling faintly
> through the universe and faintly falling, like the descent of their
> last end, upon all the living and the dead. (59)

As the reader reaches the last ending of the fifteen stories that make up
Dubliners, all written in what is usually described as a realistic style, Gabriel Conroy hears and apparently recognizes the ubiquity of the snow
that is mentioned regularly earlier in the story. He apparently recognizes as well, because of the snow, the connection between the living
and the dead. But in order to understand that recognition, if indeed
that is what it is, the reader needs to understand the sentence, which
poses some interpretive difficulties that are hard to ignore and that cannot be resolved entirely, although their character can be clarified.

The oddities of this sentence are numerous. In fact, they are so
abundant and persistent that the sentence successfully resists being reduced to a simple paraphrase. How, for example, can we fix for interpretation the oscillations of the closing words, "the dead," which occur
within the narration as its ending, earlier in the penultimate paragraph
in the phrase "vast hosts of the dead," and on the narrative's border as
the title? In their role as a title these words initiate our experience of the
story, but as a closing they do the opposite. As a title their source is an
ambiguous figure, either the author or the narrator, who does not participate in the narrative action. As an ending their source is the
character's mind, or the narrator's, or both. The technique of free indirect discourse, in which the character's language and the narrator's are
often ambiguously mixed, prevents the reader from readily deciding
who speaks the final phrase. This is generally true of the story's last
pages, not just of the final sentence, but it becomes particularly evident
at the end because that sentence cannot be translated into a univocal
statement that is indisputably either Gabriel's or the narrator's. It is
worth noting that problems of this sort keep the reader from adopting

a single position. We are invited to stand in two places at once as the recipient of what may be the character's private language, addressed to no one except himself, and as the recipient of the narrator's public language, addressed to us. By experiencing the character's unspoken thoughts, we undergo a partial displacement from being ourselves. When at the end of that experience the closing words repeat the title, whose origin and position are also ambiguous, the sentence becomes the locus of thorny issues for any reader who claims to be able to explain its meaning and the story that it closes. As in *Finnegans Wake,* the ending of the narrative sends us back to its beginning in a spiraling movement that is at once forward out of the text and backward to its earliest moment.

That movement involves the perplexing relations of part to whole, for we move from a part of the story, a single phrase in the narration, to the identical phrase that names the story taken as a whole. It would seem that, as in the *Wake,* "a part so ptee does duty for the holos" (18.36–19.01), but the exact relations of a part so petite (and perhaps in the *Wake* petty) to the whole and of ending to beginning, as of character to narrator and of narrator to author, are anything but clear. The final sentence's phrasing evokes the puzzling relation of parts to wholes in other ways as well. The snow, which prior to the final paragraph seemed to be primarily a detail within realistic scenes composed of contiguous elements, has become something much larger. It is no longer one item, however important, among many, for it falls not just through the air of Dublin or of Ireland or of the British Isles but through the "universe." This universalized snow covers everything, as the word "all" in the passage emphasizes, including "the dead," presumably not just those who are buried in the earth but "the dead" in all the senses that can reasonably be assigned to the title. The dead would include Gabriel and all the other characters who are presented as literally alive in the story but who can be said to be figuratively dead. In such a reading Gabriel could be described as imagining himself as dead, either as literally dead or as one of the living dead, within the context of the now universalized snow. The possibility that someone living could imagine himself as dead brings us to a limiting point in language's ability to portray unambiguously the contents of someone's mind since with death language stops. This would be a point at which consciousness projects itself as what it cannot literally be — dead — if in fact it continues to be consciousness. That fact adds another puzzling dimension to a sentence in which a part of the narrative, the snow, has now become the totalizing context for understanding the phrase, "the dead," which

is at once a part of the story, the name of the whole, and the trace of an
experience that would seem to lie outside language's potential for coherent expression.

The narrator's perspective and the character's have been subtly
mingled and merged in the sentence by a style that mediates between an
internal and an external view. The style signals the merger because it
uses the third person, an ostensibly *external* point of view, to present
not only what occurs *within* the character (in words that appear at times
to mimic the character's language), but also the swooning of his soul
(whatever that may be) and his act of hearing something that apparently
lies *outside* himself. That act of perception, like the style, mediates between internal and external, and it may cause the swooning that takes
place along with it. The swooning soul aside, what the sentence suggests may at first seem clear enough, but the closer we look at its details,
the stranger it appears to be. One of the main oddities is its assertion
that Gabriel could be *hearing* the snow as it falls. That assertion need
not be read realistically. We may sometimes hear the wind during a
snowstorm or hear snow mixed with rain or sleet when it strikes a window. At the beginning of the final paragraph, Gabriel apparently has
such an experience, whose uncanny, repetitive character I shall return
to, but snow is in many situations virtually soundless. The closing statement would be less odd had the narrator repeated the phrase "upon the
pane" from the paragraph's opening, but instead of snow falling against
something, now it is falling "through the universe." It is not evident
how snow that is doing that could be audible even though snow under
some other circumstances might be. The snow that Gabriel is said to
hear at the end is clearly not literal snow, and the sentence cannot mean
by the predicate "heard" what that word might denote in some other
situations. Such language, which is figurative, not referential, strenu-
ously resists being translated as a single meaning. Its potential for being
understood in several ways, a potential that cannot be separated from
our response to the rest of the story, is a central factor contributing to
the divergence among interpretations.

Understanding the sentence's implications is not just a matter of
reading semantically. It involves also recognizing the ambiguous relations of literal to figurative, part to whole, internal to external, living to
dead, and narrator to character that enable the sentence's words to carry
implications that they might not carry in other contexts. Because of so
many doublings and linkages, any one of which would complicate interpretation, potentially meaningful connections among the sentence's
words develop for the reader in surprising ways. These connections con-

tribute to the sense we make of the sentence's main elements: Gabriel, the snow, and the living and the dead, which are also central elements in the story. To interpret the sentence is also to interpret a small version of the story, a part that can represent the whole because of the presence of these elements and because of the sentence's position. When we look closely at some of the sentence's internal relations, we find links between Gabriel and the snow on the one hand and between him and the dead on the other. He becomes aligned with both the snow that falls and what it falls upon. The double relation, which suggests a blurring or merger of subject and object, makes it difficult to translate Gabriel's experience into more determinate language than the sentence provides.

Gabriel perceives as if with his ears the snow falling "faintly," that is, feebly or perhaps "softly," a word used earlier in the paragraph. But "faintly" suggests the way in which he hears it, barely, and it would be more idiomatic to attach the word to Gabriel's way of perceiving than to use it to describe the manner in which the snow falls. Because swooning means fainting, the word, "faintly," that is predicated of the snow's falling, besides being relevant to Gabriel's hearing, bears a relation to what is happening to Gabriel, who, if he is swooning along with his "soul," might be described as falling in a faint. In addition to these potential cross-predications, the two words, *swoon* and *faintly*, viewed historically evoke the conceptual dissonance in the story that results in antithetical readings. The origin of *swoon* is an Anglo-Saxon word, while the origin of *faintly* is Latin. The Anglo-Saxon word suggests suffocation, and therefore death, while the Latin word from which *faint* derives develops from an Indo-European root that means "to build" or "to form"; that root gives rise as well to our words *figure*, as in figure of speech, *feign*, a word that once indicated imaginative activity, and *fiction*.[1] From this etymological perspective, the contrary interpretations of Gabriel, on the one hand, breaking down as if he were dying and, on

---

[1] I take these etymologies from *The American Heritage Dictionary*, including the "Indo-European Roots Appendix." Skeat, a source that Joyce knew, gives similar information about *faint* but says that the Anglo-Saxon precursor for *swoon* was predicated of wind and meant "to move or sweep along noisily." If we accept Skeat, the opposition in the words' meanings does not disappear but becomes the difference between something comparatively noisy and something comparatively quiet. It is worth mentioning that Joyce uses a similar vocabulary in crucial passages of *A Portrait of the Artist as a Young Man*, especially at the ends of sections. *Fall* and *swoon* occur in various forms either individually or together at the ends of parts one, two, and four. At the end of part four, just before Stephen's "soul" swoons into sleep, there is a passage that sets "to fall" in apposition with "to create life out of life." This gloss for "fall" emphasizes the renewal that I see implied in the history of *faint*. Joyce's use of the same vocabulary in the later text is an important form of repetition in literature that lies beyond the scope of this essay.

the other, as developing a new, more resilient, honest, and compassionate form of selfhood have counterparts of a general sort in words from
the sentence that are linked semantically in modern English but that
have markedly different histories. Anglo-Saxon and Latin, suffocation
and building are antipodes in the sentence that are also connected.

The link between Gabriel's swooning and the snow's "falling
faintly" indicates that subject and object, consciousness and material reality, have merged in some sense or become parallel, but not in the way
that Gabriel had earlier imagined when he stood in the window embrasure and looked out at the snow. There he ascribed a comforting character to the snow; here he becomes assimilated because of the snow to
the dead and is also reduced to the snow's inorganic, falling state. Gabriel is not entirely distinct from the snow that he imagines hearing or,
differently considered, the snow that having been heard now becomes
part of his imaginings. When we learn after the second occurrence of
"faintly" that the snow's falling is like a descent, it is not clear whether
Gabriel or the narrator is the primary source of this simile, which may
render Gabriel's understanding of the snow's meaning. The simile begins as a tautology since the words *fall* and *descent* can be synonymous.
Falling snow would literally descend on the organic and the inorganic
alike, and the word "descent" by itself could present the snowfall as
merely literal. This snow, however, descends not just literally but like a
"last end," including both death and apocalypse, for both living and
dead, a group that necessarily includes Gabriel himself. By blurring a
distinction that might seem easy to maintain, the compound closing
phrase, "the living and the dead," reinforces the link between subject
and object, thinking being and inorganic world. The links among
swoon, falling faintly, and *descent* align Gabriel with the snow that is
descending on himself and on all things. They do so at the end of a story
that has involved various kinds of descent, including Gabriel's descent
from the living and dead relatives whom he either visits or remembers,
the lowering in self-esteem that he suffers as a result of the story's
events, and the recognition expressed in the final sentence that he, like
all others who live and die, is one with the descending, blanketing snow
that has in some way become audible to him.

The repetition of sounds in the final sentence is as remarkable and as
revealing of the story's curious double antithetical character as are the
other elements I have mentioned. In this regard, the sentence is more
thoroughly echoic than we might have anticipated, particularly by contrast with much of the language that occurs before the final paragraph.
The sentence's echoic language includes, for example, a great deal of

sibilance ("*s*oul *s*wooned *s*lowly . . . *s*now . . . univer*s*e . . . de*s*cent"), numerous repetitions of liquid consonants ("sou*l* . . . s*l*ow*l*y . . . fa*ll*ing faint*l*y . . . faint*l*y fa*ll*ing, *l*ike . . . *l*ast . . . a*ll* . . . *l*iving"), examples of assonance ("s*ou*l . . . sl*o*wly . . . sn*o*w"), and an instance of chiasmus ("falling faintly . . . faintly falling"). Any sentence that possesses this kind of phonetically echoic character, which we expect in lyric poetry but not in realistic stories, enables a reader to generate meanings that may not be evident or that may not be emphasized semantically.

At the center of the sentence, conceptually and literally, is the chiasmus, a figure of speech involving reversal and repetition in which the elements occur first in one order and then in reversed order. The language of a chiasmus is structurally double and antithetical because of the repetition and reversal. Karl Marx uses chiasmus regularly because it provides a convenient rhetorical device for evoking two quite different but linked aspects of his conception of history.[2] On the one hand, it can express the self-destructive character of bourgeois society, which in Marx's view behaves in certain ways that will eventually have an effect opposite to what was intended. Chiasmus in this form is a figure that can communicate self-undoing, as in Marx's evocations of the self-destructive, contradictory tendencies of the bourgeoisie. On the other hand, it can also express the course of revolution, in which the elements of an old order are dismantled and then reconfigured into something quite different and better. Chiasmus in this form is a figure of renewal.

Readers have understood "The Dead" according to both these potentials of chiasmus: as a narrative in which the central character destroys himself and as a narrative in which he begins to renew himself. The interlocking character of destruction and renewal is, of course, central to Joyce's later writing, especially *Finnegans Wake*. The chiasmus of "The Dead"'s closing sentence is a double antithetical echoic counterpart for the two divergent readings of the story that I have mentioned. The emphasis created by centering the chiasmus in the sentence is reinforced because it echoes the earlier chiasmus, "falling softly . . . softly falling," that occurs only two sentences before it in the middle of the closing paragraph. And, as we shall see, that paragraph contains as well

[2] Marx and Engels's well-known definition of history in *The German Ideology* provides an example of chiasmus used conceptually and rhetorically to emphasize both continuity and radical change, repetition and reversal: "History is nothing but the succession of the separate generations, each of which exploits the materials . . . handed down to it . . . and thus, on the one hand, continues the traditional activity in completely changed circumstances and, on the other, modifies the old circumstances with a completely changed activity" (172).

an event, the tapping of the snow on the window, that creates and completes uncannily a chiasmus in the action. "The Dead" involves crossovers, the blurring of boundaries, mergers, and exchanges of position, as in a chiasmus. As a consequence, attempts to formulate determinate directions for the story are likely to slight the contrary directions and implications that also contribute to the story's oscillations.

The fluctuations of meaning in "The Dead" occur in one obvious way through repetitions. The much remarked repetition of the snow, for instance, cannot be reduced to a formula because every occurrence carries its own particular connotations that differ in small or large ways from every other occurrence. The references to the snow at the story's end, which occur seven times in the final paragraph (as "snow," "flakes," and "it") can even change retrospectively our response to the earlier references and to earlier portions of the narrative by sending us back to them with a heightened sensitivity to the particular repetitions and to repetition in general. The flurry of closing references crystallizes our sense that snow has been mentioned frequently. Without those insistent repetitions, the references in nine earlier passages would not seem so pervasive or emphatic.

"The Dead" contains repetitions from beginning to end besides the snow. They start in the first paragraph, when Lily's repeated action of greeting guests at the door and then dealing with the men's overcoats is described as almost Pavlovian in character; when the bell rings, she hurries again back down the hall from the pantry to greet another guest. We learn in the next paragraph that the narrative concerns a dance that has been given annually for "years and years" without ever having "fallen flat." Habit is in many ways dominant in the story, which concerns a social event whose participants know their parts virtually by rote. Gabriel, Lily, and others make the event what it has always been by doing again what they have done before in this situation or in others. Freddy Malins, for example, speaks with an "habitual catch in his voice." And Gabriel, who goes on a European cycling tour "every year," performs roles in the party's ritual that have been his for some years. Not only does he carve the goose "as usual"; like Lily he repeats himself immediately when he begins carving "second helpings as soon as he had finished the first round." And the after-dinner speech, a central event in the narrative, is his duty annually. At the conclusion of that speech, the story's second part is punctuated by the repeated singing in unison of refrains from a pluralized version of "For He's a Jolly Good Fellow" and by an "acclamation" that is "renewed time after time." The participants are like grandfather Patrick Morkan's horse, Johnny, who is described in the story's third section as circling round and round a monument because he is used to performing that particular task. The crucial difference between the horse and the party-goers is that, like the snow, the horse repeats himself in a way that exposes the limits of human control.

After his unpleasant encounter with Miss Ivors and after rebuffing Gretta's suggestion that he travel to the west of Ireland, Gabriel retires to the window embrasure to think about his speech (34). He meditates there on the snow in a scene whose elements are repeated twice later, in a passage that occurs just before he delivers his speech and again in the final paragraph. His meditation involves what Fitzgerald calls "retiring into an infantile dream" (75), but the later iterations, especially the last one, indicate that Gabriel cannot escape having "contacts with the world" (75) and recognizing what those contacts mean. In the embrasure Gabriel "tapped" the window pane with "trembling fingers" and imagined the pleasure of escaping from the table to be alone outside, where the snow covered the trees and the top of the Wellington Monument (34). Gabriel here indulges in a momentarily comforting but deluded fantasy that an aspect of nature could be more companionable than the people at the party. The snow seems to him to coincide more perfectly with his desires than they do. The fantasy appears harmless enough in some respects, but it forms part of a pattern of habitual thinking that marks and mars Gabriel's relations with others. In particular, Gabriel overlooks the fact that his partner, whether servant, colleague, spouse, or nature, can act independently of his wishes and his will. He ignores his own limits and, in effect, denies his own mortality. His experience with his wife reveals clearly the deluded character of that denial, but so does his perception of the snow at the story's end.

I mentioned earlier that coincidences in a narrative can sometimes ruffle the realistic texture of a story. But coincidence in another sense is of the essence in realism, the coincidence, or one-to-correspondence, of words and things that supports our sense that a story's language is coincident with events that might take place in actuality. In "The Dead" Gabriel wants the world in which he lives to coincide with his sense of who he is and with his desires. His desire for control is clear in the series of encounters with Lily, Miss Ivors, and Gretta. And it is also clear in his meditation on the snow as his ally. Gabriel's delusion about his relations with nature is continuous with his desire for control and coincidence in his social relations. In neither case can his desires be fulfilled.

Gabriel's longing for coincidence is patent in his thoughts about Gretta before he learns about Michael Furey. Those thoughts concern the past's connection to the present, specifically the possibility of a perfect repetition of the past. Gabriel is filled with "[m]oments of their secret life together," which he "longed to recall to her. . . . For the years, he felt, had not quenched his soul or hers" (52). When he thinks of a love letter that he had written her, the words concerning her name "written years before were borne towards him from the past" (52), and he wants to be alone with Gretta to actualize them by calling her name in the same way that the snow is later said to be falling, "softly." When they enter a cab, Gabriel imagines that they are "again" in a cab from the past, "galloping to catch the boat, galloping to their honeymoon" (52). The realities of the situation, however, do not correspond to his fantasies. The horse gallops "wearily" under a "murky" sky while "dragging his old rattling box after his heels" (52). Recalling ecstatic moments to Gretta means also forgetting "the years of their dull existence together" (52). And all the while Gretta is thinking not about secret moments that they shared together, moments that no one else knows about, but about secrets she has not shared with him, moments he knows nothing of.

Gabriel's repeated scenes of discomfort with women, in which he behaves in flustered, defensive, and angry ways, all arise because he habitually resists admitting that his desires and reality do not and cannot coincide. With Gretta he wants to restore a fullness of love that turns out not ever to have been there in the form in which he mistakenly conceived and experienced it. He wants things to be again as he thought they once were, but he discovers that his sense of the past as a perfect merger and coincidence of two people, upon which he had built his conceptions of the present and the future, is faulty and cannot be recaptured. He learns that exact repetition, unchanged by the passage of time, is not only impossible because of time's passage, it is impossible because the original to be repeated never existed. Gabriel is mastered by this lesson with a vengeance; he even wonders, churlishly but also reasonably, after Gretta has fallen asleep, whether her words coincided entirely with the facts, some of which she may have left out of her account (58).

The character of the mistake that motivates Gabriel's habitual attitudes and his repeated behavior involves a misunderstanding about what the snow is and his relations with it. When we hear in the final paragraph that "it had begun to snow again," the word "again" means something different than it does when Gabriel thinks about "again" being on a honeymoon with Gretta. Despite the fact that one can never step into the same snowstorm twice, the snow appears to be closer to a state of absolute repetition than human action can ever achieve. Like the wild swans that Yeats imagines returning each year to Coole Park, the new snowfall enables the person experiencing it to recognize a difference between nature and people that includes nature's resistance to some human desires. The snow, of course, varies in amount from year to year. The snowfall that occurs during the party is the heaviest in thirty years, perhaps heavier than it has ever been earlier in the period of this party's annual repetition. But it is "general" in the broadest possible sense, the sense projected by the final sentence. Gabriel Conroy lives as though, by means of his will and his habits, he can actualize the perfect repetition of the past in the present and the full coincidence of desire and reality. He even thinks that the snow can contribute to the enhancing of his pleasure. He discovers, however, that, instead of being a compliant element in a context of experience that he defines, the snow defines him and his experience as mere elements in its unyielding context. The snow as a form of repetition, not repetition motivated by human agency and desire, establishes the limits of possibility as well as the shape of necessity in Gabriel's world and his life.

We see this reversal emerging in the passages that repeat elements of the scene in the window embrasure. The repetitions take the form of a chiasmus in the narrative in which Gabriel and the snow change places. The elements are either the same or related in each scene: Gabriel, a window, snow, and tapping. In the second scene, just before beginning his speech, Gabriel leans on the table with the same "trembling fingers" (42) that he used to tap the window in the first scene. But instead of tapping, we now hear "patting" as "a few gentlemen patted the table" (42) to bring the guests to attention. Curiously, "pat" and "tap" bear a chiastic relation to each other in a literal, orthographic way. Patting repeats tapping but with a reversal. The snow, repeated here three times in the four sentences of Gabriel's thoughts, again caps Wellington's Monument, but now it flashes "westward" (42), anticipating the final paragraph's reference to traveling "westward." He again thinks positively about the outside, where the air is "pure" and people may be looking at the "windows" (42). Especially considering Gabriel's close relation to the snow in the earlier and later parallel passages, we can understand the beginning of his speech as providing terms that apply as well to the snow: " — It has fallen to my lot this evening, as in years past" (42). It is, of course, the snow that has fallen as in years past in a repetition that provides the context for understanding how Gabriel has been involved in a falling that is more general than repetition driven by the human will.

The description of the second scene might seem labored or fanciful were it not that the third passage and the final paragraph as a whole take us beyond the limits of realism. It is no coincidence, in particular no coincidence of past and present, desire and actuality of the sort that Gabriel hoped to have with his wife, when a tapping reoccurs in the story's closing. That tapping on the pane that lets Gabriel know that the snow has started again repeats Gabriel's earlier tapping but with a reversal. The snow is now tapping at Gabriel, who must attend to its presence. Such a scene, in which an action involving a person and inanimate nature is repeated with a reversal in agency, does not accord with our expectations for realism any more than does the substitution of "pat" for "tap" in an intermediate scene that anticipates the later, more substantive reversal. There is also no realistic reason why Gabriel should have tapped on the window in the first scene. His doing so seems inexplicable except as part of a pattern that exists to be reversed in order to create a chiasmus in the action. The snow's tapping can mean various things, including especially that the snow with its repetitions, not Gabriel with his, is the more "general." Like his tears, mentioned in the penultimate paragraph of the story, Gabriel may be "generous," as Gretta says that he is, but he is not "general." The tapping also resembles Michael Furey's throwing gravel at Gretta's window (57). Gabriel's tapping was a sign of alliance; the tapping that he hears is a sign of eventual, if not impending, death that lacks the expression of love in Michael Furey's action and the sense of pleasure that accompanied Gabriel's own tapping.

In the story's final pages, the events express noncoincidence when the earlier scene is repeated with a reversal and when Gabriel expresses the possible lack of correspondence between his wife's words and the whole truth. In those pages as well, the style presses against and beyond the limits of realism, with its promise of believable, determinate representations, because its language, the free indirect discourse in general and the last sentence's convolutions in particular, cannot be translated in just one way. The final sentence repeats as echoic language the chiastic structure of repeated, reversed scenes that represents Gabriel's relations to the snow. Its language is a rhetorical mirror that reflects in small the repetitions and reversals that are central to the story's transformations.

Gabriel resists recognizing that his own purposive, habitual actions and his desire for coincidence in his social and personal relations do not take the implications of the snow, itself a form of recurrence, adequately into account. At the end Gabriel has been assimilated to the snow as an ineluctable form of repetition; or he has assimilated the snow and its meanings sufficiently so that he understands and accepts as part of his thinking and his future behavior what it represents and why it is important. Gabriel may be overwhelmed and even silenced for a moment as he recognizes his place in a general process of leveling that is not absolutely self-destructive because it allows him to continue functioning. Or the experience may be a defining, totalizing one in which Gabriel, unable to continue in any way, breaks down. These two possibilities and other cognate oppositions are referred to the reader in, among other places, the final sentence. They are referred to us not for adjudication but as elements to be taken up into our own process of recognition, in which we can see things in more than one way because of the story's style and its repetitions. This process provides one antidote for the self-delusion that contributes to the swoon that Gabriel brings on himself by refusing to face his mortality but that he also ultimately cannot avoid any more than he can ignore the uncanny tapping of the snow. It taps for him.

WORKS CITED

American Heritage Dictionary of the English Language. 3rd ed. Boston: Houghton, 1992.

Fitzgerald, F. Scott. *The Crack-Up.* Ed. Edmund Wilson. 1931. New York: New Directions, 1956.

Joyce, James. *Finnegans Wake.* New York: Viking, 1939.

Skeat, W. W. *An Etymological Dictionary of the English Language, New Edition Revised and Enlarged.* 1879–1882. Oxford: Oxford UP, 1989.

Tucker, Robert C., ed. *The Marx-Engels Reader,* 2nd ed. New York: Norton, 1978.

Glossary of Critical
and Theoretical Terms

Most terms have been glossed parenthetically where they first appear in the text. Mainly, the glossary lists terms that are too complex to define in a phrase or a sentence or two. A few of the terms listed are discussed at greater length elsewhere (feminist criticism, for instance); these terms are defined succinctly and a page reference to the longer discussion is provided.

AFFECTIVE FALLACY First used by William K. Wimsatt and Monroe C. Beardsley to refer to what they regarded as the erroneous practice of interpreting texts according to the psychological responses of readers. "The Affective Fallacy," they wrote in a 1946 essay later republished in the *Verbal Icon* (1954), "is a confusion between the poem and its *results* (what it *is* and what it *does*). . . . It begins by trying to derive the standards of criticism from the psychological effects of a poem and ends in impressionism and relativism." The affective fallacy, like the intentional fallacy (confusing the meaning of a work with the author's expressly intended meaning), was one of the main tenets of the New Criticism, or formalism. The affective fallacy has recently been contested by reader-response critics, who have deliberately dedicated their efforts to describing the way individual readers and "interpretive communities" go about "making sense" of texts.

See also: Authorial Intention, Formalism, Reader-Response Criticism.

AUTHORIAL INTENTION Defined narrowly, an author's intention in writing a work, as expressed in letters, diaries, interviews, and conversations. Defined more broadly, "intentionality" involves unexpressed motivations, designs, and purposes, some of which may have remained unconscious.

The debate over whether critics should try to discern an author's intentions (conscious or otherwise) is an old one. William K. Wimsatt and Monroe C. Beardsley, in an essay first published in the 1940s, coined the term "intentional fallacy" to refer to the practice of basing interpretations on the expressed or implied intentions of authors, a practice they judged to be erroneous. As proponents of the New Criticism, or formalism, they argued that a work of literature is an object in itself and should be studied as such. They believed that it is sometimes helpful to learn what an author intended, but the critic's real purpose is to show what is actually in the text, not what an author intended to put there.

See also: Affective Fallacy, Formalism.

BASE *See* Marxist Criticism.

BINARY OPPOSITIONS   *See* Oppositions.

BLANKS   *See* Gaps.

CANON   Since the fourth century, used to refer to those books of the Bible that the Christian church accepts as being Holy Scripture. The term has come to be applied more generally to those literary works given special status, or "privileged," by a culture. Works we tend to think of as "classics" or the "Great Books" produced by Western culture — texts that are found in every anthology of American, British, and world literature — would be among those that constitute the canon.

Recently, Marxist, feminist, minority, and Third World critics have argued that, for political reasons, many excellent works never enter the canon. Canonized works, they claim, are those that reflect — and respect — the culture's dominant ideology and/or perform some socially acceptable or even necessary form of "cultural work." Attempts have been made to broaden or redefine the canon by discovering valuable texts, or versions of texts, that were repressed or ignored for political reasons. These have been published both in traditional and in nontraditional anthologies. The most outspoken critics of the canon, especially radical critics practicing cultural criticism, have called into question the whole concept of canon or "canonicity." Privileging no form of artistic expression that reflects and revises the culture, these critics treat cartoons, comics, and soap operas with the same cogency and respect they accord novels, poems, and plays.

See also: Cultural Criticism, Feminist Criticism, Ideology, Marxist Criticism.

CONFLICTS, CONTRADICTIONS   *See* Gaps.

CULTURAL CRITICISM   A critical approach that is sometimes referred to as "cultural studies" or "cultural critique." Practitioners of cultural criticism oppose "high" definitions of culture and take seriously popular cultural forms. Grounded in a variety of continental European influences, cultural criticism nonetheless gained institutional force in England, in 1964, with the founding of the Centre for Contemporary Cultural Studies at Birmingham University. Broadly interdisciplinary in its scope and approach, cultural criticism views the text as the locus and catalyst of a complex network of political and economic discourses. Cultural critics share with Marxist critics an interest in the ideological contexts of cultural forms.

DECONSTRUCTION   A poststructuralist approach to literature that is strongly influenced by the writings of the French philosopher Jacques Derrida. Deconstruction, partly in response to structuralism and formalism, posits the undecidability of meaning for all texts. In fact, as the deconstructionist critic J. Hillis Miller points out, "deconstruction is not a dismantling of the structure of a text but a demonstration that it has already dismantled itself." See "What Is Deconstruction?" pp. 206–215.

DIALECTIC   Originally developed by Greek philosophers, mainly Socrates and Plato, as a form and method of logical argumentation; the term later came to denote a philosophical notion of evolution. The German philosopher G. W. F. Hegel described dialectic as a process whereby a thesis, when countered by an antithesis, leads to the synthesis of a new idea. Karl Marx and

Friedrich Engels, adapting Hegel's idealist theory, used the phrase "dialectical materialism" to discuss the way in which a revolutionary class war might lead to the synthesis of a new social economic order. The American Marxist critic Fredric Jameson has coined the phrase "dialectical criticism" to refer to a Marxist critical approach that synthesizes structuralist and poststructuralist methodologies.

See also: Marxist Criticism, Structuralism, Poststructuralism.

DIALOGIC See Discourse.

DISCOURSE Used specifically, can refer to (1) spoken or written discussion of a subject or area of knowledge; (2) the words in, or text of, a narrative as opposed to its story line; or (3) a "strand" within a given narrative that argues a certain point or defends a given value system.

More generally, "discourse" refers to the language in which a subject or area of knowledge is discussed or a certain kind of business is transacted. Human knowledge is collected and structured in discourses. Theology and medicine are defined by their discourses, as are politics, sexuality, and literary criticism.

A society is generally made up of a number of different discourses or "discourse communities," one or more of which may be dominant or serve the dominant ideology. Each discourse has its own vocabulary, concepts, and rules, knowledge of which constitutes power. The psychoanalyst and psychoanalytic critic Jacques Lacan has treated the unconscious as a form of discourse, the patterns of which are repeated in literature. Cultural critics, following Mikhail Bakhtin, use the word "dialogic" to discuss the dialogue *between* discourses that takes place within language or, more specifically, a literary text.

See also: Cultural Criticism, Ideology, Narrative, Psychoanalytic Criticism.

FEMINIST CRITICISM An aspect of the feminist movement whose primary goals include critiquing masculine-dominated language and literature by showing how they reflect a masculine ideology; writing the history of unknown or undervalued women writers, thereby earning them their rightful place in the literary canon; and helping create a climate in which women's creativity may be fully realized and appreciated. See "What Is Feminist Criticism?" pp. 178–185.

FIGURE See Metaphor, Metonymy, Symbol.

FORMALISM Also referred to as the New Criticism, formalism reached its height during the 1940s and 1950s but it is still practiced today. Formalists treat a work of literary art as if it were a self-contained, self-referential object. Rather than basing their interpretations of a text on the reader's response, the author's stated intentions, or parallels between the text and historical contexts (such as the author's life), formalists concentrate on the relationships *within* the text that give it its own distinctive character or form. Special attention is paid to repetition, particularly of images or symbols, but also of sound effects and rhythms in poetry.

Because of the importance placed on close analysis and the stress on the text as a carefully crafted, orderly object containing observable formal patterns, formalism has often been seen as an attack on Romanticism and impressionism, particularly impressionistic criticism. It has sometimes even been called an "objective" approach to literature. Formalists are more likely than certain other critics to believe and say that the meaning of a text can be known objectively. For instance, reader-response critics see meaning as a function either of each reader's experience or of the norms that govern a particular "interpretive community," and deconstructors argue that texts mean opposite things at the same time.

Formalism was originally based on essays written during the 1920s and 1930s by T. S. Eliot, I. A. Richards, and William Empson. It was significantly developed later by a group of American poets and critics, including R. P. Blackmur, Cleanth Brooks, John Crowe Ransom, Allen Tate, Robert Penn Warren, and William K. Wimsatt. Although we associate formalism with certain principles and terms (such as the "Affective Fallacy" and the "Intentional Fallacy" as defined by Wimsatt and Monroe C. Beardsley), formalists were trying to make a cultural statement rather than establish a critical dogma. Generally Southern, religious, and culturally conservative, they advocated the inherent value of literary works (particularly of literary works regarded as beautiful art objects) because they were sick of the growing ugliness of modern life and contemporary events. Some recent theorists even suggest that the rising popularity of formalism after World War II was a feature of American isolationism, the formalist tendency to isolate literature from biography and history being a manifestation of the American fatigue with wider involvements.

See also: Affective Fallacy, Authorial Intention, Deconstruction, Reader-Response Criticism, Symbol.

GAPS   When used by reader-response critics familiar with the theories of Wolfgang Iser, refers to "blanks" in texts that must be filled in by readers. A gap may be said to exist whenever and wherever a reader perceives something to be missing between words, sentences, paragraphs, stanzas, or chapters. Readers respond to gaps actively and creatively, explaining apparent inconsistencies in point of view, accounting for jumps in chronology, speculatively supplying information missing from plots, and resolving problems or issues left ambiguous or "indeterminate" in the text.

Reader-response critics sometimes speak as if a gap actually exists in a text; a gap is, of course, to some extent a product of readers' perceptions. Different readers may find gaps in different texts, and different gaps in the same text. Furthermore, they may fill these gaps in different ways, which is why, a reader-response critic might argue, works are interpreted in different ways.

Although the concept of the gap has been used mainly by reader-response critics, it has also been used by critics taking other theoretical approaches. Practitioners of deconstruction might use "gap" when speaking of the radical contradictoriness of a text. Marxists have used the term to speak of everything from the gap that opens up between economic base and cultural superstructure to the two kinds of conflicts or contradictions to be found in literary texts. The first of these, they would argue, results from the fact that texts reflect ideology, within which certain subjects cannot be covered, things that cannot be said, contradictory views that cannot be recognized as contradictory. The second kind of conflict, contradiction, or gap within a text results from the fact that works don't just reflect ideology: they are also fictions that, consciously or unconsciously, distance themselves from the same ideology.

See also: Deconstruction, Ideology, Marxist Criticism, Reader-Response Criticism.

GENRE   A French word referring to a kind or type of literature. Individual works within a genre may exhibit a distinctive form, be governed by certain conventions, and/or represent characteristic subjects. Tragedy, epic, and romance are all genres.

Perhaps inevitably, the term "genre" is used loosely. Lyric poetry is a genre, but so are characteristic *types* of the lyric, such as the sonnet, the ode, and the elegy. Fiction is a genre, as are detective fiction and science fiction. The list of genres grows constantly as critics establish new lines of connection between individual works and discern new categories of works with common characteristics. Moreover, some writers form hybrid genres by combining the characteristics of several in a single work.

Knowledge of genres helps critics to understand and explain what is conventional and unconventional, borrowed and original, in a work.

HEGEMONY Given intellectual currency by the Italian communist Antonio Gramsci, the word (a translation of *egemonia*) refers to the pervasive system of assumptions, meanings, and values — the web of ideologies, in other words — that shapes the way things look, what they mean, and therefore what reality *is* for the majority of people within a given culture.

See also: Ideology, Marxist Criticism.

IDEOLOGY A set of beliefs underlying the customs, habits, and/or practices common to a given social group. To members of that group, the beliefs seem obviously true, natural, and even universally applicable. They may seem just as obviously arbitrary, idiosyncratic, and even false to outsiders or members of another group who adhere to another ideology. Within a society, several ideologies may coexist, or one or more may be dominant.

Ideologies may be forcefully imposed or willingly subscribed to. Their component beliefs may be held consciously or unconsciously. In either case, they come to form what Johanna M. Smith has called "the unexamined ground of our experience." Ideology governs our perceptions, judgments, and prejudices — our sense of what is acceptable, normal, and deviant. Ideology may cause a revolution; it may also allow discrimination and even exploitation.

Ideologies are of special interest to sociologically oriented critics of literature because of the way in which authors reflect or resist prevailing views in their texts. Some Marxist critics have argued that literary texts reflect and reproduce the ideologies that produced them; most, however, have shown how ideologies are riven with contradictions that works of literature manage to expose and widen. Still other Marxists have focused on the way in which texts themselves are characterized by gaps, conflicts, and contradictions between their ideological and anti-ideological functions.

Feminist critics have addressed the question of ideology by seeking to expose (and thereby call into question) the patriarchal ideology mirrored or inscribed in works written by men — even men who have sought to counter sexism and break down sexual stereotypes. New historicists have been interested in demonstrating the ideological underpinnings not only of literary representations but also of our interpretations of them. Fredric Jameson, an American Marxist critic, argues that all thought is ideological, but that ideological thought that knows itself as such stands the chance of seeing through and transcending ideology.

See also: Cultural Criticism, Feminist Criticism, Marxist Criticism, New Historicism.

IMAGINARY ORDER One of the three essential orders of the psycho-analytic field (see Real and Symbolic Order), it is most closely associated with the senses (sight, sound, touch, taste, and smell). The infant, who by compari-son to other animals is born premature and thus is wholly dependent on others for a prolonged period, enters the Imaginary order when it begins to experience a unity of body parts and motor control that is empowering. This usually occurs between six and eighteen months, and is called by Lacan the "mirror stage" or "mirror phase," in which the child anticipates mastery of its body. It does so by identifying with the *image* of wholeness (that is, seeing its own image in the mirror, experiencing its mother as a whole body, and so on). This sense of oneness, and also difference from others (especially the mother or primary care-taker), is established through an image or a vision of harmony that is both a mirroring and a "mirage of maturation" or false sense of individuality and inde-pendence. The Imaginary is a metaphor for unity, is related to the visual order, and is always part of human subjectivity. Because the subject is fundamentally separate from others and also internally divided (conscious/unconscious), the apparent coherence of the Imaginary, its fullness and grandiosity, is always false, a *mis*recognition that the ego (or "me") tries to deny by imagining itself as coherent and empowered. The Imaginary operates in conjunction with the Real and Symbolic and is not a "stage" of development equivalent to Freud's "pre-oedipal stage," nor is it pre-linguistic.

See also: Psychoanalytic Criticism, Real, Symbolic Order.

IMPLIED READER A phrase used by some reader-response critics in place of the phrase "the reader." Whereas "the reader" could refer to any idio-syncratic individual who happens to have read or to be reading the text, "the implied reader" is *the* reader intended, even created, by the text. Other reader-response critics seeking to describe this more generally conceived reader have spoken of the "informed reader" or the "narratee," who is "the necessary coun-terpart of a given narrator."

See Reader-Response Criticism.

INTENTIONAL FALLACY *See* Authorial Intention.

INTENTIONALITY *See* Authorial Intention.

INTERTEXTUALITY The condition of interconnectedness among texts. Every author has been influenced by others, and every work contains ex-plicit and implicit references to other works. Writers may consciously or uncon-sciously echo a predecessor or precursor; they may also consciously or uncon-sciously disguise their indebtedness, making intertextual relationships difficult for the critic to trace.

Reacting against the formalist tendency to view each work as a freestanding object, some poststructuralist critics suggested that the meaning of a work only emerges intertextually, that is, within the context provided by other works. But there has been a reaction, too, against this type of intertextual criticism. Some new historicist critics suggest that literary history is itself too narrow a context and that works should be interpreted in light of a larger set of cultural contexts.

There is, however, a broader definition of intertextuality, one that refers to the relationship between works of literature and a wide range of narratives and discourses that we don't usually consider literary. Thus defined, intertextuality could be used by a new historicist to refer to the significant interconnectedness between a literary text and nonliterary discussions of or discourses about contemporary culture. Or it could be used by a poststructuralist to suggest that a work can only be recognized and read within a vast field of signs and tropes that is *like* a text and that makes any single text self-contradictory and "undecidable."

See also: Discourse, Formalism, Narrative, New Historicism, Poststructuralism, Trope.

MARXIST CRITICISM An approach that treats literary texts as material products, describing them in broadly historical terms. In Marxist criticism, the text is viewed in terms of its production and consumption, as a product *of* work that does identifiable cultural work of its own. Following Karl Marx, the founder of communism, Marxist critics have used the terms "base" to refer to economic reality and "superstructure" to refer to the corresponding or "homologous" infrastructure consisting of politics, law, philosophy, religion, and the arts. Also following Marx, they have used the word "ideology" to refer to that set of cultural beliefs that literary works at once reproduce, resist, and revise.

METAPHOR The representation of one thing by another related or similar thing. The image (or activity or concept) used to represent or "figure" something else is known as the "vehicle" of the metaphor; the thing represented is called the "tenor." In other words, the vehicle is what we substitute for the tenor. The relationship between vehicle and tenor can provide much additional meaning. Thus, instead of saying, "Last night I read a book," we might say, "Last night I plowed through a book." "Plowed through" (or the activity of plowing) is the vehicle of our metaphor; "read" (or the act of reading) is the tenor, the thing being figured. The increment in meaning through metaphor is fairly obvious. Our audience knows not only *that* we read but also *how* we read, because to read a book in the way that a plow rips through earth is surely to read in a relentless, unreflective way. Note that in the sentence above, a new metaphor — "rips through" — has been used to explain an old one. This serves (which is a metaphor) as an example of just how thick (another metaphor) language is with metaphors!

Metaphor is a kind of "trope" (literally, a "turning," that is, a figure that alters or "turns" the meaning of a word or phrase). Other tropes include allegory, conceit, metonymy, personification, simile, symbol, and synecdoche. Traditionally, metaphor and symbol have been viewed as the principal tropes; minor tropes have been categorized as *types* of these two major ones. Similes, for instance, are usually defined as simple metaphors that usually employ "like" or "as" and state the tenor outright, as in "My love is like a red, red rose." Synecdoche involves a vehicle that is a *part* of the tenor, as in "I see a sail" meaning "I see a boat." Metonymy is viewed as a metaphor involving two terms commonly if arbitrarily associated with (but not fundamentally or intrinsically related to) each other. Recently, however, deconstructors such as Paul de Man and J. Hillis Miller have questioned the "privilege" granted to metaphor and the metaphor/metonymy distinction or "opposition." They have suggested that all metaphors are really metonyms and that all figuration is arbitrary.

See also: Deconstruction, Metonymy, Oppositions, Symbol.

METONYMY The representation of one thing by another that is commonly and often physically associated with it. To refer to a writer's handwriting as his or her "hand" is to use a metonymic "figure" or "trope." The image or thing used to represent something else is known as the "vehicle" of the metonym; the thing represented is called the "tenor."

Like other tropes (such as metaphor), metonymy involves the replacement of one word or phrase by another. Liquor may be referred to as "the bottle," a monarch as "the crown." Narrowly defined, the vehicle of a metonym is arbitrarily, not intrinsically, associated with the tenor. In other words, the bottle just happens to be what liquor is stored in and poured from in our culture. The hand may be involved in the production of handwriting, but so are the brain and the pen. There is no special, intrinsic likeness between a crown and a monarch; it's just that crowns traditionally sit on monarchs' heads and not on the heads of university professors. More broadly, "metonym" and "metonymy" have been used by recent critics to refer to a wide range of figures and tropes. Deconstructors have questioned the distinction between metaphor and metonymy.

See also: Deconstruction, Metaphor, Trope.

NARRATIVE   A story or a telling of a story, or an account of a situation or of events. A novel and a biography of a novelist are both narratives, as are Freud's case histories.

Some critics use the word "narrative" even more generally; Brook Thomas, a new historicist, has critiqued "narratives of human history that neglect the role human labor has played."

NEW CRITICISM   *See* Formalism.

NEW HISTORICISM   One of the most recent developments in contemporary critical theory, its practitioners share certain convictions, the major ones being that literary critics need to develop a high degree of historical consciousness and that literature should not be viewed apart from other human creations, artistic or otherwise. See "What Is the New Historicism?" pp. 150–158.

See also: Authorial Intention, Deconstruction, Formalism, Ideology, Poststructuralism, Psychoanalytic Criticism.

OPPOSITIONS   A concept highly relevant to linguistics, since linguists maintain that words (such as "black" and "death") have meaning not in themselves, but in relation to other words ("white" and "life"). Jacques Derrida, a poststructuralist philosopher of language, has suggested that in the West we think in terms of these "binary oppositions" or dichotomies, which on examination turn out to be evaluative hierarchies. In other words, each opposition — beginning/end, presence/absence, or consciousness/unconsciousness — contains one term that our culture views as superior and one term that we view as negative or inferior.

Derrida has "deconstructed" a number of these binary oppositions, including two — speech/writing and signifier/signified — that he believes to be central to linguistics in particular and Western culture in general. He has concurrently critiqued the "law" of noncontradiction, which is fundamental to Western logic. He and other deconstructors have argued that a text can contain opposed strands of discourse and, therefore, mean opposite things: reason *and* passion, life *and* death, hope *and* despair, black *and* white. Traditionally, criticism has involved choosing between opposed or contradictory meanings and arguing that one is present in the text and the other absent.

French feminists have adopted the ideas of Derrida and other deconstructors, showing not only that we think in terms of such binary oppositions as male/female, reason/emotion, and active/passive, but that we also associate reason and activity with masculinity and emotion and passivity with femininity. Because of this, they have concluded that language is "phallocentric," or masculine-dominated.

See also: Deconstruction, Discourse, Feminist Criticism, Poststructuralism.

PHALLUS The symbolic value of the penis that organizes libidinal development and which Freud saw as a stage in the process of human subjectivity. Lacan viewed the Phallus as the representative of a fraudulent power (male over female) whose "law" is a principle of psychic division (conscious/unconscious) and sexual difference (masculine/feminine). The Symbolic order (see Symbolic) is ruled by the Phallus, which of itself has no inherent meaning *apart from* the power and meaning given to it by individual cultures and societies, and represented by the name of the father as lawgiver and namer.

POSTSTRUCTURALISM The general attempt to contest and subvert structuralism initiated by deconstructors and certain other critics associated with psychoanalytic, Marxist, and feminist theory. Structuralists, using linguistics as a model and employing semiotic (sign) theory, posit the possibility of knowing a text systematically and revealing the "grammar" behind its form and meaning. Poststructuralists argue against the possibility of such knowledge and description. They counter that texts can be shown to contradict not only structuralist accounts of them but also themselves. In making their adversarial claims, they rely on close readings of texts and on the work of theorists such as Jacques Derrida and Jacques Lacan.

Poststructuralists have suggested that structuralism rests on distinctions between "signifier" and "signified" (signs and the things they point toward), "self" and "language" (or "text"), texts and other texts, and text and world that are overly simplistic, if not patently inaccurate. Poststructuralists have shown how all signifieds are also signifiers, and they have treated texts as "intertexts." They have viewed the world as if it *were* a text (we desire a certain car because it *symbolizes* achievement) and the self as the subject, as well as the user, of language; for example, we may shape and speak through language, but it also shapes and speaks through us.

See also: Deconstruction, Feminist Criticism, Intertextuality, Psychoanalytic Criticism, Semiotics, Structuralism.

PSYCHOANALYTIC CRITICISM Grounded in the psychoanalytic theories of Sigmund Freud, it is one of the oldest critical methodologies still in use. Freud's view that works of literature, like dreams, express secret, unconscious desires led to criticism that interpreted literary works as manifestations of the authors' neuroses. More recently, psychoanalytic critics have come to see literary works as skillfully crafted artifacts that may appeal to *our* neuroses by tapping into our repressed wishes and fantasies. Other forms of psychological criticism that diverge from Freud, although they ultimately derive from his insights, include those based on the theories of Carl Jung and Jacques Lacan. See "What Is Psychoanalytic Criticism?" pp. 85–96.

READER-RESPONSE CRITICISM An approach to literature that, as its name implies, considers the way readers respond to texts, as they read. Stanley Fish describes the method by saying that it substitutes for one question,

"What does this sentence mean?" a more operational question, "What does this sentence do?" Reader-response criticism shares with deconstruction a strong textual orientation and a reluctance to define a single meaning for a work. Along with psychoanalytic criticism, it shares an interest in the dynamics of mental response to textual cues. See "What Is Reader-Response Criticism?" pp. 125–133.

REAL One of the three orders of subjectivity (see Imaginary and Symbolic), the Real is the intractable and substantial world that resists and exceeds interpretation. The Real cannot be imagined, symbolized, or known directly. It constantly eludes our efforts to name it (death, gravity, the physicality of objects are examples of the Real), and thus challenges both the Imaginary and the Symbolic orders. The Real is fundamentally "Other," the mark of the divide between conscious and unconscious, and is signaled in language by gaps, slips, speechlessness, and the sense of the uncanny. The Real is not what we call "reality." It is the stumbling block of the Imaginary (which thinks it can "imagine" anything, including the Real) and of the Symbolic, which tries to bring the Real under its laws (the Real exposes the "phallacy" of the Law of the Phallus). The Real is frightening; we try to tame it with laws and language and call it "reality."

See also: Imaginary Order, Psychoanalytic Criticism.

SEMIOLOGY, SEMIOTIC *See* Semiotics.

SEMIOTICS The study of signs and sign systems and the way meaning is derived from them. Structuralist anthropologists, psychoanalysts, and literary critics developed semiotics during the decades following 1950, but much of the pioneering work had been done at the turn of the century by the founder of modern linguistics, Ferdinand de Saussure, and the American philosopher Charles Sanders Peirce.

Semiotics is based on several important distinctions, including the distinction between "signifier" and "signified" (the sign and what it points toward) and the distinction between "langue" and "parole." *Langue* (French for "tongue," as in "native tongue," meaning language) refers to the entire system within which individual utterances or usages of language have meaning; *parole* (French for "word") refers to the particular utterances or usages. A principal tenet of semiotics is that signs, like words, are not significant in themselves, but instead have meaning only in relation to other signs and the entire system of signs, or langue.

The affinity between semiotics and structuralist literary criticism derives from this emphasis placed on langue, or system. Structuralist critics, after all, were reacting against formalists and their procedure of focusing on individual words as if meanings didn't depend on anything external to the text.

Poststructuralists have used semiotics but questioned some of its underlying assumptions, including the opposition between signifier and signified. The feminist poststructuralist Julia Kristeva, for instance, has used the word "semiotic" to describe feminine language, a highly figurative, fluid form and discourse that she sets in opposition to rigid, symbolic masculine language.

See also: Deconstruction, Feminist Criticism, Formalism, Poststructuralism, Oppositions, Structuralism, Symbol.

SIMILE *See* Metaphor.

SOCIOHISTORICAL CRITICISM *See* New Historicism.

STRUCTURALISM A science of humankind whose proponents attempted to show that all elements of human culture, including literature, may be understood as parts of a system of signs. Structuralism, according to Robert Scholes, was a reaction to " 'modernist' alienation and despair."

Using Ferdinand de Saussure's linguistic theory, European structuralists such as Roman Jakobson, Claude Lévi-Strauss, and Roland Barthes (before his shift toward poststructuralism) attempted to develop a "semiology" or "semiotics" (science of signs). Barthes, among others, sought to recover literature and even language from the isolation in which they had been studied and to show that the laws that govern them govern all signs, from road signs to articles of clothing.

Particularly useful to structuralists were two of Saussure's concepts: the idea of "phoneme" in language and the idea that phonemes exist in two kinds of relationships: "synchronic" and "diachronic." A phoneme is the smallest consistently significant unit in language; thus, both "a" and "an" are phonemes, but "n" is not. A diachronic relationship is that which a phoneme has with those that have preceded it in time and those that will follow it. These "horizontal" relationships produce what we might call discourse or narrative and what Saussure called "parole." The synchronic relationship is the "vertical" one that a word has in a given instant with the entire system of language ("langue") in which it may generate meaning. "An" means what it means in English because those of us who speak the language are using it in the same way at a given time.

Following Saussure, Lévi-Strauss studied hundreds of myths, breaking them into their smallest meaningful units, which he called "mythemes." Removing each from its diachronic relations with other mythemes in a single myth (such as the myth of Oedipus and his mother), he vertically aligned those mythemes that he found to be homologous (structurally correspondent). He then studied the relationships within as well as between vertically aligned columns, in an attempt to understand scientifically, through ratios and proportions, those thoughts and processes that humankind has shared, both at one particular time and across time. One could say, then, that structuralists followed Saussure in preferring to think about the overriding langue or language of myth, in which each mytheme and mytheme-constituted myth fits meaningfully, rather than about isolated individual paroles or narratives. Structuralists followed Saussure's lead in believing what the poststructuralist Jacques Derrida later decided he could not subscribe to — that sign systems must be understood in terms of binary oppositions. In analyzing myths and texts to find basic structures, structuralists tended to find that opposite terms modulate until they are finally resolved or reconciled by some intermediary third term. Thus, a structuralist reading of *Paradise Lost* would show that the war between God and the bad angels becomes a rift between God and sinful, fallen man, the rift then being healed by the Son of God, the mediating third term.

See also: Deconstruction, Discourse, Narrative, Poststructuralism, Semiotics.

SUPERSTRUCTURE *See* Marxist Criticism.

SYMBOL A thing, image, or action that, although it is of interest in its own right, stands for or suggests something larger and more complex — often an idea or a range of interrelated ideas, attitudes, and practices.

Within a given culture, some things are understood to be symbols: the flag of the United States is an obvious example. More subtle cultural symbols might be the river as a symbol of time and the journey as a symbol of life and its manifold experiences.

Instead of appropriating symbols generally used and understood within their culture, writers often create symbols by setting up, in their works, a complex but identifiable web of associations. As a result, one object, image, or action suggests others, and often, ultimately, a range of ideas.

A symbol may thus be defined as a metaphor in which the "vehicle," the thing, image, or action used to represent something else, represents many related things (or "tenors") or is broadly suggestive. The urn in Keats's "Ode on a Grecian Urn" suggests many interrelated concepts, including art, truth, beauty, and timelessness.

Symbols have been of particular interest to formalists, who study how meanings emerge from the complex, patterned relationships between images in a work, and psychoanalytic critics, who are interested in how individual authors and the larger culture both disguise and reveal unconscious fears and desires through symbols. Recently, French feminists have also focused on the symbolic. They have suggested that, as wide-ranging as it seems, symbolic language is ultimately rigid and restrictive. They favor semiotic language and writing, which, they contend, is at once more rhythmic, unifying, and feminine.

See also: Feminist Criticism, Metaphor, Psychoanalytic Criticism, Trope.

SYMBOLIC ORDER   One of the three orders of subjectivity (see Imaginary Order and Real), it is the realm of law, language, and society; it is the repository of generally held cultural beliefs. Its symbolic system is language, whose agent is the father or lawgiver, the one who has the power of naming. The human subject is commanded into this preestablished order by language (a process that begins long before a child can speak) and must submit to its orders of communication (grammar, syntax, and so on). Entrance into the Symbolic order determines subjectivity according to a primary law of referentiality that takes the male sign (phallus, see Phallus) as its ordering principle. Lacan states that both sexes submit to the Law of the Phallus (the law of order, language, and differentiation) but their individual relation to the law determines whether they see themselves — and are seen by others to be — either "masculine" or "feminine." The Symbolic institutes repression (of the Imaginary), thus creating the unconscious, which itself is structured like the language of the symbolic. The unconscious, a timeless realm, cannot be known directly, but it can be understood by a kind of translation that takes place in language — psychoanalysis is the "talking cure." The Symbolic is not a "stage" of development (as is Freud's "oedipal stage") nor is it set in place once and for all in human life. We constantly negotiate its threshold (in sleep, in drunkenness) and can "fall out" of it altogether in psychosis.

See also: Psychoanalytic Criticism, Imaginary Order, Real.

SYNECDOCHE   *See* Metaphor, Metonymy.

TENOR   *See* Metaphor, Metonymy, Symbol.

TROPE   A figure, as in "figure of speech." Literally a "turning," that is, a turning or twisting of a word or phrase to make it mean something else. Principal tropes include metaphor, metonymy, simile, personification, and synecdoche.

See also: Metaphor, Metonymy.

VEHICLE   *See* Metaphor, Metonymy, Symbol.

Case Studies in Contemporary Criticism

SERIES EDITOR: Ross C Murfin, *University of Miami*

JAMES JOYCE
The Dead

Complete, Authoritative Text with
Biographical and Historical Contexts,
Critical History, and Essays from
Five Contemporary Critical Perspectives

EDITED BY

Daniel R. Schwarz
Cornell University

International College
2654 E. Tamiami Trail
Naples, FL 33962

Bedford Books *of* **St. Martin's Press**
BOSTON • NEW YORK

For Bedford Books

Publisher: Charles H. Christensen
Associate Publisher/General Manager: Joan E. Feinberg
Managing Editor: Elizabeth M. Schaaf
Developmental Editor: Stephen A. Scipione
Production Editor: Heidi Hood
Text Design: Sandra Rigney, The Book Department
Cover Design: Richard Emery Design, Inc.

Library of Congress Catalog Card Number: 93–85157
Copyright © 1994 by Bedford Books *of* St. Martin's Press

All rights reserved. No part of this book may be reproduced, stored in a retrieval system, or transmitted by any form or by any means, electronic, mechanical, photocopying, recording, or otherwise, except as may be expressly permitted by the applicable copyright statutes or in writing by the Publisher.

Manufactured in the United States of America.

8 7 6 5 4
f e d c b a

For information, write: St. Martin's Press, Inc.
175 Fifth Avenue, New York, NY 10010

Editorial Offices: Bedford Books *of* St. Martin's Press
29 Winchester Street, Boston, MA 02116

ISBN: 0–312–08073–5 (paperback)
ISBN: 0–312–12082–6 (hardcover)

Published and distributed outside North America by:

MACMILLAN PRESS LTD.
Houndmills, Basingstoke, Hampshire RG21 2XS and London
Companies and representatives throughout the world.

ISBN: 0–333–61849–1

Acknowledgment

The text of "The Dead" is reprinted from the Viking Critical Library edition of *Dubliners* (1969), edited by Robert Scholes and A. Walton Litz.

About the Series

Case Studies in Contemporary Criticism provide college students with an entrée into the current critical and theoretical ferment in literary studies. Each volume reprints the complete text of a classic literary work and presents critical essays that approach the work from different theoretical perspectives, together with the editors' introductions to both the literary work and the critics' theoretical perspectives.

The volume editor of each *Case Study* has selected and prepared an authoritative text of the classic work, written an introduction to the work's biographical and historical contexts, and surveyed the critical responses to the work since its initial publication. Thus situated biographically, historically, and critically, the work is examined in five critical essays, each representing a theoretical perspective of importance to contemporary literary studies. These essays, prepared especially for undergraduates by exemplary critics, show theory in praxis; whether written by established scholars or exceptional young critics, they demonstrate how current theoretical approaches can generate compelling readings of great literature.

As series editor, I have prepared introductions, with bibliographies, to the theoretical perspectives represented in the five critical essays. Each introduction presents the principal concepts of a particular theory in their historical context and discusses the major figures and key works that have influenced their formulation. It is my hope that these introductions will reveal to students that good criticism is informed by a set of coherent assumptions, and will encourage them to recognize and examine their own assumptions about literature. Finally, I have compiled a glossary of key terms that recur in these volumes and in the discourse of contemporary theory and criticism. We hope that the *Case Studies in Contemporary Criticism* series will reaffirm the richness of its literary works, even as it introduces invigorating new ways to mine their apparently inexhaustible wealth.

Ross C Murfin
Series Editor
University of Miami

About This Volume

The text of "The Dead" reprinted here follows that of the Viking critical edition of *Dubliners* (1969). A revision of the 1958 Viking edition, it was prepared by Robert Scholes in consultation with Richard Ellmann, and incorporated additional suggestions by Jack P. Dalton. Now recognized as the authoritative text, it observes Joyce's desire that dashes be used to introduce direct dialogue and that italics be used for speech employed within direct dialogue.

Part One reprints "The Dead" preceded by my biographical and historical introduction. Part Two begins with my critical history of "The Dead" and includes five essays written from different theoretical perspectives: psychological (mine), reader-response (Peter Rabinowitz), new historical (Michael Levenson), feminist (Margot Norris), and deconstructive (John Paul Riquelme). Each of these essays — written especially for this volume and placed in theoretical context by Ross Murfin's introductions — addresses both the experience of reading "The Dead" and the critical, scholarly, and pedagogical issues that "The Dead" presents to the contemporary critical mindscape. I chose the four other contributors because for years I have been learning from their work. Each of them plays an important role in the dialogue within the profession and is recognized as a master teacher by students and colleagues. That the contributors often address similar issues from different perspectives creates a community of inquiry that teachers and students will surely wish to enter.

Acknowledgments

For the textual notes, I am indebted to Marvin Magalaner, *Time of Apprenticeship: The Fiction of Young James Joyce* (New York: Abelard-Schulman, 1959, 147–71); Don Gifford, *Joyce Annotated* (2nd ed., rev. and enlarged, Berkeley: University of California Press, 1982, 110–26); and Robert Scholes and A. Walton Litz, *Dubliners: Text, Criticism, and Notes* (New York: Viking, 1969, 500–04). Readers are also referred to Terence Brown's recent edition of *Dubliners* (New York: Penguin, 1992).

My close friend and colleague Phillip L. Marcus has provided generous editorial advice on textual matters. It has been a pleasure working with the four contributors: Michael Levenson, Margot Norris, Peter Rabinowitz, and John Paul Riquelme. At every stage of the project, the secretarial assistance of Phillis Molock has been essential and superb. My long collegial relationship with Ross Murfin, general editor, helped make the project a delight. At Bedford Books, Steve Scipione provided guidance and direction and Heidi Hood's input has been invaluable; I also thank Charles Christensen, Joan Feinberg, Elizabeth Schaaf, and Laura McCready. As always I want to acknowledge the input of my Cornell students from whom I have continually learned over the past twenty-five years when teaching "The Dead," as well as the stimulation of my five NEH summer seminars for college teachers and four NEH summer seminars for secondary school teachers. I would be remiss if I did not thank the University of Hawaii, where I held the Visiting Citizen's Chair in 1992–93, and especially the English Department Chair, Glenn Man, for the generous support of my professional activities.

Daniel R. Schwarz
Cornell University

About the Contributors

THE VOLUME EDITOR

Daniel R. Schwarz is professor of English at Cornell University. His books include *Narrative and Representation in the Poetry of Wallace Stevens* (1993); *The Case for a Humanistic Poetics* (1991); *The Transformation of the English Novel, 1890–1930* (1989); *Reading Joyce's "Ulysses"* (1987); *The Humanistic Heritage: Critical Theories of the English Novel from James to Hillis Miller* (1986); *Conrad: The Later Fiction* (1982); *Conrad: "Almayer's Folly" through "Under Western Eyes"* (1980); and *Disraeli's Fiction* (1979). He has lectured widely in the United States and abroad and is currently working on a study of the relationship between literature and the visual arts within the modernist tradition.

THE CRITICS

Michael Levenson is professor of English at the University of Virginia. He is the author of *A Genealogy of Modernism: A Study of English Literary Doctrine, 1908–1922* (1984) and *Modernism and the Fate of Individuality: Character and Form from Conrad to Woolf* (1991).

Margot Norris is professor of English and comparative literature at the University of California, Irvine, where she teaches modernism and modern intellectual history. She is author of *The Decentered Universe of "Finnegans Wake"* (1976); *Beasts of the Modern Imagination: Darwin, Nietzsche, Kafka, Ernst, and Lawrence* (1985); and *Joyce's Web: The Social Unraveling of Modernism* (1992). Her current research explores the discourses of modern mass warfare.

Peter J. Rabinowitz, professor of comparative literature at Hamilton College, divides his time between music and narrative theory. Author of *Before Reading: Narrative Conventions and the Politics of Interpretation* (1987) and co-editor, with James Phelan, of *Understanding Narrative* (1994), he is currently completing, with composer Jay Reise, a book on the act of listening. His published articles cover a wide range of subjects, from Dostoyevsky to Mrs. E.D.E.N. Southworth, from detective fiction to the ideology of musical structure, from Mahler to Scott Joplin. He is also an active music critic and a contributing editor of *Fanfare.*

John Paul Riquelme is professor and chair in the English Department at Boston University, where he teaches late nineteenth-century and early twentieth-century British and Irish literature. His books include *Teller and Tale in Joyce's Fiction: Oscillating Perspectives* (1983) and *Harmony of Dissonances: T. S. Eliot, Romanticism, and Imagination* (1991). He is at work on a study dealing with Thomas Hardy and Oscar Wilde.

THE SERIES EDITOR

Ross C Murfin, general editor of *Case Studies in Contemporary Criticism,* is dean of the College of Arts and Sciences and professor of English at the University of Miami. He has taught at Yale University and the University of Virginia and has published scholarly studies on Joseph Conrad, Thomas Hardy, and D. H. Lawrence.